The Archaeology and Historical Ecology of Small Scale Economies

UNIVERSITY PRESS OF FLORIDA

Florida A&M University, Tallahassee
Florida Atlantic University, Boca Raton
Florida Gulf Coast University, Ft. Myers
Florida International University, Miami
Florida State University, Tallahassee
New College of Florida, Sarasota
University of Central Florida, Orlando
University of Florida, Gainesville
University of North Florida, Jacksonville
University of South Florida, Tampa
University of West Florida, Pensacola

The Archaeology
and Historical Ecology
of Small Scale Economies

⊷⟋⟋⊷

Edited by Victor D. Thompson and James C. Waggoner Jr.

UNIVERSITY PRESS OF FLORIDA

Gainesville / Tallahassee / Tampa / Boca Raton

Pensacola / Orlando / Miami / Jacksonville / Ft. Myers / Sarasota

This book may be available in an electronic edition.

First cloth printing, 2013
First paperback printing, 2019

24 23 22 21 20 19   6 5 4 3 2 1

A record of cataloging-in-publication data is available from the Library of Congress.
ISBN 978-0-8130-4242-8 (cloth)
ISBN 978-0-8130-6415-4 (pbk.)

The University Press of Florida is the scholarly publishing agency for the State University
System of Florida, comprising Florida A&M University, Florida Atlantic University, Florida
Gulf Coast University, Florida International University, Florida State University, New College
of Florida, University of Central Florida, University of Florida, University of North Florida,
University of South Florida, and University of West Florida.

University Press of Florida
2046 NE Waldo Road
Suite 2100
Gainesville, FL 32609
http://upress.ufl.edu

Contents

Figures

Tables

Preface

This book grew out of a symposium that Jamie Waggoner and I organized for the 74th annual Society for American Archaeology meetings in Atlanta, Georgia. Our goal with this symposium, originally entitled "Footprints on the Landscape: the Historical Ecology of Hunter-Gatherers," was to bring together scholars working in different environments around the world to elicit a discourse on the nature of human-environmental interactions among groups practicing small scale economies (e.g., hunter-gatherers, fishers, and/or limited horticulturists). Both Jamie and I had had a keen interest in ecology and anthropology since our early undergraduate days at the University of Georgia, where we became lifelong friends. This symposium was a way for us to not only work on a project together as friends, but also a forum to engage colleagues working on similar issues and to explore the commonalities and differences among the various regions represented. Working on this with Jamie was truly exciting as we began to invite people to the symposium and decide what themes needed to be addressed by the participants.

Unfortunately, that summer before the Society for American Archaeology meeting, I got a call from Jamie while I was in the field in central Florida. He informed me that he was at the hospital and the doctors had discovered a brain tumor. Due to Jamie's illness, he was not able to write his paper for the symposium or a chapter subsequently for this book. Jamie's condition did not improve, and he eventually succumbed to the cancer on September 23, 2009. He was 38 years old. I decided to carry on with our project, although at times I must admit I wanted to abandon it for emotional reasons. Although Jamie passed away before we could really begin work on this enterprise, he served as a driving force for me to finish the book. For me, this volume represents the last intellectual dialogue I had with my best friend. His memory continues to inspire me in my work, in my friendships with others, and simply to be a good human being.

Victor D. Thompson

Acknowledgments

This book could not have been completed without the aid and support of a number of individuals. I would like to thank my wife, Amanda Roberts Thompson, for her unending emotional support and understanding of my work on this project. She provided a much-needed sounding board for ideas and encouraged me to finish the project. My graduate and undergraduate student assistants Julia Giblin, Randee Hunter, Kimberly Swisher, and Ellen Burlingame Turck also provided support formatting the text code on the chapters. John Turck also provided helpful comments and typographical editing on the introductory chapter, as well as endlessly entertaining conversations on the subject of historical ecology. While I was in the department of anthropology at the Ohio State University, Clark Spencer Larsen provided additional support for this book.

Over the years, there have been a number of colleagues who have influenced mine and Jamie's thinking regarding the subject of historical ecology. I would be remiss if I did not mention these individuals here. First, Jamie's dissertation advisor, Ken Sassaman, is recognized for the role he played in helping Jamie finalize his dissertation so that he could graduate. I know that Jamie truly appreciated the knowledge that Ken imparted to him, particularly on the subject of fire ecology. Likewise, Richard Jefferies, who served as my mentor, deserves many thanks for all the insightful conversations and guidance he has provided me over the years. Finally, we thank the following individuals, in no particular order, for their general academic and intellectual support and friendship: Tom Pluckhahn, John Chamblee, Maureen Meyers, Neill Wallis, Michelle LeFebvre, Asa Randall, Keith Stephenson, Deborah Mullins, Jason Burns, Stephen Kowalewski, David G. Anderson, Christopher Morehart, Richard Yerkes, William A. Parkinson, John Worth, Julie Field, Kristen Gremillion, Rob Cook, Chris Rodning, Merryl Alber, Clark Alexander, Erv Garrison, Fred Andrus, Deborah Keen, David Hurst Thomas, Christopher Pool, Tom Dillehay, Jose Iriarte, David Hally, William

Marquardt, Karen Walker, Elizabeth Reitz, Matthew Reynolds, and finally, last but not least, Mark Williams, who started us both on our journey in archaeology. This volume is dedicated to our parents: Marjorie Waggoner and Dr. James C. Waggoner and Marie Rose Thompson and the late William Emory Thompson.

1

Whispers on the Landscape

VICTOR D. THOMPSON

Mighty things from small beginnings grow.
John Dryden, "Annus Mirabilis"

During the latter half of the twentieth century, anthropology began to integrate explicit notions of ecology and the environment as central themes in the study of human societies (e.g., McCay and Acheson 1987; Moran 1990; Rappaport 1984; Steward 1977). The theoretical implications of these viewpoints influenced a host of subsequent studies across the subdisciplines of anthropology. In archaeology, such work was key in bringing about the new archaeology (e.g., Binford and Binford 1968) as well as those studies that would presage its development (e.g., Caldwell 1958). This research would also lead to the development of new methods in archaeology (e.g., flotation, fine screening, etc.) to accommodate the growing theoretical interest in human-environmental interactions (see Trigger 2006 for a history).

Ecologically focused anthropological research continues to be a central topic at the start of the twenty-first century, especially in archaeological studies. Recent archaeological literature concerning socio-ecological systems follows several key themes. By far the most predominant subject among these themes relates to impacts that lead to a collapse or destabilization of the human socioeconomic system (Dean 2010; Diamond 2005; Redman 1999; Redman et al. 2004:1). Another theme focuses on the depression of biodiversity and/or the extinction of certain species (James 2004; Kirch 1997, 2004). Finally, the other major theme is the large-scale transformation of environments by intensive agriculturalists and urban societies (Gunn et al. 2004 ; Redman 1999, 2004). These avenues of research are not mutually exclusive, of course, and contribute significantly to our understanding of socio-natural systems.

Historical ecology is one of the more prevalent theoretical frameworks that deals with issues such as those previously mentioned. The purpose of this introduction is to consider the ideas of historical ecology in the context of the study of small-scale societies. That is, how can a historical ecology approach to the study of hunters and gatherers and limited horticulturists inform us about the nature of human-environmental relationships? In order to explore this, I first provide a brief outline of the core tenets of historical ecology and explore its implications for archaeology. My brief review of historical ecology here draws heavily on the works of Balée (1998, 2006), Balée and Erickson (2006), and Crumley (1994a), who have, over the past two decades, worked to define historical ecology as a research program. Next, I discuss the relevance of studies of small-scale economies for the historical ecology research framework. Specifically, I briefly summarize the major themes of other previously published volumes on historical ecology and contrast them with the ones presented here. Finally, I outline and comment on the future of historical ecology with regards to the last three chapters. These final chapters offer both a consideration of the unifying themes of the case studies, as well as broader observations on historical ecology.

Core Concepts

While historical ecology is related to its theoretical predecessors, such as cultural ecology, evolutionary ecology, and behavioral ecology, among others, it differs in a few fundamental ways (Balée 1998:2; Balée and Erickson 2006:3; see also Balée 2006). Specifically, there are two key aspects of historical ecology that set it apart from other frameworks. As defined by Balée and Erickson (2006:1, 5), historical ecology takes the view that humans are a keystone species and thus primary drivers of ecological change. Changes or alterations by humans to the environment can be small or large in scale and can stem from intentional and/or unintentional actions (see Balée 1998). The second key distinguishing aspect of historical ecology is that, in terms of analysis, it takes as its focus the landscape, but also recognizes that such an understanding is only possible by linking together multiple scales of analysis that range from the local to the regional (Balée 1998; Balée and Erickson 2006:12; Crumley 1994b:10, 2007:16–17; Erickson 2008:158). This explicit focus on multiple temporal and spatial scales sets it apart from other theoretical frameworks.

While historical ecology built upon the theoretical base of ecological anthropology, its more nuanced approach to human-environmental inter-actions, outlined previously, has elicited a major movement in archaeology. Indeed, use of this framework is becoming increasingly common among researchers interested in central problems regarding issues directly related to human impacts, management of past ecosystems, baselines for contem-porary ecosystems, and human agency.

The development of historical ecology as an organizing structure is im-pacting the way in which archaeologists think about the past. Specifically, this has resulted in three main developments: addressing the relevance of past baseline studies of ecosystems; understanding that research must en-compass the totality of its subject; and, finally, realizing that humans are agents of environmental change and management. While these three devel-opments were, to varying degrees, already present in Americanist archaeol-ogy, it was only with the inception of historical ecology that they became explicitly articulated with ecology and the environment.

The first major impact of historical ecology was its forcing archaeolo-gists to consider the implications of their research beyond reconstruct-ing past life ways. Specifically, historical ecology compels us to reflect on how archaeological research comes to bear on problems and issues facing contemporary ecosystems and the role of humans in the management of such ecosystems. The most obvious contribution of such studies is that they provide baseline data on how these ecosystems changed over time, and the nature of the impact that humans had in shaping these systems.

One example of this is Erlandson and Rick's (2008) edited volume, *Hu-man Impacts on Ancient Marine Ecosystems: A Global Perspective,* which exemplifies studies of past impacts and key baseline studies for modern ecosystems. In their introduction to the case studies, they argue that we can learn much from the past regarding our understanding of contempo-rary environments. In fact, there is much evidence to suggest that human populations have impacted the distribution, size, and population structure of many marine species (Erlandson and Rick 2008:5). These case studies go on to demonstrate how and to what degree humans have impacted these ecosystems. Further, such research illustrates how attitudes toward modern fisheries have changed in recent years. The ocean was once thought to be a vast inexhaustible resource; however, we are now beginning to appreciate the fragility of ocean and coastal ecosystems (Jackson et al. 2001; see also Erlandson and Rick 2008). This realization comes not only from studies of modern ecosystems, but is also based on research of past societies.

The second impact of historical ecology is its focus on totalities. That is, we must approach the subject under consideration as a whole and not simply examine its parts (Patterson 1994: 230; see also Gragson 2005). This approach is favored because totalities are particular configurations that are the products of historical circumstances at specific points in time (Patterson 1994:230). For archaeology, especially for those studies that encompass time frames for which there are no written records, such analyses start with the landscape as their focus. This has led to a specific conceptualization of landscape, which has been somewhat of a nebulous concept in archaeological studies (see Kowalewski 2008:251). While there are a myriad of different permutations of landscape archaeology, for historical ecologists the landscape is similar to a text that tracks human actions, natural processes, and the ongoing interaction between the two (Balée 2006:77; Balée and Erickson 2006:2; Crumley 1994a:9; Marquardt and Crumley 1987). In essence the landscape is "a form of the built environment, often having been intentionally designed as architecture or as some other symbolic appropriation of the nature that has patterned, physical underpinnings" (Balée and Erickson 2006:2).

Intertwined with the focus on landscape is the view of humans as intentional actors and agents of environmental change. As Balée (2006) notes, this aspect of the historical ecology program is one of the central themes that sets it apart from other frameworks. Deeply embedded notions of ancient peoples as reactors to, rather than causes of, environmental change, stability, degradation, and increased biodiversity pervade the ecologically focused anthropological literature. Likewise, research in the natural sciences has tended to ignore or marginalize ancient and contemporary "traditional" peoples in their studies of ecosystems, although this is changing. The subtext of this view is that past peoples have largely been thought of as having only a limited or "light" impact on modern ecosystem services, if any.

In contrast and in reaction to these ecocentric bodies of literature is the explicitly anthropocentric view of historical ecology (Balée 2006:79). That is, humans, as stated earlier, are a keystone species that actively manipulate the environment for various purposes. These manipulations have both intended and unintended effects at both long- and short-term time scales. Thus, the implication for archaeological practice is that we view past peoples, in many cases, as active managers of the landscape. *Management* used in this sense is not quite the same as its modern usage. Indeed, there is not one single modern definition of environmental management (Barrow 1999:3). However, many of the perspectives on modern environmental management involve such issues as value of resources and regulatory mechanisms, developmental strategies, scientific and policy development, sustainability issues, control of human impacts, and systems-oriented natural science (Barrow 1999: Box 1.1). While certainly there is some degree of overlap with the aforementioned issues, historical ecology explicitly views management as manipulations of the biotic and abiotic components of ecosystems that increase biodiversity (Balée 1994:117; Erickson 2008:160).

As outlined above, historical ecology as a research program has impacted archaeological theory. That is, it has affected the way in which we think about the past and structured the way in which we question the archaeological record. Similar to previous paradigm shifts, the culminating effect of this for archaeology is that we are currently refining our methods and working at scales necessitated by the questions derived from a historical ecology perspective. Specifically, one of the concerns of the historical ecology program is qualitatively and quantitatively measuring the degree, scale, and kinds of human impacts on the landscape. In addition, we must understand how and why humans are manipulating the landscape and assess the degree of intentionality in such actions as well as the historical circumstances of such actions. The implications of this are that the kinds of archaeological data that we collect must be amenable to analysis through the lens of action, practice, and structure. In addition, such data must also be empirical in terms of a quantifiable impact or alteration on the "natural" landscape. Often the latter requires an interdisciplinary approach and entails collaboration with natural scientists, ecologists, etc. (e.g., Briggs et al. 2006). Methodologically, the most important facet of this work is that there are new approaches to disentangle natural changes in the environment with those that are intentionally and unintentionally induced by humans (e.g., Erlandson et al. 2005; Kirch 1997; McGovern et al. 2008; Reitz et al. 2009). Understanding and being able to define these processes and how they interact is the key to addressing the larger, substantive issues of historical ecology as well as being able to examine it in its totality of relationships.

The Significance of Small Scale Economies

The publication of several edited volumes as well as the historical ecology series by Columbia University Press has significantly increased the visibility of historical ecology as a research program. Foremost among these are William Balée's (1998) *Advances in Historical Ecology* and Carole Crumley's (1994a) *Historical Ecology: Cultural Knowledge and Changing Landscapes.* These two volumes serve as the cornerstone of historical ecology research. Both outline many of the core principles of the historical ecology research program. Further, both volumes bring together cultural anthropologists and archaeological anthropologists to explore the nature of human-environmental interactions within a historical schema.

More recently Balée and Erickson's (2006) *Time and Complexity in Historical Ecology* expands on many of the ideas put forth in the earlier volumes. The case studies in the book apply concepts of historical ecology and focus specifically on the Neotropical lowlands and include case studies on the Maya of the Petén region of Guatemala, coastal Peru, and various parts of the Amazonia. Many of the chapters in the volume focus on agriculture to some degree or in some fashion, in terms of domestication, earthworks and intensification projects, species diversity as an effect of agriculture, etc. (see Cormier 2006 for an exception).

As previously discussed, the chapters in Erlandson and Rick's (2008) recently edited volume also focus on many aspects germane to historical ecology. However, in contrast to the other previously mentioned volumes, the key, unifying theme of these studies is human impacts on fisheries from a global perspective. Both Rick and Erlandson's (2008) and Balée and Erickson's (2006) thematic volumes illustrate the value of focused themed collections centering on historical ecology. Both of these volumes bring to the forefront issues and situations that address commonalities either within a specific environment or with regards to specific resources. If one of our goals is to construct a global historical ecology, then volumes such as these are the first steps in facilitating such a broad understanding of not only the past, but also implications for the future of our world.

The structure of this book follows the theme set by the more recent volumes on historical ecology. That is, its purpose is to follow a common theme that engenders ideas and discussion regarding broader issues related to this theoretical framework. The unifying topic of the case studies in this book is that they deal with groups that are pursuing small-scale economies. I use the term *small-scale economies* to refer to groups primarily making their living by hunting, gathering, fishing, or through limited agricultural endeavors. Most of the chapters in the book specifically examine foraging societies; however, several of the case studies either straddle transitional periods in subsistence economies (e.g., from foraging to farming) or describe situations where the primary subsistence is rooted in hunting and gathering, but is supplemented by the use of cultigens. The fundamental point, however, is that these groups were not involved in intensive agriculture or industrialized subsistence endeavors.

There are several reasons why a focus on such small-scale economies is important to understanding a global historical ecology. First, it is widely recognized that modern and past state-level polities practice intensive and extensive subsistence economies that altered the landscape in fundamental ways, such as shifting the flow of water and landscape structure for agricultural production (see Scarborough 2003 for an excellent discussion of water management). Less understood is the degree and extent to which foraging and limited agricultural practices modify the landscape. Recent studies, such as the one examining the use of fire by Martu Australian groups (Bliege Bird et al. 2008), are beginning to document the implications that such practices have for the subsistence systems, as well as for the management and sustainability of the ecosystem in general. However, we are still a long way from understanding the variability of relationships that such economies and their concomitant ideologies have for various environments.

While major earth moving projects, urbanization, and large-scale public works all leave an obvious mark on the landscape, methodologically the traces of small-scale societies are subtler and more nuanced (see Balée, this volume). The title of this chapter, "Whispers on the Landscape," takes its name directly from this idea. While not always the case (e.g., Poverty Point; see Kidder, this volume), many alterations by foraging societies and similar small-scale societies are in effect not as obvious in the archaeological record. However, simply because these relationships are not as obvious on the landscape does not mean that their impact or legacy must always be proportional. Indeed, recent work by Briggs et al. (2006:180) in the American Southwest has shown that, in some cases, "non-intensive, short term" agriculture can have lasting legacy effects on certain ecosystems. The main point of this is that we should not assume a priori that small-scale economies are sustainable and in harmony with "nature," while large-scale economies are destructive and ultimately lead to degradation (see Erickson 2006:160). As Balée and Erickson (2006:9) caution, we should take care not to uncritically assign "value-laden terms such as beneficial, enhancing, sustainable, destruction and degrading to human activities past and present."

The ideas discussed previously also have implications for interdisciplinary approaches to historical ecology (see Pennings, this volume). The visible (e.g., buildings, temples, agricultural fields, road systems) aspects of societies with grand economies often help archaeologists make the case for the importance and inclusion of past societies in ecological studies, providing tangible evidence for collaborating natural scientists. However, making the argument for the inclusion of foraging societies and similar small-scale economies can be considerably more difficult. This line of thinking is a variant of what Denevan (1992) refers to as the "pristine myth." That is, there is no such thing as pristine Holocene environments (see also Crumley 1994c:239). I refer to this variant as the *myth of the moderns*. Briefly, this concept refers to the belief by some social and natural scientists alike that if past impacts are not directly observable (i.e., with their eyes) on the landscape, then their impact is somewhat minimal. For those anthropologists whose research pertains to past foraging populations and the like, such views, particularly when coupled with often lingering Rousseauan ideas of "noble savages," can make convincing natural scientists of their impacts difficult. Further, there is also a perspective that nature has some sort of reset button, and that such activities, which may have played a role in shaping the ecosystem during their operation, now do not really concern us since enough time has elapsed for nature to restore the impacted area to its original form. Thus, research regarding the nature of environmental relationships and their impacts regarding small-scale economies is crucial to combating such unsubstantiated viewpoints.

Lastly, the study of small-scale economies is important because these types of economies have pervaded most of the past and continue to operate in areas still today. For over 99 percent of human history, we pursued a foraging mode of production (Panter-Brick et al. 2001:5). And, even when we humans began to domesticate plants, in many areas of the world food production remained at low levels and was more of a supplement to the hunting and gathering that had sustained populations prior to domestication (Smith 2001). Further, in some regions it was not until considerable time had passed that large-scale agriculture became the dominant economy (Smith 2001).

We now recognize, as Kidder (1998:143; see also this volume) states, that ever since the emergence of those animals we assign to the genus *Homo*, we have been altering "subtly and not so subtly" the ecology of our worlds. And since this time, the scale and distribution of our impact on the landscape has increased. By the late Pleistocene, foraging groups had colonized all but one of the major continents. During the Holocene, populations grew, the new environments that accompanied the fluctuating climate were exploited, monument construction became widespread, and permanent settlements were established (see Anderson et al. 2007 for a global review). In some regions these changes were accompanied and facilitated by large-scale agricultural economies; in other areas foraging and low-level food production supported these cultural shifts. Therefore, as we reflect on the history of small-scale economies, the remaining view is one of tremendous time depth and variability. In many instances, people following these economies were capable of both transforming and domesticating entire landscapes. The chapters in this volume are an exploration of these variations from an explicitly historical ecological point of view.

Structure of the Volume

This volume is divided into two sections. Part I consists of historical ecology case studies of small-scale economies from various regions around the world. As economy is the unifying theme of these studies, effort was made to bring in researchers working in a wide variety of climates, as well as time frames. To this end, these case studies encompass a temporal scale that begins in the late Pleistocene and extends to modern-day groups. Further, a wide range of climatic environments is included in the volume. The climates covered in the case studies include temperate mountain (Zedeño), arid (Gilman, Toney, and Beale), California Island Mediterranean (Rick), humid subtropical (Thompson, Turck, and DePratter), oceanic (Milner), temperate continental (Habu and Hall), and tropical (Fish, Fish, DeBlasis, and Gaspar). In Part II, three scholars—a cultural anthropologist (Balée), an archaeologist (Kidder), and an ecologist (Pennings)—provide short commentary on the broader themes and implications of the volume as a whole.

The case studies deal with many of the various aspects of historical ecology discussed in the introduction. Many of the chapters focus on the relationships that people have with specific species or how subsistence practices impacted the landscape and how such practices relate to and are influenced by cultural, political, and ideological structures, although the reader will notice that both topics are present in all the chapters.

In chapter 2, Nicky Milner explores the impact that gathering had on shellfish populations during the Mesolithic (Ertebølle culture, c. 5400–3900 cal. BC) and Early Neolithic (Early Funnel Beaker culture, c. 3900–3300 cal. BC) at the famous kitchenmiddens sites in Denmark. In this chapter, Milner evaluates whether natural processes or human impacts are responsible for size changes in shellfish collections observed in these midden sites. Such methodological considerations are key in studies of historical ecology, and she rightly points out several confounding factors in such analyses. Through careful study, however, Milner is able to trace a complex history of impacts due to exploitation as well as possible recovery events for the shellfish populations.

Rick's (chapter 3) study of the California Channel Islands similarly examines the relationship of people to specific species. However, in contrast to Milner's study, his work documents dispersal events that were most likely facilitated by Native American hunter-gatherers in the region. Specifically, he makes the case that Native groups were responsible for the introduction of at least three of the islands' extant endemic mammals—the island fox, deer mice, and harvest mice. In addition, they may have also aided in the dispersal of island spotted skunk, Catalina Island ground squirrels, and shrews. Such introductions, especially of apex predators, have overall ecosystem implications, and Rick stresses that to really understand such changes we must work to better integrate archaeology, paleontology, and modern biological and ecological information. In order to achieve such a synthesis, we must be willing to work collaboratively and across traditional disciplinary boundaries.

In the next study, Habu and Hall (chapter 4) examine overall changes in Middle Jomon land use, climate, and cultural trajectories. Specifically, they discuss the possible changes in land use that accompanied the transition from the Middle Jomon period. They point out that the rise of Middle Jomon was linked to an economy reliant on mast nut trees, such as the chestnut. They hypothesize that such long-term tending and utilization of forests in the regions not only affected the landscape, but also more than likely altered people's perception of it. Such perceptions may be reflected in ritual and ceremonial practices, such as the growth and decline of figurine production. Habu and Hall conclude that while climate data show interesting correlations with overall cultural changes during Jomon time frames, the broader context of historical ecology provides a more encompassing view of these transitions.

In chapter 5, Thompson, Turck, and DePratter examine the long-term impact of small-scale economies on the Georgia coastal ecosystem. Their thesis is that the collection and deposition of shellfish by hunter-gatherer-fishers from 4500 to 250 BP fundamentally altered coastal areas by creating and modifying upland habitats. They argue that humans were not only keystone species, but they created keystone structures without which the past and modern ecosystem of the Georgia coast could not have been sustained. Further, they point out that such habitats are no longer being created and that this could have dire implications for the health of the current system.

The previous studies focus on the effects that humans had on the population and distribution of specific species and the work on cultural trajectories and the overall landscape impact. Gilman, Toney, and Beale's (chapter 6) research provides a nice contrast to this. They focus their study on early agriculture in Southwest North America and Northwest Mexico. Agriculture is often assumed to have engendered major changes in the environment compared to hunter-gatherer economies. Their study of the Tucson Basin, Cerro Juanaqueña, and the San Simon Basin bring to light the fact that different types of agriculture can have different effects and that some forms may not be radically different, in terms of environmental disturbance, than previous periods in the same region, where subsistence was primarily based in hunting and gathering.

In chapter 7, Fish, Fish, DeBlasis, and Gaspar examine the idea of persistent places situated within a historical ecology framework for the sambaquis of coastal Brazil. Specifically, they examine these large shell mounds, one of which is over 30 m tall, regarding arguments related to their primary function. They challenge previous interpretations of these sites as large middens or platforms to permit dry habitation in their wetland lagoon setting. Instead, they suggest that the sambaquis are more properly thought of as "symbolically charged and highly visible monuments." Their interpretation of the sambaquis shell mounds as monumental places, however, hinges upon the concept of persistent place and the role that both human agency and ecology had in the creation of such landscapes.

In the final case study, Zedeño (chapter 8) examines the history, ideology, and persistence of hunting ethos as a core value among the Blackfeet Native American group of (western) North America. Unlike the other chapters in this volume, her work centers on not only the past, but also its presence among contemporary peoples. She shows how the Blackfeet persevered as hunters despite dramatic changes in the ecology of the regions, as well as the geopolitical conditions surrounding such practices. She argues that this hunting ethos has aided in the Blackfeet's adaptation to reservation life.

In Part II, Pennings, Kidder, and Balée offer their thoughts and perspectives on the themes in the volume as a whole. Pennings (chapter 9) presents his ideas on how ecologists and archaeologists can more productively collaborate. He sees ways to link the narratives of archaeological work with more traditional biological approaches to ecosystem science. He also points out and suggests potential ways to overcome the inherent difficulties of scale in linking archaeological and ecosystem science data sets.

Kidder (chapter 10) takes on the central theme of the book, regarding the nature, impact, and dynamic interaction that societies following small-scale economies have with the environment. He suggests that humans have been altering their environment since the "dawn of humanity," perhaps as far back as two million years. He challenges us to explore the intentionality and microhistories of these changes. In other words, the "history" in historical ecology. He provides this commentary and perspective from his considerable work at Poverty Point, one of the largest hunter-gatherer archaeological sites in the world.

Finally, Balée (chapter 11), one of the founders of the historical ecology movement, provides an epilogue to the volume. He considers the book within the context of time, scale, the concept of nature, and views on ancient hunter-gatherers. He poses the question of what we can learn from such studies that can be applied to a modern context—in essence, an applied historical ecology.

A Program for the Future

What good is it to study the micro and macrohistories of past peoples? Why should we concern ourselves with the variations of how past societies modified, shaped, created, unintentionally degraded, intentionally made more productive, protected, managed, ritualized, domesticated, and otherwise interacted with their environments? Perhaps part of the answer to these questions can be found in Sir Grahame Clark's book *Aspects of Prehistory.* Clark (1970:51), famous for his early environmentally based work at Star Carr, a hunter-gatherer Mesolithic site in northern Europe, wrote "Our survival depends on, among other things, our ability to view one another in a historical context appropriate to a world that shrinks in size and grows in potential danger." He goes on to state that history "is something which to a large degree determines how we behave." Clark's justification for the study of world "prehistory," although written more than 40 years ago, seems still relevant today, considering the looming environmental problems that we face. The contributors of this volume have made an attempt to provide insight into the inner histories of past societies' interactions with their environments, and the volume as a whole considers the relevance of such inquiry with respect to our own interactions with the environment. Although the focus of the chapters in this book varies, each represents a departure point from which other researchers may continue to explore these topics, developing more detailed historical and processual understandings of such issues. Therefore, I see this volume as a beginning rather than an end in refining the concepts of historical ecology, discovering and revealing the histories of past peoples, and contemplating its relevance for modern society. By gaining a deeper appreciation, which includes the historical contingencies that people faced in their interaction with certain environments, climates, resource bases, etc., we are better able to view our own behavior in a broader context, and hopefully make informed decisions that will not only preserve our world, but also our species.

I

Case Studies

2

Human Impacts on Oyster Resources at the Mesolithic–Neolithic Transition in Denmark

NICKY MILNER

Human impacts on the environment are particularly pertinent in today's world. The aim of this chapter is to consider the extent to which humans impacted shellfish populations in the past, and specifically in Denmark toward the end of the Mesolithic period (Ertebølle culture, c. 5400–3900 cal. BC) and into the Early Neolithic period (Early Funnel Beaker culture, c. 3900–3300 cal. BC). This is a period of important cultural change, with the introduction of domesticates such as grain, sheep, and cattle appearing in Denmark at about 3900 cal. BC. Stable isotopes on human bone from around Europe suggest a major, rapid transformation in economy from heavily marine to terrestrial at this time (Richards and Hedges 1999; Richards et al. 2003; Schulting and Richards 2002), with some even suggesting a taboo on marine foods (Thomas 2003). However, the shell middens, also called kitchenmiddens, in Denmark provide evidence that in fact marine consumption did continue into the Early Neolithic period (see Bailey and Milner 2002; Milner et al. 2004 for discussion).

These shell middens are excellent resources for a historical ecology approach because they accumulate over centuries and thus can provide a *longue durée* perspective (Balée 2006). Two important observations can be made of the Danish Mesolithic–Neolithic shell middens: (1) there is a clear shift in shellfish composition from predominantly oysters to cockles at the Mesolithic–Neolithic transition at many middens; (2) there is a visible decline in the size of oyster shells over time.

Rowley-Conwy (1984) attributes the decline in oysters at the beginning of the Early Neolithic, c. 3900 cal. BC, to lowered salinity and argues that the decline in oysters created an economic crisis, which led to the adoption of agriculture. The hypothesis has had its critics, and has been rejected on the basis that oysters would not have been a significant enough resource to have such a major impact on the economy, i.e., the adoption of agriculture (e.g., Price 2000). A further criticism might be that the hypothesis assumes that hunter-gatherers were *affected by* an environmental change but does not explore in detail the *interaction between* humans and the environment.

This paper will examine three Danish shell midden sites with Mesolithic and Neolithic stratified deposits, and investigate the changing shellfish composition and sizes in relation to the environment and gathering strategies.

Theoretical Discussion

Shell middens are present around the world and are frequently the subject of study concerning the impacts of humans on marine shellfish populations (e.g., recent studies include: Bailey and Craighead 2003; Bailey and Milner 2008; Bailey et al. 2008; Erlandson et al. 2008; Faulkner 2009; Mannino and Thomas 2001, 2002; Morrison and Hunt 2007; Milner et al. 2007; Rick and Erlandson 2008).

There are three main observations in the literature that are used in order to suggest intensive or overexploitation (Claassen 1998:45; Faulkner 2009:822; Mannino and Thomas 2001, 2002):

1. Mean shell length decreases over time (usually observed as from the bottom to the top of the midden).
2. The modal size of the archaeological shells will be significantly smaller than an unexploited population of the same species.
3. Less easily procured species will increase in number through time.

It has, however, been argued that there are serious limitations with such studies. One possible confounding factor may be cultural choice; for instance, people might start to exploit a new species for reasons other than energy and nutrition. These may include shellfish, which are perhaps less easily procured or processed, but which are collected because of their taste and/or because they are hard to collect and so endow prestige on the gatherers and consumers. An example of this type of cultural choice, which goes against "common sense," is the fishing of the goose barnacles (*Policepes cornucopia*) in Portugal and Spain. Although they are considered a delicacy, the gathering of them is dangerous work involving climbing down treacherous cliffs or swimming from boats onto the rocks in order to do the collecting (Baptista 2001; *Times Online* 2008).

It has also been argued that environmental factors are far more likely to play a role in shellfish size change than human gathering. Claassen (1998:47–49) explores a number of environmental events that may impact natural populations, including predation by animals, negative environmental effects on spawning, larvae survival, juvenile survival and growth, increased sedimentation, changing water temperature, changing salinity, pollutants, and storms and hurricanes. It is also demonstrated that problems in sampling the data set may reveal changes, which are a product of statistical artifacts. Claassen (1998:51) calls for the consideration of multiple hypotheses for such observed trends and states that the assumption that decreasing shell size or numbers results from human exploitation is bad science.

Campbell (2008) has also suggested that the assumption that smaller average sizes equate to greater human exploitation is "simplistic," because the average size of a species of shellfish varies considerably across a shore and over time. This has been demonstrated in various studies, including ethnographic and ecological analyses of shellfish gathering by the people of Transkei (Lasiak 1992). Here, different zones were exploited, including an area where gathering had previously been prohibited and another that had long been exploited. The data on shellfish size varied between species and some shellfish from the long-exploited region were actually smaller than those from the area that had previously been inaccessible. However, it is important to note that the kinds of archaeological sequences that are studied are usually stratified and cover long periods of time. The importance of these sequences is that they are time-averaged and so tend to filter out short-term "noise" (Mannino and Thomas 2001:1110).

Although these criticisms have some validity, they appear to give preference to the environment over human impact. In fact, Campbell states that "When explaining changes over time in either natural or archaeological accumulations of shellfish, human exploitation must take its place behind climate change, natural predation, and catastrophic events (such as frosts, storms, disease, or apex predator loss)" (Campbell 2008:119). But, if animal predation on shellfish can cause negative effects, why should not human predation have similar effects in certain circumstances? After all, humans have produced huge mounds of shell all over the world, many of which contain thousands of millions of shells. In addition, there are further human actions that may have an effect on the landscape and in turn an indirect effect on the marine ecology. In a case study from Western Fiji (Morrison and Cochrane 2008), it is argued that variation in the Natia Beach shellfish assemblage cannot be explained solely through human predation, but that local natural and cultural landscape changes led to coastal progradation and substantial increase in terrestrial deposition, which adversely affected some species of shellfish.

Case Study

The shell middens, or Køkkenmøddinger, of Denmark are a special type of coastal settlement, where shell waste is a primary component. In among the shell there is also much cultural debris, including flint, bone, charcoal, pottery, hearths, fire-cracked stones, and sometimes features including pits, stake holes, and even graves or scattered human bone (Andersen 2000). The composition of the middens means that there is generally good preservation and the organics that survive, such as fish and animal bone, provide important information on subsistence and seasonality. The most well-known middens are the Late Mesolithic ones that belong to the Ertebølle culture and date to around 5400–3900 cal. BC. The Mesolithic–Neolithic transition occurs at around 3900 cal. BC with the introduction of new types of pottery (Funnel Beaker) and domesticated grain and animals. Many of the middens continue to accumulate for a couple of centuries into the Early Neolithic (3900–3700 cal. BC).

The exploitation of oysters from three sites—Havnø, Norsminde, and Krabbesholm—will be examined in detail in this section (figure 2.1). They are all shell middens that span the Late Mesolithic and Early Neolithic periods and have visible changes in stratigraphy at the transition from a predominance of oysters to cockles, as well as obvious changes in oyster size from very large oysters at the base to very small oysters within the Neolithic layers.

As well as using size data and species change in this analysis, it is also important to consider the age of the shells. Without age data it is much harder to say whether the size is declining or increasing because of human predation or a change in environment. Size, as has already been discussed, may vary due to location on the shore or fluctuations in the ambient environment in temperature or salinity, which may reduce or increase growth rates. Age is related to growth, and so a decline in size coupled with a decline in age suggests that a population is being intensively exploited (by humans or animals), thereby altering the age profile and reducing the average age.

Oysters grow incrementally, and through the study of modern controls,

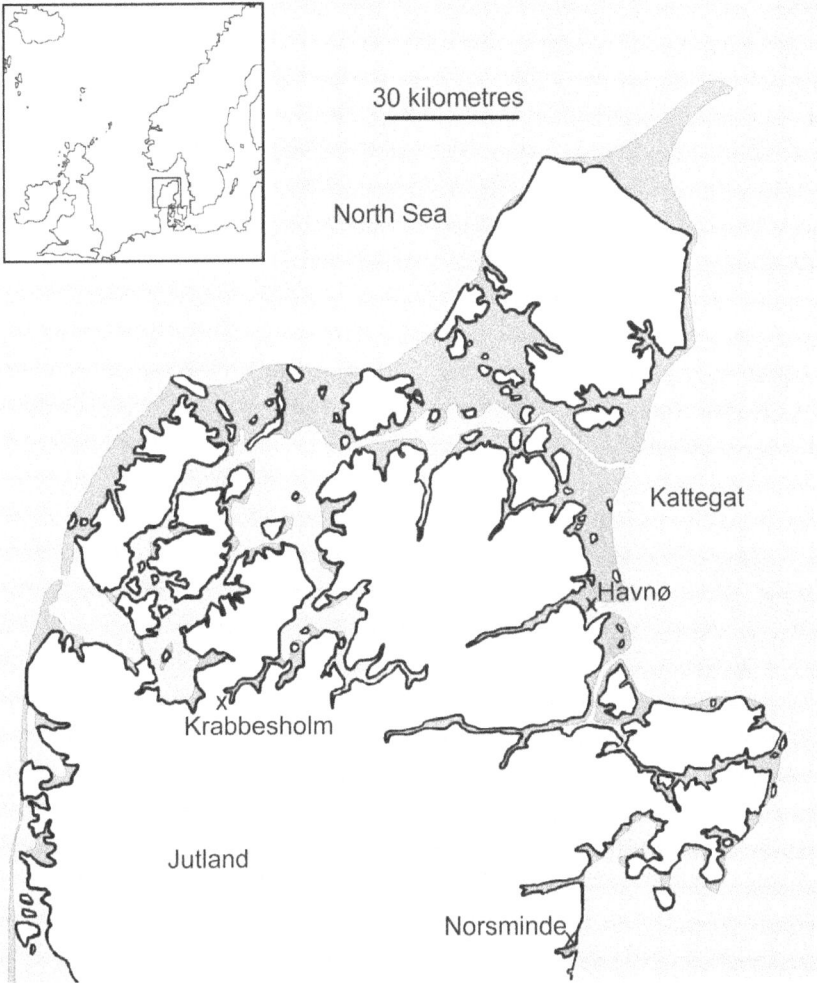

Figure 2.1. Map of Denmark with sites located.

it has been demonstrated that they form growth breaks, or lines, in the spring, around March–April, when temperatures begin to rise and growth resumes after the colder months of the winter (figure 2.2) (Milner 2002). Through thin sectioning of the oyster hinges, the growth structures can be examined in detail under the microscope.

The season in which oysters are harvested may also have an impact (Claassen 1998:49), so it is important to ascertain what time of the year people were collecting the shellfish in order to see whether a change in harvesting practice may have contributed to a change in population de-

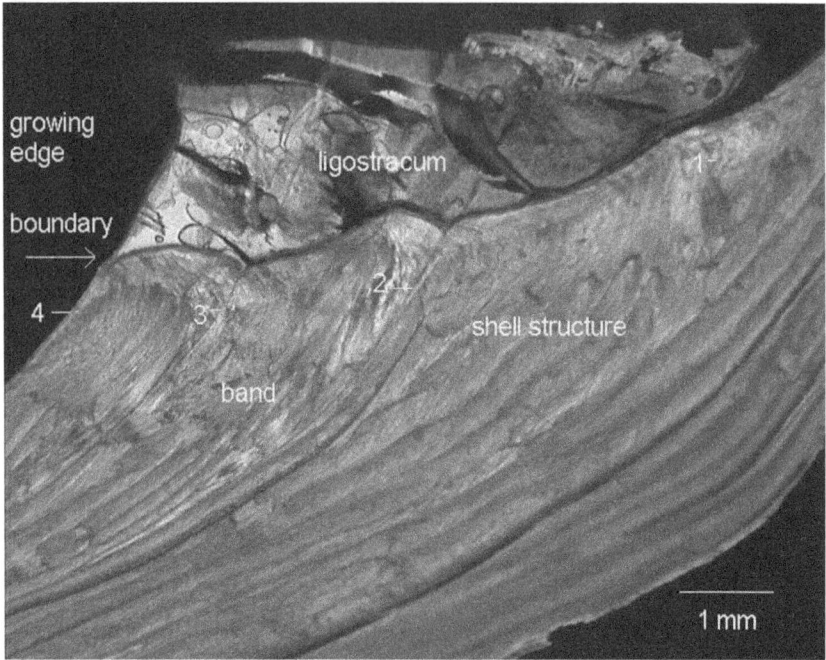

Figure 2.2. A thin section of an oyster from the modern control sample, collected in May. Four annual lines have been identified, with number 4 having just formed on the edge.

mographics. Seasonality in oysters is assessed by examining the amount of growth that has occurred since the last growth line. An oyster that has been gathered in May should have a very thin band of shell formed after the last line (see figure 2.2) (see Milner 2002 for further explanation).

It is important to state that, as with many other scientific analyses, there are some caveats. For instance, the oyster hinges are measured to provide size data because sometimes the shells have been broken, but the hinges may also have the tip missing or they may have grown on a skew. In as many cases as possible, only the best hinges have been measured. It is also worth noting that the oyster shell tends to be approximately 10 times the size of the hinge, so a measurement of 2 mm means the complete valve was about 2 cm in size. This is useful when considering the changes in the size of oysters from various parts of the midden stratigraphy.

The age of the oyster can be very hard to assess in older shells because growth slows significantly in old oysters and lines can occur close together, making them hard to count. In the past old oysters have not been sectioned because they are so large they are difficult to saw, as well as being hard to age. Unfortunately, this then skews the age data at the base of the middens (where oysters are largest) toward younger shells; this will be noted below. Because of slower growth, older oysters can also be harder to assess for season of death. Very young oysters are also harder to analyze for season of death, because if they are only one or two years old, there are no previous years of growth to compare back to. However, the ages and seasonal assessments are not made if there is any doubt about the structure, and blind testing and correspondence testing is carried out between two people in order to have confidence in the results.

Havnø Midden

Havnø is around 70 m long and c. 35 m wide with a shell depth of about 90 cm. In the Mesolithic period, it was located on an island at the mouth of the Mariager Fjord and would have been an excellent location for marine hunting, fishing, fowling, and shellfish gathering. The site was first investigated by the Second Kitchenmidden Committee in 1894 and the results were published by Madsen et al. in 1900. More recently, since 1995, the site has been excavated by Søren H. Andersen (figure 2.3) (Andersen 2008). Radiocarbon dating and dating through the presence of cultural artifacts demonstrates both a gradual and horizontal accumulation of shell midden

Figure 2.3. Excavations at Havnø (photo by the author 2009).

material with the C^{14} dates placing occupation between 4500 and 3800 cal. BC, i.e., spanning the transition from the Late Mesolithic to Early Neolithic. The midden appears to have accumulated fairly consistently, although at present it is not possible to be sure whether there was a hiatus.

A pilot assessment of oyster seasonality was undertaken in 1997 (Milner 2002) and the thin sections revealed clear growth structures that demonstrated the potential for further work. More recently, further samples were obtained in order to conduct a more fine-grained analysis of both size change and seasonality. Samples were taken from within three different levels of the midden. Layer 1 comes from near the top of the midden at the youngest level and is associated with the Early Neolithic. Layer 2 is located at the top of the Mesolithic layers and dates to the Late Mesolithic. Layer 3 is located at the oldest part of the midden at the base and is also Late Mesolithic in date.

The shells from this midden were exceptionally large compared to other shell middens previously analyzed. In addition, like other middens, it was very clear simply looking by eye at the oysters that they get smaller in size through the sequence from bottom to top. This can be demonstrated by measuring the hinge lengths of those shells that had been sampled for sectioning and is clearly shown in figure 2.4. Here, the average size of the largest oysters at the base of the midden is enormous, with many exceeding 15 cm in total length (15 mm along the hinge). This is explained by the ages, which at the base are as old as 15 years (figure 2.5), and some of the oysters look to have been even older—some of the particularly large ones were not collected because they are so hard to section and age. Oysters have been shown to reach a maximum age of 14 years from the analysis of growth lines in wild populations, with an average age range of two to six years (Richardson et al. 1993). Therefore, it is highly likely that the excavation has revealed a patch of oysters that represents a previously unexploited population.

Unfortunately, we do not know where on the shore oysters were collected for any of these sites. However, the European oyster (*Ostrea edulis*) is a sub-littoral species and the oyster beds may be partially exposed at low tides, but it has been demonstrated that growth ceases if they are exposed for more than 30 percent of the time (Walne 1958). This means that they may be harvested at low tide, but if the beds are constantly submerged, people wanting to exploit them may have had to gather them from shallow waters. This has important implications. Often it is assumed in shell-gathering studies that larger, older individuals are preferentially gathered, but in these circumstances a range of sizes may be removed. In the case of

Havnø, this appears to be true, and the hunter-gatherers who found this oyster bed appear to have picked out a wide range of sizes and ages (from four years to at least 15 years).

From the decrease in average size and age in Layer 2, it can be suggested that the oyster-gathering activities had an impact on the natural

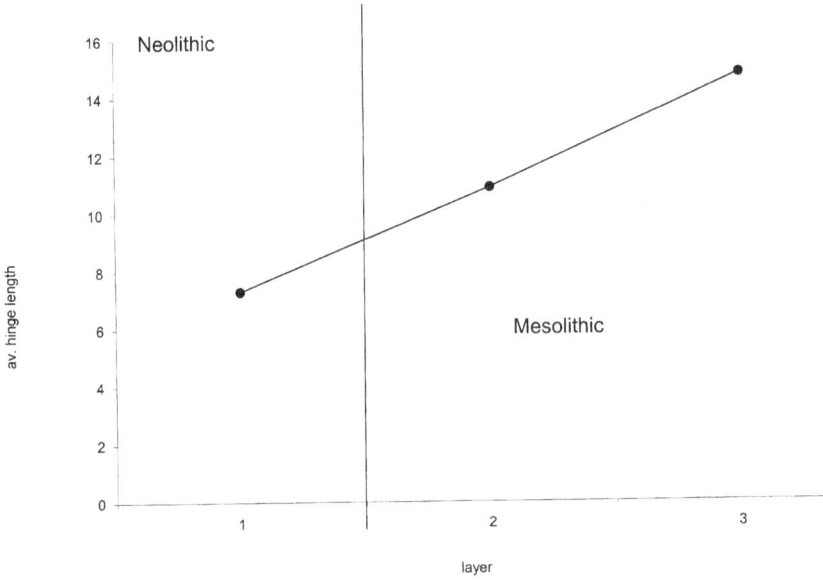

Figure 2.4. Average length of oyster hinge in millimeters.

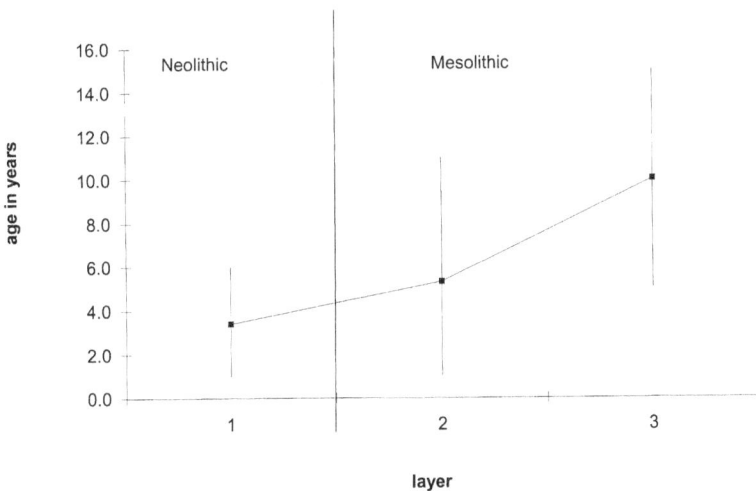

Figure 2.5. Average age in years of the oysters at Havnø from Layers 1–3 showing the average as the black square and the range of ages.

shell bed community. These measurements continue to decrease through time into the Neolithic in Layer 1, where the average age has reduced to 3.4 years. This is a major difference when compared with the average age of 10 years in Layer 3, and the age ranges between Layers 1 and 3 barely overlap.

In terms of seasonality information, the two Mesolithic layers are very similar to each other, with a predominance of spring gathering and a small amount of summer and autumn/winter gathering (figure 2.6). From the pattern within the shells there seem to be two distinct groupings: the shell patterns either show a line about to form or formed already (a clear signal of spring), or they appear to have produced a significant band since the last line, suggesting possibly a second season of gathering in the late summer/early autumn. The pattern from the Layer 1 shells is different, however. Although spring still seems to be the main season of gathering, it appears that oyster consumption continues through the year. Ideally, more oysters are needed from this layer in order to provide a stronger interpretation. Unfortunately, many shells in this sample were too weathered or broken to be sectioned because they came from the top of the midden. However, it can be argued that there is no strongly predominant season.

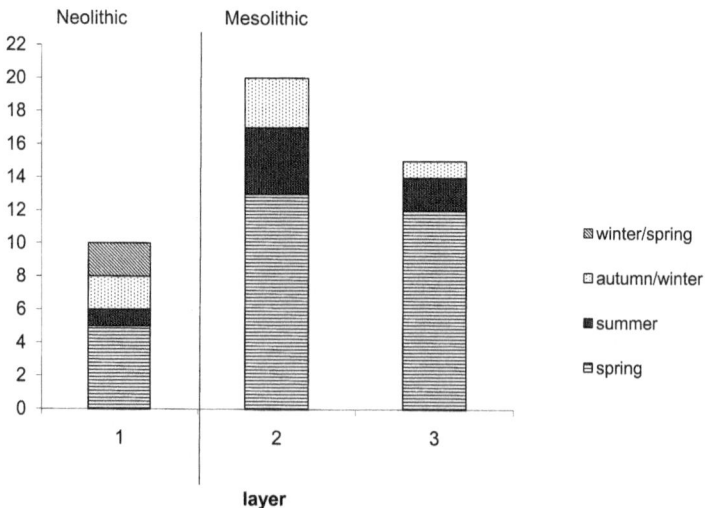

Figure 2.6. Seasonality results from Havnø. Sample size: Layer 1 (N=17), Layer 2 (N=19), and Layer 3 (N=14).

Norsminde Midden

Norsminde, in the Mesolithic period, would have been located at the mouth of an estuary. It was first discovered in 1972 and excavated from 1972–89 (Andersen 1989). The midden was oval in shape and extended about 30 m in length; it was between 5 and 12 m wide and as much as 1.5 m thick. The midden deposits appear to have been built up from west to east and then vertically at the east end. It is a stratified midden with Neolithic layers overlaying the Mesolithic layers. The layers have been dated using radiocarbon dating and analysis of the cultural material, such as flint tools and pottery types. The division between Mesolithic and Neolithic layers is clear, with a distinct change in shell composition from what appears visually to be an oyster-dominated Mesolithic midden and a cockle-dominated Neolithic midden with bands of charcoal and burnt stones (figure 2.7).

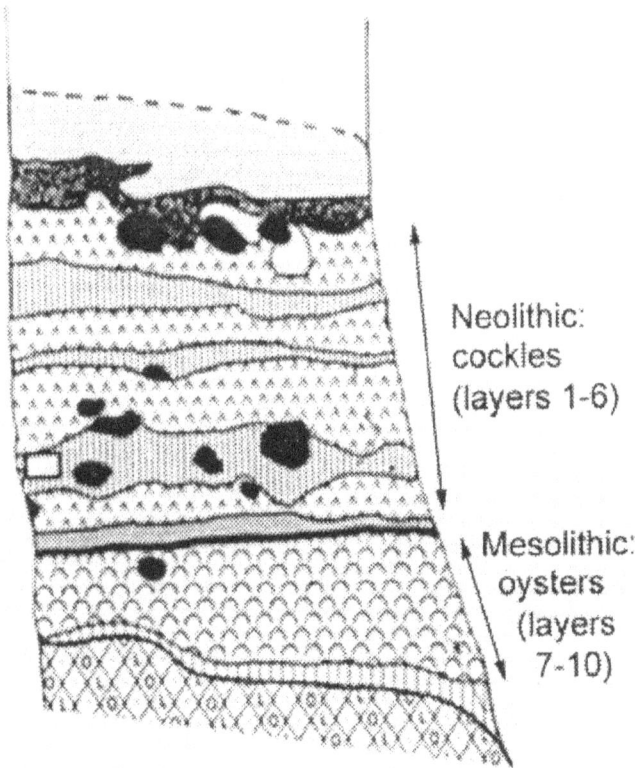

Neolithic:
cockles
(layers 1-6)

Mesolithic:
oysters
(layers
7-10)

Figure 2.7. Schematic representation of the Norsminde midden. Layer 10 is at the base of the midden and Layer 1 at the very top (adapted from Andersen 1989:18, figure 6).

In 1977 a cubic meter from the central part of the midden was excavated in 10 arbitrary spits, ca. 10 cm thick and referred to here as layers. The transition between Mesolithic and Neolithic layers occurred at the interface between Layers 7 and 6. It is thought that the Mesolithic midden and Neolithic midden represent roughly 200 years of accumulation each (Søren H. Andersen, personal communication 2000).

At Norsminde the oysters from each layer were sorted, and for the Mesolithic layers, between 105 and 111 oysters from each layer were measured, and for the Neolithic layers, between 29 and 52: this change in sample size is due to the smaller numbers of oysters in the Neolithic layers. On the whole, the shellfish were much larger in the Mesolithic layers compared to the Neolithic layers. The shells in Layer 10 were particularly large (figure 2.8). They then drop slightly in size during the rest of the Mesolithic period by an average of ca. 1 cm (1 mm in the hinge) before getting larger again in Layer 6 to match the size as those in Layer 10. There is then a steady drop in size during the Neolithic, until Layer 2, where they are more than 2 cm smaller, followed by a final increase in size in Layer 1.

This information can be interpreted in a number of different ways, and it is important to identify how this corresponds with the average age of the shells as well (figure 2.9). When the sizes are compared to the average age per layer, it can be observed that there is a correlation in pattern. However, it should be noted that only 100 oysters were aged from Norsminde com-

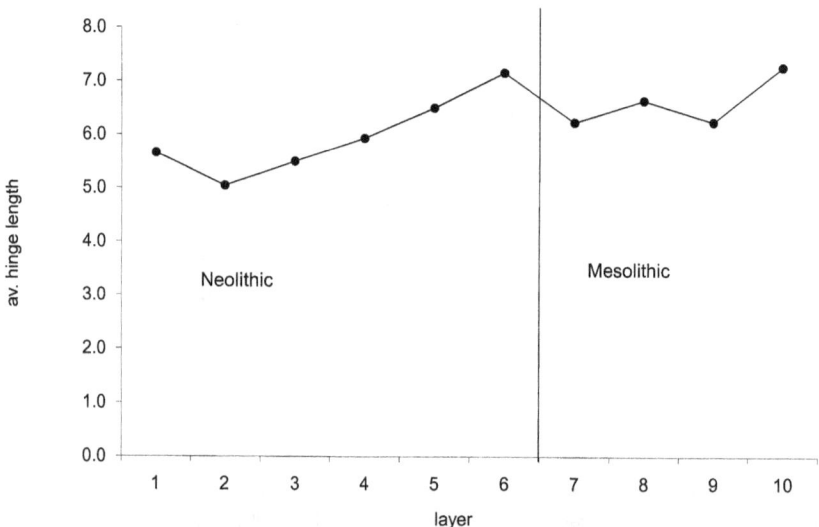

Figure 2.8. Size of oyster hinges from the Norsminde layers.

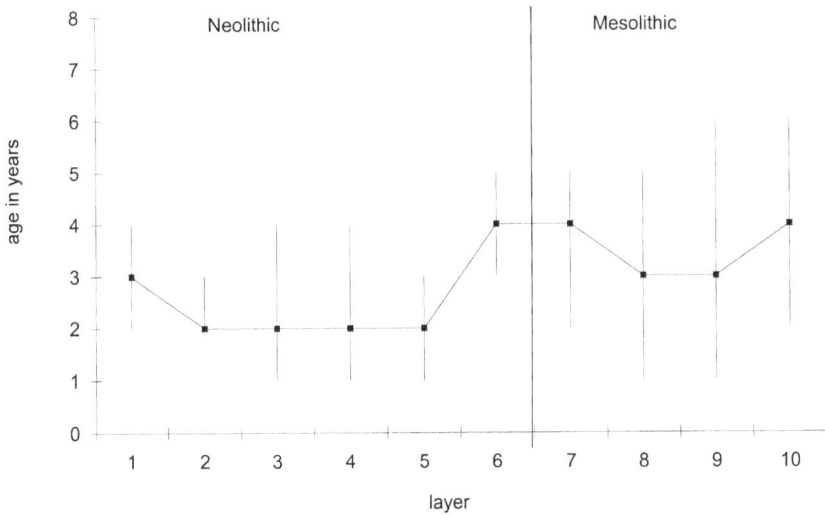

Figure 2.9. Age of oysters from the Norsminde layers.

pared with the 668 measured. The largest oysters were not sectioned because they are difficult to cut, and so the age in years for Layer 10 is probably not representative: from external analysis of some of the shells that were not sectioned, it is likely to be higher—perhaps an average of six years, with some outliers of possibly 10 years or even older. However, although similar to Havnø in that there are older and larger oysters at the base, the pattern is not the same, and these are not likely to be representative of a previously unexploited shell bed. It is possible that there is an earlier deposit elsewhere in the midden.

The oysters drop in size slightly in Layer 9 and then remain fairly constant through the rest of the Mesolithic layers, but the range of ages and the occurrence of older oysters decrease. There is a rise in average age in Layers 7 and 6, which mirrors the increase in average size, and perhaps this is indicative of a hiatus or reduction in gathering that allows the age profile to change.

There is a small rise in average age around the transition at Layers 6 and 7, but there is then a significant drop in average age at Layer 5 to two years. This drop in size through time in the Neolithic part of the midden correlates with a significant drop in age. However, analysis of the age plotted against the size, as shown in figure 2.10, also suggests some slight change in environment from the Mesolithic to Neolithic because some of the Neolithic oysters are slightly smaller than the Mesolithic oysters.

The seasonality of gathering was determined for both cockles and oysters at the site and these have been reported in more detail elsewhere (Mil-

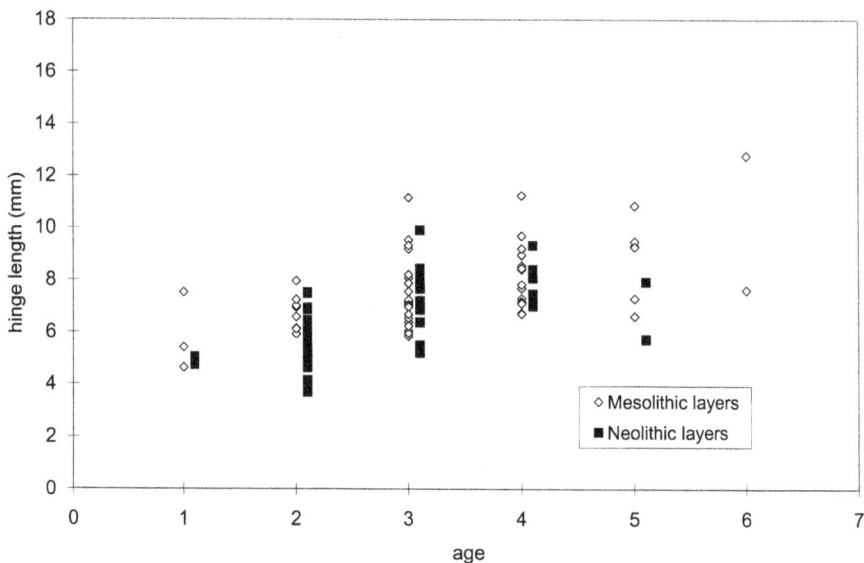

Figure 2.10. A plot to show the age of each oyster shell plotted against the hinge length in order to compare growth rates between the Mesolithic and Neolithic layers.

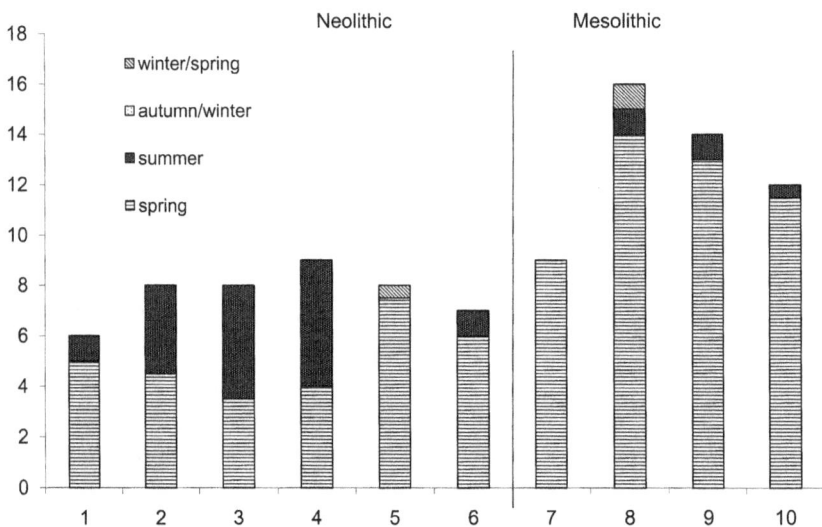

Figure 2.11. Graph to show the seasonality of oyster gathering at Norsminde in the Mesolithic and Neolithic periods. Sample size: Layer 1 (N=40), 2 (N=29), 3 (N=33), 4 (N=48), 5 (N=38), 6 (N=52), 7 (N=107), 8 (N=105), 9 (N=105), 10 (N=111).

ner and Laurie 2009). In summary, the oysters were mainly gathered in the spring in the Mesolithic and this continued into the Neolithic until Layer 4, when there was a shift to spring and summer gathering (figure 2.11).

Krabbesholm II Midden

The Krabbesholm site is located in the innermost part of the Limfjord. It contains two shell middens, known as Krabbesholm I and II, and these stretch along ca. 100 m of coastline. Krabbesholm I is the oldest registered midden in Denmark and it was excavated in 1889 by A. P. Madsen (Andersen 2005). In 2000, Søren H. Andersen started excavations across Krabbesholm II, and in 2004 a meter square column was excavated by the author through 17 layers, excavated by context; the divisions were determined by changes in the matrix, such as shell content, color, soil consistency, and inclusions (figure 2.12) (Laurie 2008). While the layers were being excavated, samples of oysters were extracted for seasonality analysis.

The dates for this midden run from the Late Mesolithic and into the Early Neolithic. This midden differs from the other two in that the Mesolithic oyster layer at the base is much thinner (Layer 16) and so only provides a snapshot of Mesolithic practices. Layer 15 appears to contain a mix of artifacts from both the Ertebølle culture and also the oldest Funnel Beaker culture. Layer 14 is a thin cleaning layer with few shells within it. The Neolithic layers extend over a longer period of time than the other middens: 3900–3700 cal. BC (for Layers 15–6) and 3600–3100 cal. BC (for Layers 5–2).

The oysters from the column sample were selected out for measuring and seasonality information. Although sample sizes from some of the layers are small, there is some patterning in size, with larger oysters being located at the base of the midden, a decline in size in Layers 13–10, and then a rise again until Layer 5 when there is a drop (figure 2.13). The age data to some extent mirror this pattern (figure 2.14). Certainly there is evidence of much older oysters at the base of the midden, as seen by the range of ages at this point with a maximum of 11 years, but like Norsminde, this is unlikely to represent the exploitation of a pristine natural oyster bed. After this point, no other oysters appear to reach this age again, although there may have been a reduction or hiatus in gathering around Layer 10–7, where the age range increases.

The seasonality data from Krabbesholm II reveals a fairly complicated picture (figure 2.15). It is highly likely that Layer 16 oysters were collected

Figure 2.12. Column excavation through the Krabbesholm II midden. Note the oysters at the base and the layers of mixed species above.

around the period in which line formation occurs, i.e., late winter/early spring. Some oysters have annual lines on their edges and some look like they are about to form: it is possible that there is a seasonal aspect to gathering in the Mesolithic around springtime. In the Early Neolithic layers

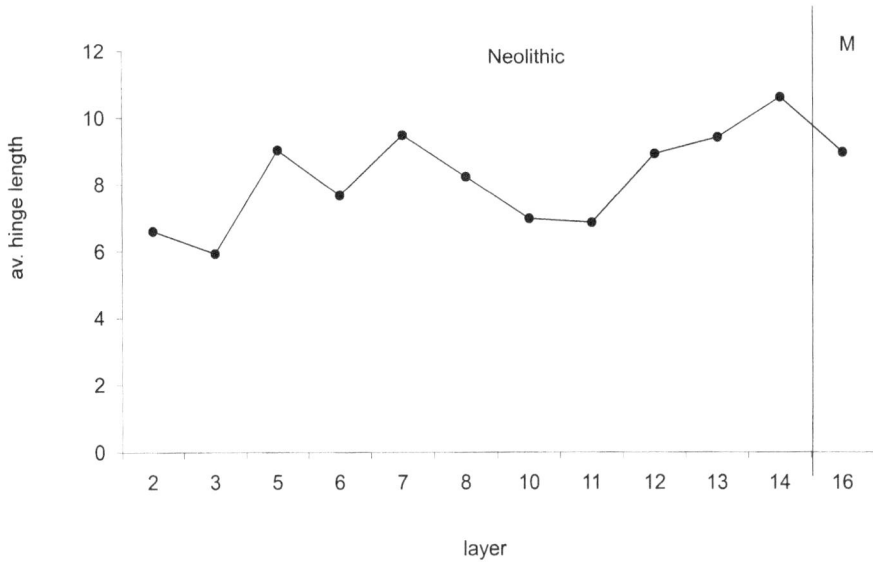

Figure 2.13. Diagram showing the average size of the oyster hinges. Layers with a sample size of fewer than five oysters have been excluded (4, 9, and 15) and Layer 1 is soil at the top of the midden.

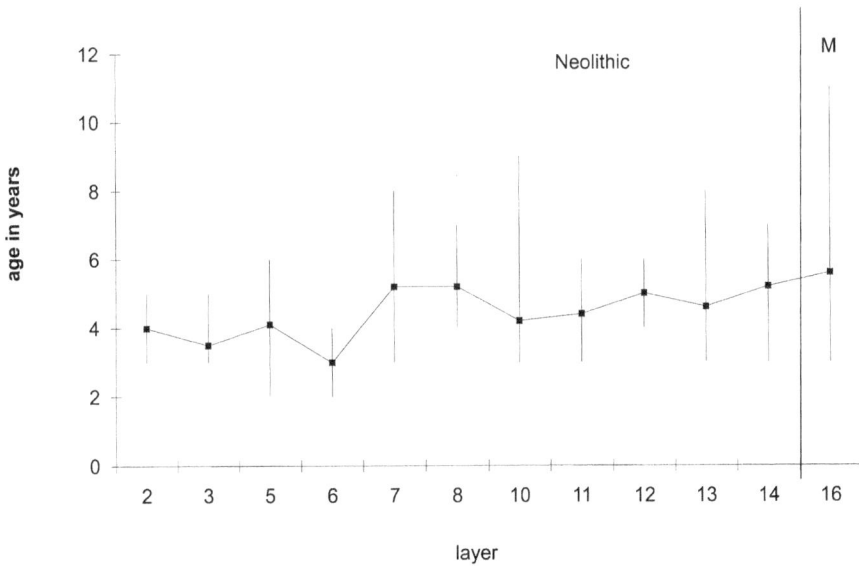

Figure 2.14. Plot to show the average age of oysters and range of ages per layer.

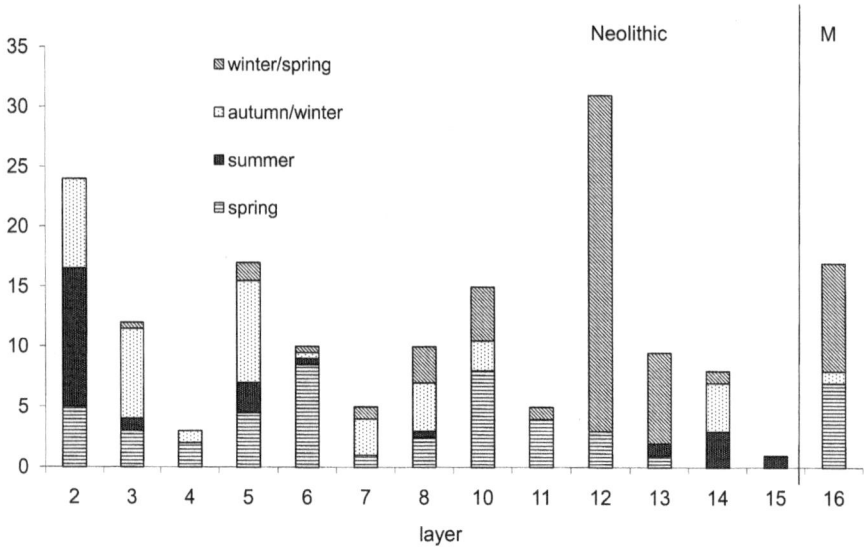

Figure 2.15. Seasonality data for the layers at Krabbesholm II. Sample size: Layer 2 (N=14), 3 (N=16), 4 (N=3), 5 (N=18), 6 (N=10), 7 (N=6), 8 (N=15), 10 (N=15), 11 (N=5), 12 (N=14), 13 (N=13), 14 (N=10), 16 (N=21).

(15–6), there appears to be a range of seasons of gathering and no consistent pattern. The later Funnel Beaker layers (5–2) demonstrate more patterning, but this is still through the seasons.

Summary

To summarize, the data on the oysters from Havnø suggest that human exploitation had an impact on the natural oyster bed, with the average age pushed down significantly over the centuries. In the Neolithic it is suggested that the season of gathering also changed, though due to the fairly coarse resolution of sampling at this site, it is unclear precisely when this may have happened. It is interesting to note that the oldest Mesolithic shells are likely to have come from a pristine bed.

At Norsminde and Krabbesholm there are also correlations between size and age, and in general an impact on the oyster beds with a lowering of average age. The lower levels do not contain shells that are as old as those at Havnø. At Norsminde there is perhaps a hiatus in the midden at around the time of the Mesolithic–Neolithic transition (and again in Layer 1) and probably some adverse change in the ambient environment in the Neolithic. The shift in the seasonality of gathering appears to occur well after the transition. At Krabbesholm there is not so much in the way of Mesolithic data, but there does seem to have been some impact on the natural oyster beds between the Mesolithic and Neolithic layers, with a significant reduction in older oysters. The seasonality information is complicated and hard to interpret without more Mesolithic samples, but there seems to be a strong seasonal spring signature in the Mesolithic with a variety of seasons in the Neolithic. There also seems to be the possibility of recovery events, perhaps related to hiatuses in gathering, in the Neolithic. Overall, there does not appear to be any clear pattern between the three sites, and like the examples of different sites in chapter 5 (Thompson et al. this volume), it is likely that each one has its own historical trajectory. It would appear that harvesting tends to occur frequently in the spring in the Mesolithic, though there is regional variation. It should also be noted that there is not necessarily a significant shift in seasonal exploitation at what is perceived to be the Mesolithic–Neolithic transition at every site; e.g., at Norsminde it seems to shift into a spring/summer harvest from Layer 4 (rather than Layer 6). At Havnø the resolution of the data is not good enough to be sure of the timing of a change, and further research is necessary. The high resolution of sampling at Krabbesholm demonstrates just how variable the results can be, and probably reflects the true complexity of gathering strategies.

It should also be noted that at all these sites, the number of gathered oysters declines in the Neolithic and cockle exploitation rises. In all likelihood this is a response to the smaller number of available oysters, but it is interesting that oysters still continue to be gathered despite the probable decrease in availability. However, at present, dating is too coarse to say whether the changes in shellfish gathering strategies, environmental events, and the oyster decline occurred slightly before or slightly after the cultural changes associated with the transition or whether this differed between sites.

Discussion

There appears to be clear evidence that human exploitation had some impact on the natural oyster beds. In all three case studies there is a significant decrease in size, which is accompanied by a decrease in age. Steady harvesting of an oyster bed will produce this pattern because the oysters are not given time to reach the older ages. However, the lowering of the average age has other potential impacts related to successful reproduction. Oysters usually start spawning during their first summer, and the age has a bearing on productivity: a one-year-old oyster will produce ca. 100,000 larvae; a two-year-old, 540,000 larvae; a three-year-old, 840,000 larvae; and, a four-year-old, 1,100,000 larvae (Walne 1974). Therefore, when the average age is pushed down from four years to two years, as it was at Norsminde, the average production of larvae is halved, which will theoretically reduce the overall size of the oyster beds by half (see Jerardino et al. 2008 for a similar example from South Africa).

The shift in seasonal gathering may also have an effect (Claassen 1998:49). In the United Kingdom, at present there is a national closed season (May 14–August 4) to protect oysters during the spawning period (Laing et al. 2006:285). The shift, therefore, to gathering more oysters in this period in the Neolithic at some of these sites may have had a further adverse effect on the population.

However, the picture is probably not that simple; environmental factors may also have had a part to play. There appears to have been rapid silting in the Early Neolithic from studies in Djursland due to changes in the tidal amplitude, though it is unclear whether this would have affected the entire Danish coastline (Petersen 1993). We should also consider whether silting may have occurred through some of the new farming practices on the land, which may have included clearance. There is evidence for a decline in elm and ivy pollen at this time, though whether this is due to climatic change, disease, foddering, or land clearance is debated (Dincauze 2000; Iversen 2002).

A recent example of a silting event occurred in January 1953 when exceptionally high tides in the south of the North Sea caused great floods in the Thames Estuary and Holland. Embankments were breached, and a combination of burial beneath silt and high levels of silt in the water led to an oyster mortality of up to 40 percent (Yonge 1960). It is possible that if silting did occur in the locations of the Danish shell middens, it may have significantly clogged up some of the oyster beds, thereby reducing the size of the natural population available for harvesting.

It is also thought that around the time of the Mesolithic–Neolithic transition, there was a reduction in salinity (Rowley-Conwy 1984). The oyster is very susceptible to changes in salinity and cannot tolerate salinities below 23 percent, although it needs to be even higher for spawning (Walne 1974). Although there is some evidence that salinity may have dropped to some degree, it is not clear to what extent this would have affected the oysters. As has been demonstrated, oysters continue to be gathered at all of these sites.

However, at Norsminde the annual growth rate may have slowed down (with evidence of smaller yearly growth bands). It should be noted that Norsminde is much farther south than the other middens and may have been more affected than the sites in the north, which are located nearer to the entrance to the Kattegat, where the salty waters enter from the North Sea.

Conclusions

There is strong evidence from the age/size data that human exploitation did have a significant impact on the oyster beds. The average age is reduced through time, and this in all likelihood had an effect on larvae production, thereby causing a decrease in size of the oyster beds. Seasonal gathering practices are slightly different between sites, but they all appear to change at, or after, the Mesolithic–Neolithic transition. Other environmental factors also come into play, and there may have been rapid silting at the transition, which may have clogged up beds and reduced them further; plus, there may have been a reduction in salinity which may be the reason for the decrease in growth rates at Norsminde.

What is also noteworthy, however, is that oysters continue to be exploited at these sites, and they do not become locally extinct. And there are a couple of periods at Norsminde and Krabbesholm where potentially there may have been a hiatus, which allowed the oyster population to recover slightly.

In conclusion, the issue of detecting human impact on the natural oyster beds is reliant on age as well as size data, but the overall study of changing size/age is also inextricably linked to changing environmental parameters. The human element cannot be divorced from the environment. Humans were part of the environment, acting directly and indirectly upon it, as well as responding to it.

Relevance to the Past and the Present

Gathering oysters, and the potential impact this may have, is an issue that is relevant in the present. Oysters used to be prevalent around the British Isles in the nineteenth and early twentieth centuries, with a boom about the 1850s. However, there was a precipitous fall between 1850 and 1880. Five hundred million oysters were sold through Billingsgate market in 1850 compared to only 40 million in 1886 (Nield 1995:55). During the twentieth century, the production and consumption reduced even further due to a number of factors, including new predators, such as the slipper limpet (*Crepidula fornicata*), brought in with American oysters, which were imported and re-laid in British waters. There was also a great mortality of oysters in the early 1920s, which is thought to be the result of an unidentified malady (Orton 1937). In addition, there were a number of extremely cold winters: 1939–40, 1946–47, and 1962–63. The extreme cold can have detrimental effects: the oysters can freeze, or due to rapid thawing of snow, estuaries can become inundated with fresh water, dramatically lowering the salinity. The worst event was in 1962–63 and it destroyed 95 percent of the stock that was to be marketed (Nield 1995: 140). But overfishing pressures are also seen as one of the major contributing factors because harvest probably exceeded biological production for much of the recorded history of exploitation (Laing et al. 2006). Native oysters in the United Kingdom have now declined to such an extent that they are the subject of a Species Action Plan as part of the government's commitment to the International Convention on Biodiversity (Laing et al. 2006).

In Scotland, native oysters are now absent from areas that previously had fisheries and mainly occur in small, isolated populations in west coast sea lochs. The major contemporary threat is understood to be unauthorized gathering (Donnan 2003). In many areas the right to gather oysters belongs solely to the Crown, but in some areas the right has been obtained by permit by individuals or institutions. As part of the reform of landownership the Scottish Law Commission has suggested that gathering shellfish from the foreshore and seabeds should be a public statutory right, but it is argued that if this is the case the native oyster populations may become eradicated by uncontrolled gathering (Smith et al. 2006).

The same issue has arisen in Strangford Lough in Northern Ireland. This area also suffered from a major decline in oysters, but new beds of oysters (probably due to the spawning of high-density commercial oysters) were observed in the 1990s and detailed annual surveys were made between 2002 and 2007. It is argued that unregulated harvesting was observed at a number of these sites and that this has posed a major threat to the stocks (Smyth et al. 2009). The population structures were examined, and oyster sizes measured revealing gradual increases in the proportion of smaller oysters and concomitant decreases in the proportion of larger individuals between 2002 and 2005. These changes are attributed to reproduction, local environmental conditions, such as heavy frosts in 2004 and siltation, and unregulated harvesting.

These examples demonstrate that concerns regarding the impacts of oyster gathering are being faced in the present, but can archaeological case studies provide any new perspectives? Oyster beds have been massively depleted over the last 150 years in Europe due to a variety of reasons, both environmental and human impact in nature. Arguably, modern overexploitation has little parallel with gathering by hunter-gatherer groups who did not have dredgers and a large commercial market. Claassen (1998) and Campbell (2008) would probably agree with this view, having suggested that human harvesting is unlikely to be responsible for declining shellfish populations. Claassen (1998:51) has stated that this view can potentially result in unfortunate public policy: "Closing shellfish beds near villages means that people are denied a free foodstuff and that traditional practices are branded illogical, environmentally unsound," which has substantial economic impacts.

However, it has been demonstrated in this chapter that the past can show us that even gathering by hunter-gatherers (which occurs on a much smaller scale than in the modern commercial world) can have a negative impact on oyster beds, especially if this is combined with negative environmental effects. This kind of exploitation is more likely to be on the kind of scale witnessed today in the west coast of Scotland and Strangford Lough. We also know from the past that this level of gathering is unlikely to wipe out the oysters completely, but nevertheless, in areas where the authorities are attempting to conserve oysters, human exploitation may well have a negative impact.

The key issue is that every situation is different, wherever the study is located and whatever the species of shellfish. There are many factors to be taken into account, including changing environmental parameters, size of the natural shellfish bed, shellfish recruitment rates, and the nature and extent of human gathering. The study of human impact on shell beds, past and present, should involve a detailed examination of as many of these issues as possible before conclusions are drawn. This is particularly important in the present because uninformed decisions may have a serious effect on the natural shellfish population.

Acknowledgments

I would like to thank Professor Søren H. Andersen for providing access to the middens and oysters and for all his support and advice. I am also grateful to Eva Laurie and Harry Robson for technical assistance, and Geoff Bailey, Jonathan Finch, Paul Lane, Terry O'Connor and Kevin Walsh for reading and commenting on earlier versions of this paper. The research for this project has been funded by AHRB grant (B/RG/AN1717/APN14658).

3

Hunter-Gatherers, Endemic Island Mammals, and the Historical Ecology of California's Channel Islands

TORBEN C. RICK

> The peculiar assemblage of land vertebrates presently on the islands thus might well be viewed as not just a random assortment when compared to the mainland fauna. Those animals are, for the most part, the sorts of animals one might associate with an Indian culture or which could have rafted to the islands.
>
> Adrian M. Wenner and Donald L. Johnson,
> "Land Vertebrates on the California Channel Islands: Sweepstakes or Bridges?"

Historical ecology has emerged as an important transdisciplinary approach for investigating the influence of ancient peoples and natural climatic changes on ecosystems and organisms over long time scales (e.g., centuries, millennia, or more) (Balée 1998, 2006; Balée and Erickson 2006; Crumley 1994a; Egan and Howell 2001; Rick and Erlandson 2008; Thompson, this volume). Integrating archaeology, ecology, paleobiology, and other disciplines, historical ecology provides context and background for understanding the structure, management, and restoration of contemporary ecosystems (see Braje 2010; Egan and Howell 2001; Jackson et al. 2001; Lyman 2006; Rick and Erlandson 2008). One of the strengths of historical ecological data is that they inform the long-term evolutionary and ecological history of plants and animals, helping discern the species that are endemic (native) to a particular region and showing how these populations have responded to climatic and anthropogenic changes in deep time.

The ancient environmental reconstructions provided by historical ecology enhance knowledge of a range of issues, including the impact of non-native species on contemporary ecosystems. Invasive non-native species are one of the great threats to contemporary ecosystems around the world, transforming our planet and requiring countless dollars for remediation, monitoring, prevention, and eradication (Davis 2009). Archaeological and paleoecological data have shown that some of the problems of invasive species seen in contemporary ecosystems have their roots deep in the human past (see Grayson 2001). Research in Melanesia has demonstrated that human-assisted introduction of mammals (e.g., the northern cuscus [*Phalanger orientalis*]) may extend back some 20,000 years (White 2004). Islands in the Mediterranean (Zeder 2008), North Atlantic (McGovern et al. 2008), and Pacific (Anderson 2009; Kirch 1997, 2004; Matisoo-Smith 2009) have had their ancient and modern landscapes fundamentally altered and transformed by the introduction of non-native animals and plants. These translocations often involve domestic species (e.g., dogs, chickens, and pigs), but there are also a number of wild species that have been translocated in prehistory (Grayson 2001; White 2004). While not all prehistoric faunal introductions to islands can be classified as "invasive" (see Davis 2009 for a definition), some can and have had a significant effect on ancient and modern environments.

Because islands are circumscribed and often separated by large water gaps, they are among the best places to evaluate the effects of non-native species and the role of humans in translocating animals (and plants) in ancient times. Islands often contain fragile ecosystems, with endemic flora and fauna losing some of their defensive capabilities, making them more susceptible to the effects of newly introduced animals and plants. The growing evidence for ancient animal and plant translocations to islands challenges us to critically examine the influence of ancient peoples on past and present ecosystems.

In this chapter, I provide an overview and analysis of the origins of the endemic mammals on California's Channel Islands, including several species that are the subject of ongoing management and conservation efforts (figure 3.1). The islands have been separated from the mainland throughout the Quaternary and have a diminished terrestrial vertebrate fauna, with extant endemic mammals limited to a small fox, a skunk, a deer mouse, a harvest mouse, a ground squirrel, and a shrew (species names are given below). Savage (1967), von Bloecker (1967), Wenner and Johnson (1980), and Johnson (1983) summarized the evidence for how some of the mammals and reptiles/amphibians may have colonized the Channel Islands, with some appearing to arrive naturally and others coming via human-assisted introduction. Here I update what we have learned in the last 25 years, test-

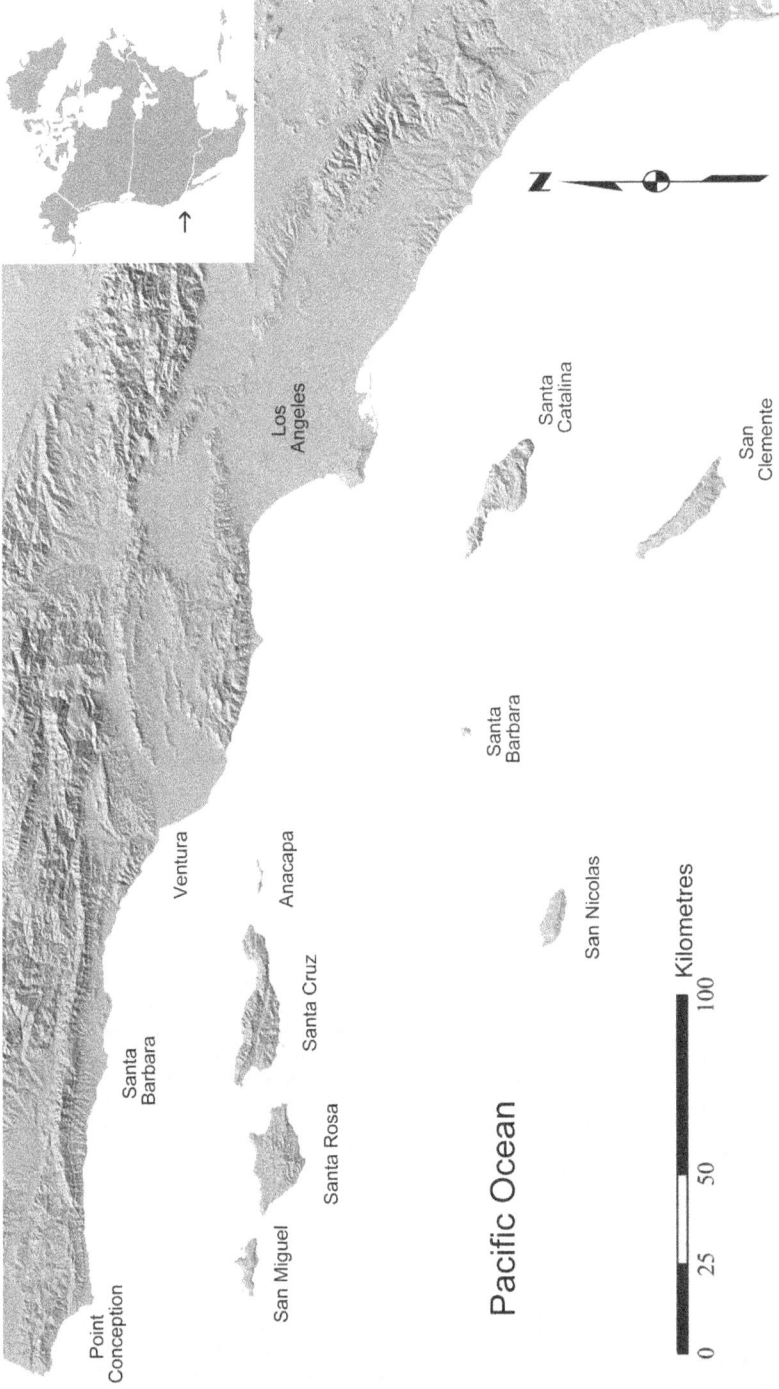

Figure 3.1. Location of the Channel Islands and Southern California coast.

ing the hypothesis that several of the island's "endemic" mammals were introduced by Native Americans, who played a significant role in shaping Channel Island ecosystems during the Holocene (Braje 2010; Erlandson and Rick 2010; Rick et al. 2008, 2009).

Background and Context

California's eight Channel Islands are located between Point Conception and San Diego off the Southern California coast. Divided into northern (Anacapa, Santa Cruz, Santa Rosa, and San Miguel) and southern (San Clemente, Santa Catalina, San Nicolas, and Santa Barbara) groups, the islands have never been connected to the mainland during the Quaternary (Johnson 1983; Kennett et al. 2008). They are currently between 20 and 98 km offshore and range in size from about 2.6 to 249 km² (table 3.1). During glacial periods of the Pleistocene, when sea levels were considerably lower than today, all of the islands were larger in size, and the four northern islands coalesced into one large superisland (Santarosae), which was only 7–8 km away from the mainland at its eastern end (Kennett et al. 2008). Recent reconstructions suggest that Anacapa separated from Santarosae

Table 3.1. General attributes of the Channel Islands and extant endemic terrestrial mammals

Island	Area (km²)	Max elevation (m)	Distance from mainland km)	Endemic mammals (extant species only)
NORTHERN ISLANDS				
Anacapa	2.9	283	20	Island deer mouse
Santa Cruz	249	753	30	Island fox, island skunk, harvest mouse, island deer mouse
Santa Rosa	217	484	44	Island fox, island skunk, island deer mouse
San Miguel	37	253	42	Island fox, island deer mouse
SOUTHERN ISLANDS				
Santa Barbara	2.6	149	61	Island deer mouse
Santa Catalina	194	648	32	Island fox, Catalina Island ground squirrel, harvest mouse, island deer mouse, ornate shrew
San Nicolas	58	277	98	Island fox, island deer mouse
San Clemente	145	599	79	Island fox, island deer mouse

Note: See Schoenherr et al. (1999). Does not include bats.

around 10,900 cal BP, Santa Cruz around 9300 cal BP, and Santa Rosa and San Miguel separated from one another around 9000 cal BP (Kennett et al. 2008:2532). The southern islands were more dispersed, remained farther from the mainland, and were never connected to one another during glacial periods of the Pleistocene.

All of the islands have a relatively mild, Mediterranean climate. Summers are generally warm and dry, while winters are cooler and wetter. Rainfall averages about 356 mm on the islands, with most of it falling during the winter and spring. The area is characterized by strong winds and foggy conditions, but there is considerable variability between islands and even locations on individual islands. El Niño, La Niña, droughts, and other climatic patterns are common in the region. Local marine environments are very productive, with rich shellfish, finfish, marine mammal, and seabird populations found throughout the islands.

Due to their relative isolation, the Channel Islands contain unique terrestrial ecosystems that are diminished when compared to the adjacent mainland (Johnson 1983; Schoenherr et al. 1999). Oak and other woodlands, for example, are confined primarily to the larger and more topographically diverse islands (i.e., Santa Cruz, Santa Rosa, and Santa Catalina). Terrestrial mammals, reptiles, and amphibians are also greatly reduced, consisting of a fraction of the animals found on the mainland (see Johnson 1983; Savage 1967; Schoenherr et al. 1999; Wenner and Johnson 1980). Endemic mammals on the islands include the island fox (*Urocyon littoralis*), island spotted skunk (*Spilogale gracilis amphiala*), Catalina Island ground squirrel (*Otospermophilus beecheyi nesioticus*), deer mice (extant and extinct forms; *Peromysucs maniculatus* and *P. nesodytes*), harvest mouse (*Reithrodontomys megalotis;* but see Collins and George 1990), ornate shrew (extinct and extant forms; *Sorex ornatus*), San Miguel Island vole (extinct; *Microtus miguelensis*), and Columbian and pygmy mammoths (extinct; *Mammuthus columbi* and *M. exilis*). Conspicuously absent until historical times are the large deer, lagomorphs (rabbits and hares), and carnivores found on the mainland. The reptile and amphibian fauna are slightly more diverse, with lizards, snakes, salamanders, etc. found around the islands (Savage 1967; Schoenherr et al. 1999).

This diminished fauna helped confirm that the islands had long been separated from the mainland by a water gap, which has prompted investigations into how and when these animals colonized the Channel Islands (Agenbroad 2002a; Collins 1991a, 1991b; Collins and George 1990; Johnson

1983; Rick et al. 2009; Vellanoweth 1998; Wenner and Johnson 1980). For several of the animals, there is no consensus on how they first reached the islands, with the possibility of human-assisted, natural, or combined dispersal. Part of the problem lies in the fact that the fossil and archaeological records for the various species are fragmentary or nonexistent and have not been adequately synthesized or analyzed. Once land bridges connecting the mainland and islands had been ruled out, many early studies argued that most animals reached the islands naturally via debris rafts in a sweepstakes colonization (see Savage 1967; Schoenherr et al. 1999). Such overwater sweepstakes colonization is a dispersal mechanism posited for other areas around the world, with survival rates dependent on currents, time at sea, and other variables (Ali and Huber 2010; Johnson 1983; Wenner and Johnson 1980). Scholars have also noted the role that Native Americans may have played in bringing many of the mammals and some of the reptiles/amphibians to the islands (Collins 1991a, 1991b; Collins and George 1990; Johnson 1983; Rick et al. 2009; Vellanoweth 1998; Walker 1980; Wenner and Johnson 1980). Genetic analysis of Channel Island fauna is greatly improving our understanding of the diversity and affinities of island mammals (Aguilar et al. 2004; Ashley and Wills 1987; Floyd et al. 2011; Gill 1980; Maldonado et al. 2001; Pergams and Ashley 2002; Wayne et al. 1991a, 1991b), but these data are often not well integrated with archaeological or paleontological studies.

Chumash and Tongva (Gabrielino) peoples, who occupied the northern and southern Channel Islands, respectively, at the time of European contact, were densely populated and complex hunter-gatherers whose predecessors occupied the islands for at least the last 13,000 (northern islands) to 9,500 (southern islands) calendar years (see Erlandson et al. 2011; Johnson et al. 2002; Kennett 2005; Rick et al. 2005). Maritime voyaging is known to extend back to the earliest island colonists (Erlandson et al. 2007, 2011; Kennett 2005; Rick et al. 2005), and Late Holocene Chumash and Tongva peoples used plank canoes (*tomols* or *t'iats*), sophisticated and seaworthy boats, that transported people and a variety of goods (beads, food, dogs, etc.) in an exchange network between the islands and mainland (Arnold 1992; Gamble 2002). Given the maritime capabilities and exchange networks of the Chumash, augmented by recent confirmation of ancient animal translocations to other islands around the world (Grayson 2001), the time is right for an updated and expanded synthesis and analysis of the origins of the endemic Channel Island mammals and the influence of ancient peoples on island ecosystems.

Channel Island Endemic Mammals

Island fox (Urocyon littoralis)

The island fox is a roughly house-cat-sized diminutive relative of the gray fox (*U. cinereoargenteus*). They are found on six of the eight Channel Islands, absent only from the small islands of Anacapa and Santa Barbara. Island foxes were pushed to the brink of extinction on some of the islands and have been part of an extensive captive breeding and release program (Coonan et al. 2002, 2005, 2010). As the largest terrestrial carnivore on the islands, they are an important predator that hunts mice, reptiles, and amphibians, and eats a variety of insects, fruits, and carrion (Collins 1980; Moore and Collins 1995). Island foxes are generally docile, easily tamed, and show a lack of fear of humans (Collins 1991a, 1991b; Moore and Collins 1995).

Based partly on a few bones of an island fox found in a reportedly 16,000- to 10,000-year-old geologic context on Santa Rosa Island (Orr 1968), most researchers suggested that the island fox was a descendant of perhaps a single pregnant fox that reached the northern islands naturally via a debris raft, probably during the last glacial period when the northern islands were connected to each other and sea levels were lower (Collins 1991a, 1991b, 1993; Johnson 1983; Wenner and Johnson 1980). In this scenario, the island fox was thought to dwarf into the present-day species over an approximately 10,000-year period (Collins 1991b, 1993). Most researchers agree that Native Americans later intentionally transported the island fox to the southern islands (Collins 1991a, 1991b; Johnson 1975; Vellanoweth 1998). Vellanoweth (1998:105; see also Agenbroad (2002a:4) raised the possibility that Native Americans introduced the fox to all the islands—a proposition that was tested by direct AMS ^{14}C dating of the Santa Rosa "fossil" fox (Shelley 2001). Shelley (2001) presented a direct AMS date on the "fossil" island fox bones from Santa Rosa, noting that they were only 1,200 years old—considerably younger than the 13,000-year colonization of the islands by humans.

Despite this re-dating, a few island fox bones from San Miguel Island were found on the surface of fossil localities that were some 40,000 to 20,000 years old (Guthrie 1993). These remains consisted of nine bones from the surface of three fossil localities all representing a single individual at each locality. Rick et al. (2009) reported AMS dates from bones at each of the localities, finding that, like the Santa Rosa specimen, they were all Holocene in age with two between about 900 years old and the

Historic period and one being the oldest securely dated island fox remains at about 6,400 cal BP. Beyond these specimens, there is no pre-Holocene fossil or subfossil record of island or full-sized gray foxes on the Channel Islands, despite a number of paleontological research projects. Moreover, several island fossil localities are thought to be ancient eagle nests (Guthrie 2005), with at least one historic nest known to contain island fox remains (Collins et al. 2005). Consequently, the lack of prehuman-era fox bones is not just an issue of the agent of accumulation, but suggests that foxes may not have been present until the Holocene, after people had arrived.

Some 41 archaeological sites contain the remains of island foxes (table 3.2). Many of these are from multicomponent sites, and because of a lack of direct radiocarbon dates it is unclear precisely how old some of these foxes are. Collins (1991a, 1993) argued that on the northern Channel Islands foxes occurred in the oldest known archaeological deposits and throughout the Holocene. In the last 10 years, the chronology of human occupation on the Channel Islands has been pushed back to roughly 13,000 cal BP. Despite systematic research in numerous sites dating to between 8,000 to 13,000 years ago (Erlandson et al. 2007, 2011; Johnson et al. 2002), none of these earliest sites have produced fox remains. It remains possible that these earliest peoples did not exploit foxes, or, as Rick et al. (2009) suggested, that foxes did not appear until the Holocene.

Morphometric and genetic analyses of island foxes and mainland foxes also inform the origins and evolution of the species (Aguilar et al. 2004; Collins 1991a, 1991b, 1993; Goldstein et al. 1999; Wayne et al. 1991a, 1991b). Island foxes are morphometrically and genetically similar to gray foxes on the California mainland, but they are about 12–18 percent smaller than their mainland counterparts and have significant mainland-island and island-island variation that help uphold their taxonomic status (Collins 1993; Wayne et al. 1991a). Island foxes are morphologically distinct, but there are similarities between the island fox and the California mainland gray fox, with the tightest correlation being to foxes in central and northern California (Collins 1993:375). Morphometric and genetic analyses support the movement of island foxes from the northern Channel Islands to the southern Channel Islands by Native Americans, and possibly suggest some movement between individual islands in the northern chain by Native Americans (Collins 1993:372, 382; Wayne et al. 1991a:1864). This movement between the northern islands and between the northern and southern islands raises the possibility that Native Americans helped maintain gene flow between prehistoric island foxes (see Collins 1993:372; Vellanoweth 1998), though genetic data are needed to test this proposition. The genetic data are based on modern foxes, which suggest that each island population is a separate genetic entity (Wayne et al. 1991b). However, Vellanoweth (1998) noted that these modern foxes had probably experienced more isolation than their prehistoric ancestors because Native Americans had been absent since at least the early nineteenth century. The morphometric and genetic studies were conducted prior to the re-dating of the "fossil" foxes and all speculated on a Late Pleistocene natural rafting event for the origin of foxes on the northern Channel Islands. Wayne et al.'s (1991a:1862–63) genetic distance data leave questions about the scheme of island colonization, but they argue that island foxes colonized the northern islands before 16,000 years ago. The northern population is thought to have then colonized the southern islands, with foxes moved between the various islands.

Rick et al. (2009) recently argued that multiple lines of data support the hypothesis that humans introduced foxes to all the Channel Islands, though they are cautious in this determination. Ultimately, they cite several reasons why foxes may have been introduced by humans to the islands: (1) They are absent in the pre-Holocene fossil/subfossil record but common in archaeological sites (table 3.2); (2) There are Pleistocene–age ground-nesting colonies of flightless geese (*Chendytes lawi*), puffins (*Fratercula dowi*), and Ancient Murrelets (*Synthliboramphus antiquus*) that would have been highly susceptible to fox predation and appear to be absent after the Pleistocene (see Guthrie 1993; Guthrie et al. 2002; Rick et al. 2009); (3) Humans revered island foxes; they used their pelts, intentionally buried them, and moved them between islands (Collins 1991a, 1991b); and (4) Dwarfing may have been a result of a small founder population, possibly from human-selected breeding, and can occur relatively rapidly (i.e., less than 6,000 years; see Rick et al. 2009:97). The precise origin, timing, and mechanism of initial fox colonization of the Channel Islands is still in question, especially since no full-sized or intermediate foxes have been found. However, Native Americans moved foxes between islands prehistorically, possibly helping maintain gene flow in prehistoric populations (see Collins 1993; Vellanoweth 1998).

Table 3.2. Island fox remains in Channel Islands archaeological and paleontological sites

Site or locality[a]	Age (cal. yr. BP)	NISP	MNI	References
ARCHAEOLOGICAL SPECIMENS				
SMI-1	7140–3250	2	1	Collins 1991a
SMI-87	4790–2340	1	1	Rick et al. 2009
SMI-261	11,600–11,640	13	1	Collins 1991a
SMI-470	460-Historic	1	1	Rick et al. 2009
SMI-481	1410–920	n/a	1	Rick et al. 2009
SMI-525	3230–520	1	1	Collins 1991a
SMI-603	4570–4260	1	1	Rick et al. 2009
SRI-1	9260–2110	9	6	Collins 1991a
SRI-2	2030-Historic	>16	9	Collins 1991a, 1991b
SRI-3	8300–2360	3	2	Collins 1991a
SRI-4	7410–2130	1	1	Collins 1991a
SRI-25	n/a	2	1	Shelley 2001
SRI-41	5470–3630	2	1	Collins 1991a
SRI-365	n/a	n/a	1	Rick et al. 2009
SCRI-122	Late Holocene	2	2	Collins 1991a
SCRI-131	Late Holocene	2	2	Collins 1991a
SCRI-147	Late Holocene	>18	5	Collins 1991a
SCRI-206	n/a	1	1	Collins 1991a
SCRI-236 (aka SCRI-83)	Late Holocene	7	6	Collins 1991a
SCRI-240	Historic	5	n/a	Noah 2005
SCRI-306	670–410	n/a	n/a	Arnold 1987
SCRI-328/330	Historic	9	n/a	Noah 2005
SCRI-333 (aka SCRI-3)	6170–1260	>45	13	Collins 1991a
SCRI-474 (aka SCRI-100)	Late Holocene	>46	11	Collins 1991a
SNI-7	n/a	n/a	20	Collins 1991a, 1991b
SNI-11	5890–5660[b], 3840–510	>5	2	Collins 1991a
SNI-25	740-Historic	n/a	10	Rick et al. 2009
SNI-39	3210–2780, 1510–270	15	6	Maxwell 2006; Shelley 2001
SNI-51	2840–1840	2	1	Collins 1991a
SNI-102	2780–2150	n/a	n/a	Martz 2005
SNI-119	n/a	4	1	Collins 1991a
SNI-160	1710–930	n/a	n/a	Martz 2005
SNI-161	5440–5270	1	1	Vellanoweth 1998
SNI-162	2000–760	2	1	Maxwell 2006
SCAI-17	5920–3900; 1330–880	3	2	Collins 1991a
SCAI-45	1450–1050	3	1	Collins 1991a
SCAI-137	270–230	3	1	Collins 1991a
SCLI-43	10,210–520, 2340–2160[b]	>28	4	Collins 1991a
SCLI-48	n/a	1	1	Collins 1991a
SCLI-1215	5300–460	>2	2	Collins 1991a
SCLI-1524	2910–460	>20	9	Collins 1991a
PALEONTOLOGICAL SPECIMENS				
SRI-Tecolote Member	1480–1280[b]	3	1	Collins 1991a; Shelley 2001
SMI-Locality 7c	7160–6910[b]	1	1	Guthrie 1993
SMI-Locality 10	950–800[b]	6	1	Guthrie 1993
SMI-Locality 11	300–0[b]	1	1	Guthrie 1993

Source: Rick et al. 2009.

Notes: a. MI=San Miguel, SRI=Santa Rosa, SCRI=Santa Cruz, SCAI=Santa Catalina, SNI=San Nicolas, SCLI=San Clemente. NISP (number of identified specimens) and MNI (minimum number of individuals) based on Collins (1991a, 1991b) unless otherwise noted. For additional details, see Collins (1991a), Shelley (2001), and sources cited therein. Bones from unknown sites were excluded. A NISP of 30 fox bones presented in Colten (2001) could be from SCRI-191, -192, -240, -330, and/or -474.
b. Fox bones with direct AMS dates.

Island Spotted Skunk (*Spilogale gracilis amphiala*)

The island spotted skunk is currently found on Santa Cruz and Santa Rosa islands, with two skunk bones also reported in a poorly dated archaeological context at Daisy Cave on adjacent San Miguel Island (Johnson 1983; Walker 1980). Voy, who visited San Miguel Island around 1893, noted that an island skunk was reportedly trapped on San Miguel Island some years prior to his visit (Johnson 1972; Walker 1980:714). This may be a reference to a report by Henshaw (1876) that Captain Forney presented him a skunk specimen reportedly from San Miguel Island. Although skunks may have been present on San Miguel Island prehistorically, this account is questionable, and the two skunk bones from Daisy Cave could have been transported by an owl or other bird from Santa Rosa Island or the mainland. This is supported by the fact that the skunk bones were found in cave deposits that were likely from ancient barn owl roosts, and one of the specimens showed morphological affinities with *S. gracilis phenax* on the mainland rather than the island skunk *S. gracilis amphiala* (see Walker 1980:714).

Compared to the island fox, relatively little is known about these nocturnal and secretive animals, though a series of studies over the last 15 years have greatly informed the ecology of island spotted skunks (Crooks 1994a, 1994b, 1999; Crooks and Van Vuren 1994, 2002). Island spotted skunks are an island endemic subspecies (*amphiala*) of the western spotted skunk (*S. gracilis*), which is found throughout the mainland (Hall 1981). Western spotted skunks are smaller than striped skunks and are resource specialists that prey on mice and insects, as well as birds, carrion, and occasionally vegetable foods (Crooks 1999; Crooks and Van Vuren 1994; Van Gelder 1959, 1965). Island skunks are morphologically very similar to mainland skunks, but are characterized by a shorter tail and broader face than mainland animals (Crooks and Van Vuren 1994; Dickey 1929). As of 1994, skunks had a widespread distribution on Santa Cruz Island, but were generally rare and/or difficult to capture (Crooks and Van Vuren 1994). Skunks are common in chaparral and open grasslands and coastal sage scrub, and they excavate and use dens (Crooks 1994a; Crooks and Van Vuren 1994). With island foxes taken into a captive breeding program and following recovery of island vegetation communities, island spotted skunk populations significantly increased on the islands by about 2003–04 (Jones et al. 2008).

Based on morphological analyses, Van Gelder (1959, 1965) suggested that island spotted skunks are more similar to skunks in Oregon (*S. g. latifrons*) rather than California (*S. g. phenax*), with skunks perhaps colonizing the Channel Islands during a cool and moist period when *latifrons*-like skunks may have been present in California. Floyd et al. (2011) recently conducted a genetic analysis of 208 specimens collected from 1906 to 2002 from Oregon, the mainland California coast, Santa Rosa and Santa Cruz islands, and Lake Tahoe. Their analysis suggests that island spotted skunks show lower genetic diversity than the mainland, but the Santa Rosa and Santa Cruz island populations are as distinct genetically from one another as they are from mainland populations (Floyd et al. 2011). Though sample size was small, in contrast to Van Gelder's (1959) morphological data Floyd et al. (2011) found that *S. g. amphiala* was not closely linked to *S. g. latifrons* and was actually more similar to *S. g. phenax* on the California mainland. They concluded that spotted skunks likely arrived on the Channel Islands just prior to the breakup of Santarosae, which began around 11,000 years ago, with Santa Rosa and Santa Cruz separating only about 9,300 years ago (Kennett et al. 2008). Floyd et al. (2011) argue that it was probably a natural overwater distribution or perhaps an introduction assisted by Native Americans.

Island spotted skunks do not appear to be the best candidates for a human-assisted dispersal to the Channel Islands. Their powerful chemical defense and nocturnal behavior seem to be natural deterrents to human introduction (Van Gelder 1959, 1965). However, people today keep skunks as pets, mostly with the scent removed, and note that they are good domestic pets (Hume 1958). Moreover, Wenner and Johnson (1980) described the importance of skunks in Native American societies, including the use of the stark black and white pelts in ritual and other contexts and even the use of scent sacks. They concluded that the introduction of skunks by Native Americans "was a distinct possibility" (Wenner and Johnson 1980). According to Chumash informant Fernando Librado (Hudson et al. 1977:79–80), the Chumash had a skunk dance and song that indicates disdain for their smell. Interestingly, the song notes that skunks come from the island of Wi'ma (Santa Rosa Island). According to Librado, who apparently saw this dance in Ventura in the nineteenth or early twentieth century, the dancer's face and back were painted with white stripes. This account does not clear up the origins of skunks, but does suggest some working knowledge of skunks and some disdain for their smell.

Like island foxes, to my knowledge there is no documented case of island skunks in the fossil record. Though not as common as island fox remains, island skunks have been found in three archaeological sites on Santa Cruz, Santa Rosa, and San Miguel islands (table 3.3). The dearth of skunks

Table 3.3. Island spotted skunk, Catalina Island ground squirrel, deer mice, harvest mice, and ornate shrew remains reported in Channel Island archaeological sites

Site Number[a]	Age (cal. BP)[b]	NISP	References
ISLAND SPOTTED SKUNK (*S. GRACILIS AMPHIALA*)			
SCRI-191, -192, or -330	650–170	1	Colten 2001
SRI-2	320–250	1	Rick 2004
SMI-261	Late Holocene?	2	Walker 1980
ISLAND DEER MOUSE (*P. MANICULATUS*)			
SCLI-43	Trans-Holocene	n/a	Porcasi 1995:9
SCAI-17	5920–880	n/a	Porcasi 2002:584
SNI-39	1510–270	10	Maxwell 2006:105
SNI-73	950–730	18	Martz 2008
SNI-102	2780–2150	n/a	Martz 2008
SNI-147	~2830	3	Martz 2008
SNI-162	2000–760	1	Maxwell 2006:105
SNI-169	3690–2830	15	Martz 2008
SCRI-93	1150–800	n/a	Arnold 1987
SCRI-192 or -240[c]	Historic	9	Colten 2001
SMI-163	320–0	12	Rick 2007
SMI-261	Trans-Holocene	133	Walker 1980
SMI-468	1150–1040	1	Rick 2007
HARVEST MOUSE (*R. MEGALOTIS*)			
SCAI-45	~1450	6	Rosen 1980
EXTINCT GIANT ISLAND DEER MOUSE (*P. NESODYTES*)			
SMI-261	Trans-Holocene	341	Walker 1980
SRI-173	13,500–12,200	n/a	Johnson et al. 2002
ORNATE SHREW (*S. ORNATUS*)			
SMI-261	Mid or Late Holocene?	1	Walker 1980
CATALINA ISLAND GROUND SQUIRREL (*O. BEECHEYI NESIOTICUS*)			
SCAI-17	5920–880	17	Porcasi 2002:581
SCAI-45	~1450	25	Rosen 1980
SCAI-118	Historic	12	Rosen 1980
SCAI-137	270–30	124	Rosenthal et al. 1988
Camp Cactus Road	Late Holocene?	154	Rosenthal et al. 1988
Cottonwood Creek	1450–30	1	Bickford and Martz 1980

Notes: a. SMI=San Miguel, SRI=Santa Rosa, SCRI=Santa Cruz, SCAI=Santa Catalina, SNI=San Nicolas, SCLI=San Clemente.

b. All dates are based on radiocarbon associations, except for direct dates from SRI-173 on *P. nesdoytes*.

c. An additional 136 bones are identified as *Peromyscus* sp. from five SCRI sites dated between 1250 and 150 cal. BP (Colten 2001), with another three NISP from two SCRI sites (Noah 2005).

in archaeological sites may be due in part to the reduced overall distribution of skunks compared to foxes, a specialized ritual use that would limit their presence in domestic contexts, or because Native Americans did not generally exploit spotted skunks. One question about Floyd et al.'s (2011) genetic data is why are the Santa Rosa and Santa Cruz populations so distinct from one another, especially given a likely small founder population and at most 9,000–10,000 years of isolation? Current data suggest that a natural dispersal of skunks is possible, but there remains a chance that Native Americans may have played a role in introducing them to the northern Channel Islands. The timing and means of colonization of the island skunk remains a topic in need of further study.

Catalina Island Ground Squirrel (*Otospermophilus beecheyi nesioticus*)

The Catalina Island ground squirrel is a close relative of the Beechey ground squirrel (*Otospermophilus beecheyi nesioticus*) found on the California mainland (Hall 1981). The differences between mainland and island *Spermophilus beecheyi* are slight, including a slightly larger crania and hind feet and an apparently darker color (Elliot 1904:263–64; Grinnell and Dixon 1918:49–51; Howell 1938:160–61). Relatively few studies have investigated the ecology and natural history of Catalina Island ground squirrels (Grinnell and Dixon 1918; von Bloecker 1967). For the most part, they appear to fill the same niche as mainland ground squirrels.

Because little is known about the ecology and evolution of Catalina Island squirrels, it is difficult to determine when and how they colonized the islands. Both a natural dispersal and a human-assisted one remain possibilities. There are no fossil specimens of Catalina ground squirrels identified, but little paleontology has been conducted on Santa Catalina Island. Squirrels are present in six archaeological sites, an important finding since Santa Catalina has seen limited archaeological research compared with other Channel Islands (see Rick et al. 2005). Virtually all of these sites are very young in age, dating to the Protohistoric or Historic periods. The exception is the Little Harbor site dated to 5,920 to 880 cal BP. Porcasi (2002) reported 17 squirrel bones from this site, but it is unclear if these are from the earlier or later deposits. It is possible that some of the squirrel bones are from animals that burrowed into the deposits and subsequently died there (Rosenthal et al. 1988), though at Little Harbor Porcasi (2002:581) notes that there was no indication of burrowing in the deposits. Rosenthal et al. (1988) suggested that many of the squirrel remains they identified likely represented food consumed by Native Americans. Small amounts of burning and butchering on squirrel bones at Bullrush Canyon may support this, with squirrels perhaps filling a dietary niche supplied by rabbits on the mainland (Rosenthal et al. 1988). Unfortunately, this does not resolve when and how the animals colonized the island. Archaeological data raise the possibility that Native Americans may have played a role in introducing them to Santa Catalina Island, perhaps intentionally for food or as a stowaway. In a recent analysis of arctic ground squirrels (*S. parryii*) on islands in the North Pacific, Cook et al. (2010:1409) also raised the possibility of prehistoric human introductions of squirrels. Until more radiocarbon dating and genetic research is conducted on Catalina Island squirrels, a natural overwater dispersal also is probable.

Island Deer Mice (*Peromyscus maniculatus* and *P. nesodytes*)

The island deer mouse (*Peromysucs mainculatus*) is the only mammal present on all eight of the California Channel Islands, with each island supporting its own endemic subspecies (Collins et al. 1979; Gill 1976; Hall 1981; Pergams and Ashley 2002). *P. nesodytes,* the giant island deer mouse, is an extinct and larger mouse than the species that currently occupies the Channel Islands (Walker 1980; Wilson 1936). *P. nesodytes* has been identified in fossil deposits only on the northern Channel Islands, including San Miguel and Santa Rosa. *P. anayapensis,* an extinct and smaller form found on Anacapa Island, may be ancestral to *P. nesodytes* and perhaps very ancient (i.e., ~100,000 BP), but is known from a small number of specimens (Guthrie 1998:190; White 1966).

P. maniculatus is common and widespread on all of the Channel Islands. They are important prey for island foxes, skunks, owls, and snakes. Although they eat seeds and vegetation, they are also known to prey on eggs from small breeding seabirds. For example, Santa Barbara Island deer mice are known to prey on the eggs of the endangered Xantus's murrelet (*Synthliboramphus hypoleucus*) (Murray et al. 1983; Schwemm and Martin 2005; Schwemm et al. 2005). They may also have an impact on the recruitment of giant coreopsis, an endemic flowering plant (Schwemm and Coonan 2001).

Because *P. nesodytes* has been found in fossil deposits dated to the Pleistocene with some greater than the accuracy of radiocarbon dating (~40,000–60,000 years old), it is apparent that the giant island mouse arrived via a natural dispersal before human arrival (Guthrie 1980; Rick et al. 2012; Walker 1980). Walker (1980) argued that *P. maniculatus* arrived during the Holocene sometime prior to 8,000 years ago. In this scenario, *P. maniculatus* was introduced to the islands inadvertently as a commensal by humans well after initial human colonization at ca. 13,000 cal BP. Guthrie (2005:37) identified abundant *P. maniculatus* remains in a 7,300-year-old barn owl roost and no *P. nesodytes* after about 8,000 years ago, lending further support to Walker's conclusion. In their recent work at the Arlington Springs site, John Johnson and colleagues noted that *P. nesodytes* was the only mouse present between 13,500 to 12,200 years ago, and that *P. maniculatus* was the only mouse found in younger, overlying midden deposits dated to ca. 8,100 years ago (John Johnson, personal communication 2011). Recent research suggests that *P. maniculatus* coexisted with *P. nesodytes* until at least 1000 cal. BP when *P. nesodytes* went extinct (Ainis and Vellanoweth 2012). The cause of the extinction of *P. nesodytes* is in debate, ranging from interspecific competition between the two mice species to changes in historical landscapes (see Ainis and Vellanoweth 2012; Guthrie 1993; Rick et al. 2012; Walker 1980).

Gill (1980), Ashley and Wills (1987, 1989), Pergams et al. (2000), and Pergams and Ashley's (2002) genetic studies demonstrate variability among island deer mice DNA, but considerable overlap between mainland and island populations. Gill (1980) argued that evidence for gene flow between island mice populations could be from natural rafting or human transportation. Ashley and Wills (1987) speculated primarily about natural, chance rafting events, but because of similarity in mtDNA between three northern Channel Islands and San Nicolas Island, they noted that Native Americans may have transported mice to San Nicolas Island. Ashley and Wills (1987) and Pergams and Ashley (2001) also suggested that genetic data document a separation from mainland populations sometime less than 500,000 years ago, but perhaps much more recent. These very early dates are at odds with the fossil record, which suggests a Holocene introduction for *P. maniculatus*. Pergams and Ashley (2002) did not evaluate the dispersal of *P. maniculatus* to the Channel Islands, noting only that mice occurred deep in the past. A minimum of 5–8 dispersal events (depending on sea levels during the time of colonization) are required to get *P. maniculatus* to all the Channel Islands. This high number of dispersals and the probable Terminal Pleistocene to Holocene age of the introduction suggest that a human-assisted dispersal of *P. maniculatus* to the northern and southern islands is the most parsimonious explanation. As Walker (1980:714–716) and Wenner and Johnson (1980:514) noted, the Chumash regularly transported materials back and forth between the mainland and islands and parked boats in tule reeds and other areas where mice could easily become stowaways.

This scenario is increasingly likely and if true demonstrates that hunter-gatherers introduced *P. maniculatus,* the most widespread and common mammal on the Channel Islands, one that has an important ecological niche, and serves as prey for the two island mammalian carnivores (skunks and foxes) and for a variety of raptors and snakes. Since agriculturalists are known to have introduced rodents—including mice and rats—to a variety of islands prehistorically (e.g., Caribbean, Pacific Islands, Mediterranean, and North Atlantic; see Grayson 2001) and hunter-gatherers may have introduced deer mice (*Peromyscus* sp.) to the Queen Charlotte Islands (Haida Gwaii) prehistorically (Foster 1965:84, 93, 115), these findings illustrate that hunter-gatherers in California may have had similar influence. Future research on the aDNA of *P. maniculatus* and *P. nesodytes* should prove fruitful for helping further evaluate the origins and evolution of island mice.

Western Harvest Mouse (*Reithrodontomys megalotis*)

Western harvest mice are found on Santa Cruz, Santa Catalina, and San Clemente islands and are thought to be island endemics on all but Clemente, where they were introduced during the nineteenth century, possibly in bales of hay (Collins and George 1990; Drost et al. 2009; Von Bloecker 1967). On Santa Cruz Island, harvest mice once had a fairly limited distribution, but they have been expanding and now occur on most of the island (Drost et al. 2009). On Santa Catalina they are widespread (Ashley 1989). Collins and George (1990) provided a detailed analysis and overview of the systematics and taxonomy of island and mainland harvest mice in Southern California, noting limited differences between populations. Analysis of Santa Catalina, Santa Cruz, and mainland harvest mice mtDNA and proteins suggest that there is little to no differentiation between these populations (Ashley 1989; Collins and George 1990). According to Collins and George (1990), harvest mice were likely introduced to Santa Cruz and Santa Catalina islands inadvertently by Native Americans during the Holocene. The widespread distribution on Santa Catalina Island and the morphological variability of the Catalina population suggests that they may have been on this island longer than the Santa Cruz population (Collins and George 1990), but determining when harvest mice arrived on Catalina is difficult. Both Santa Cruz and Santa Catalina islands were heavily populated by Native Americans and were important centers of island–mainland trade (Rick et al. 2005), which lends further support to an unintentional human-assisted introduction of harvest mice.

Ornate Shrew (*Sorex ornatus*)

Shrews are small, venomous, and carnivorous with high metabolism rates that require incessant feeding. Their high dietary needs make them an unlikely candidate for successful translocation to islands (but see Walker 1980). The ornate shrew currently lives on Santa Catalina Island, with several fossil/archaeological specimens reported from San Miguel Island (Guthrie 1998, 2005; Walker 1980), and fossil specimens reported from Santa Rosa Island (Guthrie 1998). Guthrie (1998:190) presented two radiocarbon dates of 10,240 + 180 RYBP and 28,240 + 940 RYBP for a Santa Rosa Island fossil deposit that contained shrews, but it is unclear precisely how old the shrew remains are. At Daisy Cave on San Miguel Island, ornate shrew bones are found in Early through Late Holocene deposits, suggesting at least 9,000 years of occupation (Guthrie 1993:188). The fossil and archaeological specimens that have been reported are small in number and little is known about how they arrived on the islands. The presence of *S. ornatus* in a Late Pleistocene Santa Rosa Island fossil locality suggests that *S. ornatus* may have arrived on the northern Channel Islands via a natural dispersal prior to human arrival and the breakup of Santarosae, though this should be confirmed with additional radiocarbon dating. Ornate shrews on the northern islands may have gone extinct in the Late Holocene, possibly during the Historic period (Guthrie 1998).

Sorex ornatus willetti is the Catalina Island subspecies, which is reportedly slightly larger than its mainland counterpart, has a slightly longer skull, and has a darker coloration (Collins 1998; Von Bloecker 1941, 1967). Catalina Island shrews range widely across the island and have been found from near sea level to over 600 feet, but they are fairly rare and appear to have low population numbers (Aarhus 2005; Collins 1998). Genetic analysis of ornate shrews from Catalina Island suggests that they are very distinct from mainland specimens (Maldonado et al. 2001), perhaps indicating they may have colonized the island deep in the past and possibly prior to the human era. It is unclear exactly how and when shrews colonized Catalina Island; the genetic data suggest that shrews may have occupied the island prior to human arrival, but much remains to be learned about these animals.

Columbian and Pygmy Mammoth (*Mammuthus columbi* and *M. exilis*)

Full-sized Columbian and pygmy mammoths lived on the northern Channel Islands during the Pleistocene, with pygmy mammoths appearing some

200,000 years ago and far earlier than human colonization (Agenbroad 1998, 2009). Mammoths are generally good swimmers and various researchers have long speculated that mammoths swam to the Channel Islands and perhaps back to the mainland on multiple occasions, but the pygmy forms are known only from the islands (Agenbroad 1998, 2009; Johnson 1972, 1983). Mammoths have an extensive fossil record. Orr (1968) estimated that a minimum of 200 mammoths had been identified by the early 1960s. Agenbroad's (1998, 2002b; see also Cushing et al. 1984) surveys on Santa Rosa, San Miguel, and Santa Cruz islands through 2008 identified more than 380 mammoth localities. Despite considerable speculation that mammoths were hunted by humans (see Orr 1968), there is currently no definitive evidence that humans hunted mammoths. Although the terminal dates for mammoths and the earliest dates for a human presence on the islands are close in age and perhaps overlap, there are still questions about the extent to which humans and mammoths coexisted on the islands (see Agenbroad et al. 2005; Rick et al. 2005).

Other Mammals

A few other mammals have been reported in the Channel Island fossil record and in more recent accounts. Guthrie (1998) reported the remains of *Microtus miguelensis* (San Miguel Island vole) from two mandibles found in San Miguel Island fossil localities. Guthrie speculated that these animals lived during the Late Pleistocene before human arrival and may have died out prior to 12,000 years ago and were likely never a major component of Channel Island fauna. Native Americans introduced domestic dogs (*Canis familiaris*) to the Channel Islands more than 6,000 years ago and perhaps much earlier (Rick et al. 2008). Dogs have been found in archaeological sites on all but the two smallest Channel Islands (Anacapa and Santa Barbara) and were likely an important component of human cultural systems and island ecosystems for millennia (Rick et al. 2008).

Discussion and Conclusions

Over the years, researchers have identified some 10 terrestrial mammals (excluding bats) on the Channel Islands that are island endemics, including mammoths, a vole, and a giant mouse found in the fossil record but now extinct. These endemic mammals include small rodents (e.g., mice) that are fairly common on islands around the world and two carnivores (island fox and island spotted skunk) that are generally rare on islands. Some of these animals are present on several islands: the island fox is found on six islands and island deer mice on all eight islands. Others, such as the island spotted skunk, harvest mouse, ornate shrew, and ground squirrel, are limited to just one or at most three islands. Ultimately, these mammals are part of a depauperate terrestrial flora and fauna that make the Channel Islands distinct from the adjacent mainland and an important laboratory for investigating patterns of island biogeography and ecology.

Wenner and Johnson (1980) and Johnson (1983) provided important analyses of the means of dispersal for several animals on the Channel Islands. Their studies were fueled by recent confirmation that the Channel Islands (northern islands) were not connected during the Quaternary to the mainland by a land bridge. Wenner and Johnson (1980) raised four possibilities for how mammals, reptiles, and amphibians colonized the Channel Islands: sweepstakes (i.e., natural chance rafting events), swimming, human-assisted, or combined dispersal. These two studies also concluded that Native Americans likely had an important role in moving mammals, as well as reptiles, around on the islands. These early interpretations were limited because of often poor data from archaeological or fossil contexts, but Johnson (1983:508–10) suggested that foxes, skunks, deer and harvest mice, shrews, squirrels, and some herpetofauna (e.g., rattlesnakes and island night lizards) could have been introduced or moved between islands by Native Americans.

Since these studies, a number of research projects have been conducted on the Channel Islands, including numerous paleontological, archaeological, and recent ecological and biological research projects (see Agenbroad 2009; Erlandson et al. 2011; Guthrie 1998, 2005; Kennett 2005; Rick et al. 2005; Schoenherr et al. 1999). Some of these studies have helped clarify the origins of several of the island's endemic mammals, but questions remain for others. The dispersal of the harvest mouse to Santa Cruz Island and probably Santa Catalina is one that appears to have been a result of human-assisted colonization (Ashley 1987; Collins and George 1990). Although questions persist, Rick et al. (2009) have suggested that foxes may have been introduced by Native Americans to all six Channel Islands where they currently occur, with more definitive evidence for human-assisted introduction of island foxes to the southern Channel Islands (Collins 1991a, 1991b; Johnson 1975; Vellanoweth 1998). *P. nesodytes* reached the islands prior to human arrival, but *P. maniculatus* may have reached most or all of the islands via a human-assisted dispersal. Little is known about how and when the ground squirrel reached Catalina Island, but it could have been introduced by Native Americans or arrived naturally. Squirrels are found in Late Holocene archaeological sites, were at least occasionally a source of food for Native Americans, and could have come out intentionally or unintentionally to Catalina Island via Native American boats. Similar to the squirrel, questions persist about how and when the island spotted skunk first arrived on the northern Channel Islands (see Floyd et al. 2011). Most researchers argue that skunks are an unlikely candidate for human-assisted dispersal due to their chemical defense. Skunks could have arrived naturally via a chance rafting event or perhaps could have been brought out by Native Americans for ceremonial purposes, as pets, or even for food, though evidence supporting this proposition is limited (Wenner and Johnson 1980). Shrews are a curious animal due to their high metabolic needs, but may have been on the northern islands (Guthrie 1998) and perhaps Santa Catalina prior to the human era, though further dating of specimens is needed to help refine their antiquity and origins. The dispersal of the San Miguel Island vole appears to have occurred naturally prior to human arrival, while mammoths swam to the islands well prior to the human era.

These data demonstrate that the mammalian fauna on the Channel Islands arrived via a combination of natural chance rafting events, swimming, and human-assisted dispersal. Hunter-gatherers who occupied the Channel Islands for some 13,000 calendar years may have assisted in the introduction of three of the extant endemic mammals (not including bats) on the Channel Islands (i.e., island deer mice, harvest mice, and perhaps island foxes), moved some of these animals between islands (island foxes and perhaps deer mice), and possibly played a role in introducing two others (island spotted skunk and Catalina Island ground squirrel). To put this in broader perspective, Native Americans may have assisted in the dispersal of all of the extant endemic mammals (not including bats) on Santa Barbara, San Nicolas, San Clemente, and Anacapa, and at least one or two mammals on the other four islands. In the case of mice and foxes, ancient people played a role in not only moving an apex terrestrial predator to or between islands, but also one of their primary sources of prey. Although it's beyond the scope of this chapter, it is also possible that some of the island reptiles (e.g., rattlesnakes) and perhaps amphibians may have been introduced by Native Americans, though many of these are good candidates for natural chance rafting (see Johnson 1983). While the translocation of mice to the islands was probably unintentional, some of these introductions fall into the context of niche construction, where people actively manipulate and influence wild animals and plants for their benefit or as part of larger human ecological systems (see Smith 2007, 2011). This is likely the case with island foxes, where their ritual and cultural importance probably led people to move them around between islands and introduce them to the southern islands (see Collins 1991a; Vellanoweth 1998). Other chapters in this volume also note that hunter-gatherer modifications of the landscape may have been closely tied to ritual activities, such as the construction of sambaquis in Brazil (Fish et al., this volume).

In the mid-nineteenth century, several ranching operations were established on the Channel Islands. Euroamerican, Mexican, and American ranchers introduced scores of domesticated animals to the islands, including cattle, deer, elk, donkeys, sheep, goats, dogs, cats, rabbits, hares, rats, house mice, and other animals (Schoenherr et al. 1999). Bison, which never occurred on the islands prehistorically, were also introduced to Santa Catalina Island between 1924 and 1935 (Sweitzer et al. 2005). Together these animals greatly transformed Channel Island landscapes, in some cases causing widespread denudation of vegetation and erosion (Johnson 1972, 1980). The effects of these historical transformations are one of the primary focuses of ecological restoration and management by the National Park Service, the Nature Conservancy, the Catalina Island Conservancy, and the U.S. Navy. The animal translocations by Native Americans were on a fundamentally different scale than the transformations brought about by historically introduced domestic animals, but they illustrate that ancient hunter-gatherers also had an influence on Channel Island ecosystems for millennia. The natural, human-assisted, or combined origins of the endemic mammals on the Channel Islands also underscores that ancient and modern ecosystems are the result of a mix of anthropogenic and natural processes that incrementally shape the world on multiple time scales (annual, decade, century, millennia, etc.).

A review of archaeological and ecological literature from around the world suggests that ancient and modern peoples often introduced animals to islands, providing important context for the translocations by ancient Channel Islanders. Polynesian translocation of pigs, chickens, rats, and dogs are a particularly profound and well-documented case of ancient animal translocations that were part of a larger "domestication of the landscape" (Kirch 1997; Matisoo-Smith 2009). Norse peoples in the North

Atlantic and Neolithic peoples in the Mediterranean did much the same with their suite of domesticated animals and plants (McGovern et al. 2008; Zeder 2008). Translocations by agriculturalists in the Caribbean are also common (Newsom and Wing 2004). Examples of animal translocations by hunter-gatherers, however, are less well documented (see Grayson 2001). White (2004) noted, however, that hunter-gatherers translocated the northern cuscus to islands in the Circum Papua New Guinea archipelago some 20,000 years ago. Seri hunter-gatherers who occupied the Midriff Islands of the Gulf of California are thought to have moved reptiles between various islands, including iguanids (Nabhan 2000). On Madagascar, Blench (2007) speculated that hunter-gatherers may have occupied this island and possibly introduced a rat. Foster (1965:84, 93, 115) suggested that deer mice may have been introduced or moved between islands prehistorically in Haida canoes on the Queen Charlotte Islands, British Columbia. The Channel Islands case demonstrates that, although lacking the domesticated species (except dogs) brought by agriculturalists, hunter-gatherers were capable of animal translocations that actively altered the ecosystems around them. On the Channel Islands these translocations had positive and negative consequences for people and other insular fauna. Translocation of island foxes and dogs, for example, likely greatly affected the breeding and nesting behavior of seabirds, and perhaps seals and sea lions (Rick et al. 2008, 2009). The accidental introduction of *P. maniculatus* may have played a role in the extinction of *P. nesodytes* (see Rick et al. 2012), with deer mice also affecting plant recruitment and some bird breeding and hatching activities (Murray et al. 1983; Schwemm and Coonan 2001).

With resource managers on the Channel Islands and elsewhere around the world working to restore ecosystems to a "natural" state, the role of ancient hunter-gatherers in translocating island mammals from the mainland or moving mammals between islands challenges us to redefine what that natural state is. The ancient human-assisted dispersal or at least movement between islands of the deer and harvest mice, island foxes, and possibly other species joins other studies on the Channel Islands that demonstrate the importance of Native Americans in influencing the structure and function of island marine and terrestrial ecosystems. These include a Native American influence on the formation of island dune ecosystems (Erlandson et al. 2005); on the structure, abundance, and breeding behavior of seals and sea lions (Braje et al. 2010; Erlandson and Rick 2010; Rick 2007); on the size and abundance of island shellfish stocks (Braje et al. 2009; Erlandson et al. 2008); on the ancient breeding and roosting of seabirds (Rick et al. 2009); and a host of other issues (see Braje 2010; Erlandson and Rick 2010; Kennett 2005; Rick 2007). Collectively, these data suggest that Channel Island ecosystems, like most systems around the world, have been influenced (positively and negatively) by ancient peoples, including hunter-gatherers, deep into the human past (see Habu and Hall, this volume; Milner, this volume; Redman 1999; Thompson et al., this volume). Such findings are not only important intellectually, but provide baselines and benchmarks that can help guide the management and long-term conservation of island ecosystems and organisms. In the case of Channel Island mammals, an important component of their histories has been the interactions with ancient Native Americans that spanned millennia. Given the concerted conservation efforts devoted to the endangered island fox (Coonan et al. 2002, 2005, 2010), increased research and conservation of island spotted skunks (Jones et al. 2008), the protection of island deer mice on Anacapa Island during rat eradication (see Howald et al. 2005; Pergams and Ashley 2002), and other studies and measures aimed at preserving the island's unique fauna, historical ecology and archaeology have much to offer these efforts. The key is better integrating archaeology, paleontology, and other historical disciplines with modern biological, ecological, and evolutionary data, and working collaboratively to transcend disciplinary boundaries.

Acknowledgments

This chapter is dedicated to Phil Walker, who transformed our understanding of the ancient ecology and human history of the Channel Islands and much more. I am greatly indebted to Todd Braje, Paul Collins, Jon Erlandson, Dan Guthrie, Courtney Hofman, Jesus Maldonado, Scott Sillett, René Vellanoweth, and Phil Walker for the conversations that helped shape my understanding of Channel Islands human and animal populations. I thank Victor Thompson and Jamie Waggoner for inviting me to participate in the 2009 SAA symposium, and T. Braje, P. Collins, Tim Coonan, C. Hofman, T. R. Kidder, V. Thompson, J. Waggoner, Chris Wolff, and anonymous reviewers for their insightful comments on this manuscript. Any errors of fact or omissions are solely mine.

4

Climate Change, Human Impacts on the Landscape, and Subsistence Specialization

Historical Ecology and Changes in Jomon Hunter-Gatherer Lifeways

JUNKO HABU AND MARK E. HALL

The purpose of this chapter is to use the theoretical framework of historical ecology to discuss key factors that affected changes in Jomon hunter-gatherer lifeways. As an example of prehistoric hunter-gatherer economies, data from the Jomon period (ca. 16,000–2,500 cal. BP) of the Japanese archipelago offers a unique opportunity to examine both short- and long-term changes in human-environment interaction. A large number of rescue excavations in Japan since the 1970s have provided us with fine-grained archaeological data with which to interpret the changing Jomon landscape in relation to the environment. Available lines of evidence include: (1) distribution of various types of sites (e.g., residential bases, processing sites, and ceremonial locations) and landscape features (e.g., roads, paths, and mounds), (2) macro and micro faunal and floral remains, and (3) tool assemblages. Signs of plant cultivation have been reported (e.g., charred seeds, pollen and phytoliths of cultigens), although none of the cultigens excavated from Jomon sites seems to have been an important part of Jomon diet, at least not in terms of quantity. Scientists have also suggested that climate changes, which affected vegetation and the availability of both terrestrial and marine resources, must have been closely linked with the changes in the Jomon culture.

Previous attempts by archaeologists to understand human-environment interaction during the Jomon period have focused primarily on: (1) modeling subsistence-settlement systems in relation to resource distribution (e.g., Akazawa 1980, 1987; Habu 2001), (2) finding cultigens to argue that the Jomon people were food producers, not hunter-gatherers (e.g., Crawford 2006, 2008; Yoshizaki 1995), (3) reconstructing environmental changes on the basis of macro and micro floral data, such as pollen (e.g., Fuji 1984), and (4) discussing the impact of climate change on people's lifeways (e.g., Yasuda 1989; Yasuda and Negendank 2003; Yasuda et al. 2004). So far, very few scholars have actively investigated the importance of human impacts on the Jomon landscape at the local or regional levels.

Historical ecology (e.g., Balée 1998, 2006; Balée and Erickson 2006; Crumley 1994a; Erlandson and Rick 2008; Kirch and Hunt 1997; Thompson, this volume; see also Hayashida 2005) can provide a useful theoretical framework to investigate the changing human-environment relationships through the Jomon period. There are several reasons for this. First, historical ecology emphasizes the impacts of human activities on their surrounding environment (see, e.g., Rick, this volume). This is particularly relevant in the context of Jomon archaeology, because the Jomon people were clearly engaged in a significant level of environmental management. For example, many scholars point out that Jomon people's plant utilization affected genetic characteristics of many edible plants, including chestnuts (Sato et al. 2003), elderberries (Tsuji 2002:242), and barnyard grass (Yoshizaki 1995). Thus, when we examine the process of Jomon subsistence intensification, we cannot avoid the issue of human impacts on flora and fauna at that time.

Second, historical ecology also emphasizes historically unique trajectories of human sociopolitical and economic systems in different parts of the world. Given that the long-term change in the Jomon culture does not necessarily fit into the traditional model of unilinear development from simple to complex (Habu 2004), understanding the Jomon historical trajectory is relevant in the context of recent discussions in historical ecology.

Third, with its ties to the French historical school Annales, historical ecology can deal with the concept of processes operating among temporal scales of varying duration: *événement* (event), *conjuncture* (cycle), and *longue durée* (long-term history) (Balée 2006:80). The investigation of culture change during the Jomon period requires the examination of archaeological data with varying time scales, from short-term events and changes within a single pottery phase or several decades to long-term changes that cover periods of several hundreds and more than 1,000 years (e.g., Habu 2001, 2002, 2004).

Data from Sannai Maruyama (Early to Middle Jomon; ca. 5900–4300 cal. BP) and its neighboring sites in Aomori in the Tohoku region of northern Japan provide an excellent opportunity to examine changing human-environmental relationships with varying time scales. Using the perspective of historical ecology, this chapter examines key factors in the debate over the growth and decline of large Middle Jomon sites in this region. Three factors will be discussed: climate change, human impacts on the landscape, and subsistence specialization. Through these discussions, it is suggested that the examination of the interrelation of these factors is indispensable to our understanding of the mechanisms of hunter-gatherer culture change.

Sannai Maruyama and the Middle Jomon

Located in Aomori Prefecture in northern Japan, Sannai Maruyama is currently the largest known Jomon settlement. From 1992 to 1994, the Board of Education of Aomori Prefecture conducted salvage excavation prior to the construction of a baseball stadium (Okada 2003). Results of this excavation revealed that the entire area planned for the stadium was a large Jomon settlement. Features identified from this site included more than 600 pit dwellings, post-molds of raised-floor buildings, water-logged middens, and large mounds filled with refuse deposits (for details, see Habu 2004:108–32; Okada 2003). The stadium construction was halted in 1994, and the site is currently a national historic park (Habu and Fawcett 1999, 2008).

Several lines of evidence indicate that Sannai Maruyama was occupied from the middle of the Early Jomon to the end of the Middle Jomon. In terms of typological chronology of pottery, the site occupation can be divided into 12 phases: Lower-Ento-a to -d, Upper-Ento-a to -e, Enokibayashi, Saibana, and Daigi—10 phases from the oldest to the youngest. Radiocarbon dates indicate that these 12 phases correspond to about 5900–4300 cal. BP.

Since the summer of 1997, Habu has been working on the site material with her students from the University of California, Berkeley. In collaboration with the Preservation Office of the Sannai Maruyama Site, the Berkeley team has examined excavation records and conducted collaborative field/laboratory research on faunal/floral remains, soil samples, artifacts and intra-/inter-site settlement patterns (Habu 2004, 2005, 2006, 2008; Habu and Sato 2008; Habu et al. 2001).

Reexamination of the Sannai Maruyama site is particularly important in understanding the long-term trajectory of the Jomon culture. The ending of the site occupation coincided with the timing of the abandonment of many other large Jomon settlements in northern and central Japan. Thus, examining the growth and decline of the Sannai Maruyama settlement can provide us with clues to understanding the mechanisms of the decline of the Middle Jomon culture in these regions. It is also important to note that this decline roughly coincided with the cooling climate that is said to have occurred at around 4200–4000 cal. BP (e.g., Kawahata et al. 2009; Yasuda 1989).

In examining the abandonment of large Middle Jomon sites, several key questions need to be asked. To begin with, was the cooling climate really related to the abandonment of these large settlements? If so, how? Did vegetation change caused by the cooling climate decrease or increase the total amount of available food resources? What kinds of food resources were strongly affected by the climate change? Alternatively, it is possible that other changes, such as the adoption of new subsistence strategies, were ongoing before the incidence of the cooling climate, and that they were the real cause of the decline of these large sites. In this instance, the climate change might simply have been a trigger rather than the cause. In addition, from the perspective of historical ecology, human impacts on the landscape, as well as the impacts of environmental changes on people's lifeways, should be considered. Reliable ^{14}C dates are needed to nail down the date of settlement abandonment and the onset of a cooling climate.

Answering all of these questions is obviously beyond the scope of this chapter. In the following sections, three issues that are keys to answering these questions are examined: (1) climate change, (2) human impacts on the landscape, and (3) subsistence specialization.

Climate Change

Climate change has been the most commonly cited explanation for the decrease in the number of Middle Jomon large settlements. For example, Yasuda (1989) suggests that the cooling climate at around 4,000 years ago led to the worldwide decline of prosperous cultures and civilizations, including the Middle Jomon culture of the Japanese archipelago. Archaeologists such as Okada (2003) and Kodama (2003) also support the idea that the cooling climate was the main cause of the decline of large settlements at the end of the Middle Jomon period, including the abandonment of Sannai Maruyama.

Figure 4.1 shows radiocarbon dates from Sannai Maruyama and climatic information. The bar in the top section represents the mean for each date (Kobayashi 2004; Tsuji 2006). The line below the calibrated dates shows the oxygen isotope ratios from the Greenland Ice Sheet Project (Grootes et al.

1993; Meese et al. 1994; Sowers et al. 1993; Struiver and Grootes 2000). The bottom line shows the temperature data from the Vostok ice core (Petit et al. 1999; Sowers et al. 1993). The temperature decline at around 4300–4200 cal. BP represented by the Vostok ice core data seems to correspond to the so-called Neoglaciation, the cooling climate that has been referred to by many researchers. From this diagram, the ending date of site occupation occurs shortly after the cooling climate, but the precise timings of these events are yet to be determined.

Together with their colleagues, three scholars—Sei-ichiro Tsuji, Yasu-nori Yasuda and Hodaka Kawahata—have published climate and vegeta-tion data that are relevant to the study of Sannai Maruyama. Through their analyses of pollen data from Sannai Maruyama, Tsuji (1996, 1997, 1998) and Yoshikawa and Tsuji (1998) suggest that a significant decline in *Castanea*

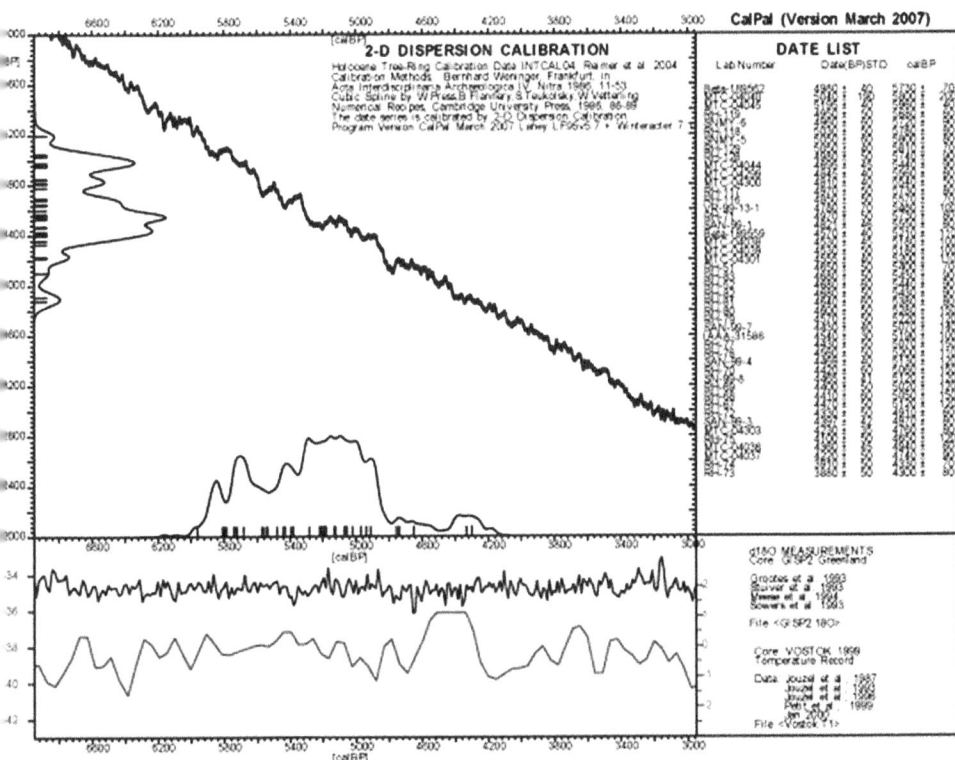

Figure 4.1. Distribution of radiocarbon determination for Sannai Maruyama and data for climate change. The top section shows radiocarbon data from Kobayashi (2004) and Tsuji (2006). The bottom section shows climate data. The top line in the section shows oxygen isotope data from the Greenland Ice Sheet Project 2 (GISP2). The bottom line is temperature data from the Vostok ice core.

(chestnut) pollen, which corresponds to a cooling climate, can be observed during the later phases of the Middle Jomon period. In their more recent publications, Tsuji (2002) and Yoshikawa et al. (2006) emphasize that the increase and decrease of the chestnut pollen at Sannai Maruyama should be seen as the direct measure of the formation and the abandonment of a large-scale chestnut orchard at the site, not as changes in natural vegetation caused by climate change. Unfortunately, the majority of their pollen samples are from the Early Jomon period, not the Middle Jomon period, and this makes it difficult to evaluate the precise timing of the chestnut pollen decline discussed in these articles.

Kitagawa and Yasuda (2004) also examine pollen data from Sannai Maruyama, with a focus on climatic fluctuations for a shorter time span of several hundred years. This fine-grained analysis was made possible by comparing their pollen data from Sannai Maruyama with climate data obtained from high-resolution analysis of annually laminated lacustrine sediments at Lake Suigetsu (Yasuda and Negendank 2003; Yasuda et al. 2004). Their results indicate that, at Sannai Maruyama, several local pollen zones with high percentages of *Castanea* pollen can be identified. In between these zones are the zones with lower percentages of *Castanea*. These latter zones include their local pollen zone III (ca. 5600 cal. BP), zone V (ca. 5400 cal. BP), zone VI (ca. 4600 BP), and zone VIII (the beginning of the Late Jomon period). (There is about an 800-year gap between zones VI and VII due to their core sample structure.) Kitagawa and Yasuda believe that the zones with abundant *Castanea* pollen represent the phases during which semi-cultivation (*hansaibai*) of chestnuts was practiced, and that these periods correspond to a warm climate.

More recently, Kawahata et al. (2009) analyzed environmental records from a marine core (KT05–7 PC-02) obtained from Mutsu Bay of Aomori Prefecture located about 20 kilometers away from the Sannai Maruyama site. Their analysis of sea surface temperature (SST) derived from C_{37} alkenone identified four high periods of SSTs (8300–7900, 7000–5900, 5100–4100, and 2300–1400 cal. BP) with mean values of 23.4, 23.4, 23.8, and 23.5 °C, and four low (?–8300, 7900–7000, 5900–5100, and 4100–2300 cal. BP) periods of SSTs with mean values of 21.6, 22.8, 22.9, and 22.7 °C, respectively. Thus, "the SST clearly fluctuated with a mean amplitude of ~1.5–2.0 °C over the last 10 kyr" (Kawahata et al. 2009:971). On the other hand, their pollen data, including the relative abundance of pollen of *Castanea* and *Quercus* subgen. *Cyclobalanopsis* (oak) seem to suggest that the terrestrial climate was relatively warm between 5900 and 4200 + 100 cal. BP. Kawahata and his colleagues state that the reason behind relatively cold temperatures during 5900–5100 cal. BP remains unclear, but that this apparent discrepancy between the SST and terrestrial temperature data may be attributed to the water column structure in the Tsugaru Straight. According to Kuroyanagi et al. (2006), the water column structure in the Tsugaru Straight before 5000 cal. BP was more stratified than at present, and this may have affected the seasonal shift of alkenone production.

We suggest that, given the fact that the change from low to high SST at 5100 cal. BP roughly coincides with the early phase of the Middle Jomon period (Upper-Ento-b and -c phases), during which significant changes occurred in archaeological data (see below), the change in the SST at around 5100 cal. BP should not be dismissed without further consideration. In particular, the potential impacts of changes in the SST on marine productivity and fishing need to be systematically examined.

Also, looking at their pollen data in more detail, an interesting pattern can be found. While *Castanea* pollen was more abundant during ca. 5900–4100 cal. BP than in the preceding and following periods, the peak of the relative abundance of *Castanea* pollen (Kawahata et al. 2009:970) was between 5900 and 5000 cal. BP. Results of our change point analysis of the *Castanea* pollen data also confirms that a major change occurred at around 5000 cal. BP, after which *Castanea* pollen began to decrease (Habu and Hall, 2010). Results of these studies indicate that climate changes reflected in pollen and other data should be examined further with a more fine-grained timescale.

In summary, while climate data show extremely interesting patterns, the causal relationships between climate change and shifts in Jomon people's lifeways need to be further examined with more data. A major problem is the scarcity of reliable radiocarbon dates that would allow us to identify the precise timing of these climate changes as well as of the changes in Jomon people's lifeways represented in archaeological data. At the same time, the possibility of examining changes in varying temporal scales, including millennium-scale changes in relation to global warming/cooling and changes in a shorter time spans such as those discussed by Kitagawa and Yasuda (2004), makes this avenue of research exciting in the context of historical ecological approaches.

Human Impacts on the Landscape

As outlined previously in this chapter, several scholars have suggested the possible importance of tending chestnut trees and/or cultivating plants at

Sannai Maruyama. Kitagawa and Yasuda (2004) link the results of their pollen analysis at Sannai Maruyama with earlier discussions on semi-cultivation (*hansaibai*) (e.g., Nakao 1976; Sakatsume 1961) during the Jomon period, and suggest that the tending of chestnut trees occurred repeatedly at the site during the warm climate phases. Their view of chestnut tending is cyclical with a timescale of several hundred years. Furthermore, they suggest that a similar practice of tending chestnut trees continued in the Aomori area through to the Final Jomon period. They also argue against Hatayama's (1997) suggestion that the fluctuation in chestnut pollen might have been caused by accidental fires.

Tsuji (2002), whose earlier work (Tsuji 1999) acknowledged the impact of cooling climate on the lifeways of Sannai Maruyama residents, and his collaborators (Yoshikawa et al. 2006) emphasize the degree of artificial alternation of the vegetation at the site, namely the establishment of chestnut orchards. Based on their pollen data, these scholars suggest that the alternation of the vegetation started shortly after the beginning of the site occupation and continued for the following 1,700 years. Furthermore, Yoshikawa et al. (2006:65–66) argue that the reduction in the relative frequency of chestnut pollen toward the end of the Middle Jomon period was not a result of the cooling climate but a reflection of site residents' intentional choice to shift their subsistence focus from chestnuts to buckeyes (*Aesculus*). They suggest that, after the Sannai Maruyama settlement was abandoned, the vegetation at the site went back to the "natural" forest of *Quercus* and *Fagus*.

From the perspective of historical ecology, the possibility of large-scale, artificial modifications of vegetation raises the question of their long-term impacts on the local and regional landscapes. Changes in vegetation reflected in pollen, diatoms, and macro-floral remains data, as well as changes in faunal assemblages, can help us understand aspects of the long-term impacts of the forest modification suggested by these scholars. It is also likely that the alternation of the vegetation affected people's perception of cultural landscapes.

Subsistence Specialization: Changes in Diversity in Staple Food

Lastly, but not least importantly, changes in settlement size, subsistence strategies, and ritual practice should be examined. The following analysis focuses on the long-term impacts of the shift in diversity of staple food.

Figure 4.2 summarizes changes through time at Sannai Maruyama in the number of pit dwellings, characteristics of stone tool assemblages, and the number of clay figurines (Habu 2008). The bar graph shows changes in the minimum number of pit dwellings identified in each phase. Some interesting trends are apparent in this diagram. First, the graph shows that only Upper-Ento-d and Upper-Ento-e phases are definitely associated with more than 50 pit dwellings. For the other 10 phases, the numbers of associated dwellings are much smaller, representing a medium or even a small settlement. Second, the graph shows fluctuations through time as opposed to a smooth and gradually increasing curve. If settlement size is correlated with strategies in securing food resources, this fluctuating pattern might support the model suggested by Kitagawa and Yasuda (2004) in which cyclical changes in subsistence activities were suggested. Despite such fluctuations, the long-term trend indicates that the high point of the Sannai Maruyama settlement can be identified at the Upper-Ento-d and -e phases.

The middle part of the diagram summarizes changes in lithic assemblage characteristics (for details, see Habu 2008:574–77). In the beginning of the site occupation, the lithic assemblage is characterized by an abundance of stemmed scrapers. They are considered to have been used for processing meat and fish. The following several phases (the Lower-Ento-b to Upper-Ento-a phases) are characterized by a mixed assemblage with arrowheads and grinding stones as well as stemmed scrapers. Arrowheads must have been used for hunting, and grinding stones are typically considered to have been plant-food processing tools. During the next three phases (the Upper-Ento-b to -d phases), the lithic assemblage is characterized by the dominance of grinding stones. This abundance of grinding stones was suddenly interrupted in the Upper-Ento-e phase, when the arrowhead became the most dominant type of lithic tool.

Assuming that characteristics in the lithic assemblage reflect subsistence activities, these archaeological patterns seem to indicate a general long-term trend in changes in subsistence strategies. Specifically, if grinding stones were a plant-food processing tool as suggested by many archaeologists, then we are observing a gradual increase in the reliance on a particular type of plant food that was processed by a single type of stone tool—the grinding stone. It is likely that this implied a significant reduction in subsistence diversity. A sudden decrease in the relative frequency of grinding stones is likely to indicate the decline of this extreme specialist type of economy.

The top part of the diagram shows changes in the number of clay figurines. To date, more than 1,600 clay figurines or figurine fragments have

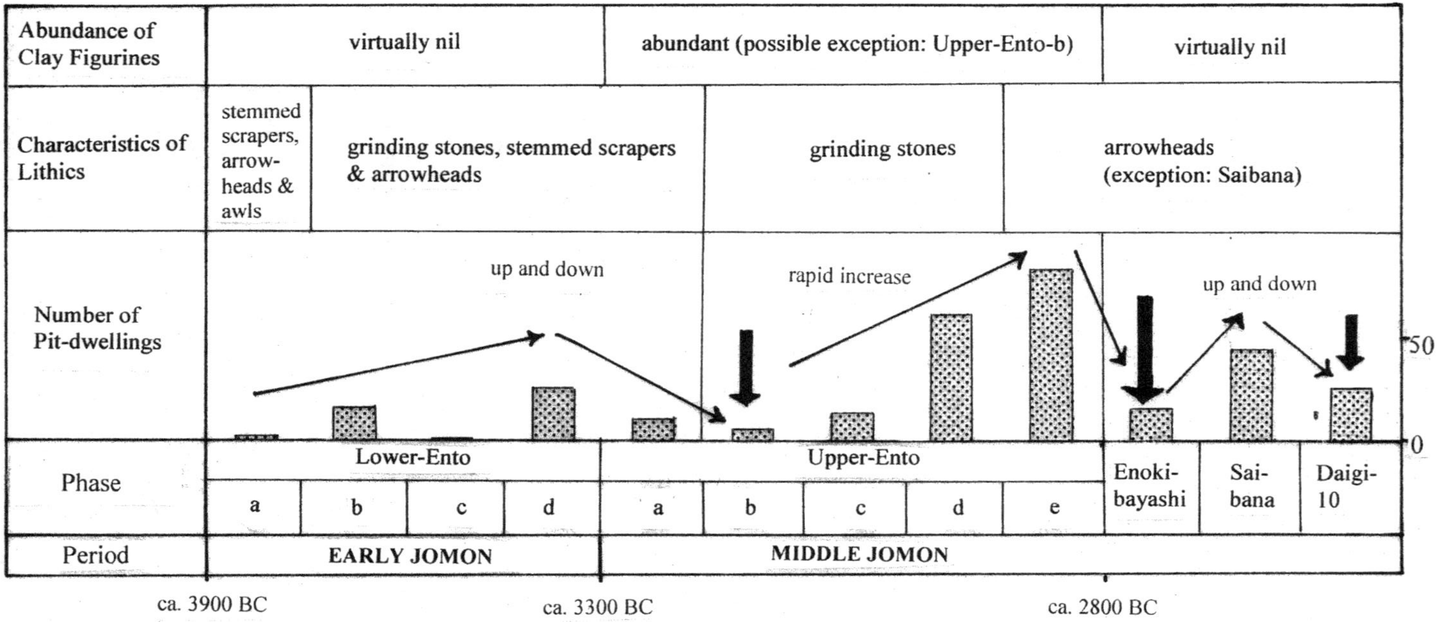
Abundance of Clay Figurines
virtually nil
abundant (possible exception: Upper-Ento-b)
virtually nil
Characteristics of Lithics
stemmed scrapers, arrow-heads & awls
grinding stones, stemmed scrapers & arrowheads
grinding stones
arrowheads (exception: Saibana)
Number of Pit-dwellings
up and down
rapid increase
up and down
50
0
Phase
Lower-Ento
Upper-Ento
a
b
c
d
a
b
c
d
e
Enoki-bayashi
Sai-bana
Daigi-10
Period
EARLY JOMON
MIDDLE JOMON
ca. 3900 BC
ca. 3300 BC
ca. 2800 BC

Figure 4.2. Summary of observed archaeological patterns at Sannai Maruyama (from Habu 2008:580).

been excavated from Sannai Maruyama. Looking at their typological characteristics, the majority of these figurines are dated to the Upper-Ento-a, -c, -d or -e phases. The number of clay figurines decreased sharply from the Upper-Ento-e to the following Enokibayashi phase. In other words, a major decline in the number of clay figurines did occur between the Upper Ento-e phase and the Enokibayashi phase, which coincided with the sharp decrease in the number of pit dwellings, as previously discussed.

In summary, an increasing reliance on plant food can be observed from the end of the Early Jomon to the middle of the Middle Jomon period. The resulting specialist type of economy was suddenly interrupted at the beginning of the Upper-Ento-e phase, after which both settlement size and the number of clay figurines decreased significantly. Thus, in terms of causal relationships, these data seem to indicate that a major change occurred first in the realm of subsistence strategies, which was then followed by changes in settlement size and ritual behavior (as represented by the number of figurines).

Based on these archaeological findings, Habu (2008) suggested a hypothesis that the increase and decrease in settlement size at Sannai Maruyama was correlated with the development and decline of subsistence intensification, with a focus on a particular type of plant food. This hypothesis by no means implies that other factors were unrelated to the growth and decline in site size at Sannai Maruyama: the observed archaeological patterns can also be a reflection of many other factors, such as changes in site function. It is important to note that, although there are numerous dwellings from the Upper-Ento-d and -e phases, the majority of these dwellings are extremely small, typically measuring only between 2.5 and 4 meters in long-axis length. These are much smaller than typical Jomon pit dwellings. Thus, during these phases, the site could have functioned as a seasonal, short-term residential base, or the place of aggregation of a large number of people for a seasonal get-together (Habu 2004:129–30).

A key issue to our understanding of the development and decline of the Middle Jomon culture in the Aomori area is the identification of the type or types of plant food that were processed using the large number of grinding stones. As discussed, many scholars suggest that the staple food for the Middle Jomon residents of the Sannai Maruyama site was the chestnut. However, preliminary results of our analysis of macro-floral remains from Sannai Maruyama and two other neighboring sites indicate that nuts utilized by the residents of these sites during the early and middle phases of the Middle Jomon period were not limited to chestnuts. A quantitative analysis of the waterlogged midden deposit of the Sannai Maruyama No. 9 Site (a small residential site located about 500 meters away from Sannai Maruyama proper) (Aomori-ken Maizo Bunkazai Chosa Center [Archaeo-logical Center of Aomori Prefecture] 2007, 2008) indicates that buckeyes were commonly used during an early phase of the Middle Jomon period, possibly as early as the Upper-Ento-a phase. Our excavation of another small residential site, Goshizawa Matsumori (Habu 2009), has revealed that the fills of a pit dwelling and two flask-shaped storage pits, all of which are dated to the Middle Jomon Upper-Ento-a phase, include a large num-ber of walnut shell fragments. Furthermore, Middle Jomon layers from Sannai Maruyama proper have also yielded a large number of walnut shell fragments (Habu 2006). Given these lines of evidence, it is too early to conclude that chestnut was the sole staple food that was associated with the rise of the Middle Jomon culture in this region. Rather, we need to think of the possibility that the development of the Middle Jomon culture in this region was based on a mixed-nut economy.

Concluding Remarks

As the next step of our research at Sannai Maruyama and its neighboring sites, we have begun our attempts to examine various lines of evidence. Sys-tematic examination of reliable ^{14}C dates from archaeological sites is indis-pensable to identify the timings of changes in subsistence, settlement, and society. In addition, obtaining new lines of evidence for climatic changes will be critical. These include pollen and phytolith analyses and oxygen iso-tope ratios of marine shells from multiple sites. Third, residue analyses of pottery and stone tools can help us greatly in obtaining information about the Jomon diet. Most importantly, we need to examine characteristics of the site in relation to changes in regional settlement patterns.

In conclusion, we have attempted to demonstrate that archaeological data from Sannai Maruyama and its neighboring sites provide us with a unique opportunity to examine changing human-environmental interac-tions in a small-scale prehistoric society. Currently available data indi-cate that subsistence specialization at Sannai Maruyama may have been the principal factor that allowed the site population to grow, but that the growth was not sustained after several hundred years. We hypothesize that a decrease in subsistence and food diversity, which was a result of subsistence specialization, made the Sannai Maruyama economic system more vulnerable to minor changes in other variables. Cooling climate may have been a factor that triggered the population decline, but we still do not have enough ¹⁴C dates to nail down the timing in relation to the archaeological sequence. In any case, examination of socioeconomic factors, as well as climate change, is critical in understanding the mechanisms of long-term human-environmental dynamics.

The link between climate change and the rise and fall of highly developed cultures has been a topic of debate in popular literature (e.g., Diamond 2005; Fagan 2000, 2004, 2008; Yasuda 2004; cf. McAnany and Yoffee 2010) as well as in environmental archaeology (e.g., Anderson et al. 2007). As demonstrated in many of these debates, climate change itself is not always a sufficient explanation for culture change. Nor did cooling climate always result in the decline or collapse of a particular culture. For example, in their discussion on the emergence of the "collector" type (*sensu* Binford 1980) of complex hunter-gatherer subsistence-settlement systems on the Northwest coast of North America, Prentiss and Chatters (2003) suggest that the Neoglacial temperature downturn shortly after 4000 uncal. BP brought new pressures upon hunter-gatherers in this region. They hypothesize that this ultimately resulted in the decimation of most other systems. In central California, the climate change at about 4500 to 4000 cal. BP seems to have triggered population movements and a resulting population increase, as well as the elaboration of burial practice (Kennett et al. 2007; Moratto 1984).

Finally, we need to ask whether the decrease in the number of large settlements at the end of the Middle Jomon period was really a "collapse" or "decline." Although the average size of settlements from the following Late Jomon period is much smaller than that of the Middle Jomon period settlements, the Late Jomon period was characterized by complex rituals, sophisticated material culture, and signs of craft specialization, such as pottery production (Habu 2004:chapter 7). Thus, the last question is tied to whether settlement size and population are valid indicators for measuring the success of a prehistoric hunter-gatherer culture.

Acknowledgments

Our research at the Sannai Maruyama and Goshizawa Matsumori sites have been conducted in collaboration with the Preservation Office of the Sannai

Maruyama Site, the Archaeological Center of Aomori Prefecture, and the Board of Education of Aomori City. The contents of this paper benefited from discussions with Kent Lightfoot, Hodaka Kawahata, and members of the above-listed organizations. We would like to thank these individuals and institutions. Financial support for the Berkeley Sannai Maruyama and Goshizawa Matsumori project was provided by the Center for Japanese Studies, the Archaeological Research Facility, the Hellman Family Faculty Fund and the Committee on Research Grants of the University of California–Berkeley, and by the Henry Luce Foundation. All opinions and views expressed in this article are those of the authors, and not the individuals or organizations listed above, the Bureau of Land Management, or the Department of the Interior.

5

Cumulative Actions and the Historical Ecology of Islands along the Georgia Coast

VICTOR D. THOMPSON, JOHN A. TURCK,
AND CHESTER B. DEPRATTER

They catch fish, gather shellfish, and build towns and villages on the strand and in small embayments. Their coastal activities have been so numerous and varied that their total effect has been significant. One of their most persistent activities has been the building of shell mounds, which are large piles chiefly of refuse resulting from various uses of shellfish. . . . they cover as much as 10 per cent of the shoreline. . . . these mounds have been instrumental both in holding the coast line against retrogression and in aiding progression.

John Davis, "Influences of Man Upon Coast Lines"

John Davis wrote the above words more than 50 years ago in a chapter in the seminal volume *Man's Role in Changing the Face of the Earth* (Thomas 1956). A professor of botany at the University of Florida at the time of its publication, Davis considered shell mounding significant enough to include in his worldwide overview of the influence of humans on coastlines. Indeed, shell accumulations that are the products of human behavior, either in the form of intentionally mounded architecture or refuse remains, occur worldwide (e.g., Bailey and Milner 2002; Erlandson 2001; Thompson and Worth 2011). While great strides in understanding shell middens and mounds have been made in the latter part of the twentieth and early twenty-first centuries (e.g., Rick and Erlandson 2008; Fish et al., this volume; Milner, this volume), we still do not fully understand the dynamic interaction between these structures in the context of human-environmental interactions in coastal environments (see Pennings, this volume).

The purpose of this chapter is to examine, in-depth, the role that preindustrial societies had in shaping coastal ecosystems and provide a preliminary case study of how small-scale economies, over time, work to transform environments (see also Rick, this volume; Milner, this volume). More specifically, we focus on the consumption and deposition of shellfish by hunter-gatherer-fishers of the southern Atlantic coast of Georgia, United States, over the past 4,500 years as a potential driving force in long-term coastal ecosystem dynamics.

Historical ecology is the primary theoretical framework that structures our research along the Georgia coast. Specifically, we focus on two key aspects of historical ecology that set it apart from other frameworks. First, as defined by Balée and Erickson (2006:1,5), historical ecology takes the view that humans are a keystone species and thus a primary driver of ecological change, whether their actions are intentional or unintentional (see Balée 1998). Second, historical ecology focuses on the landscape, while also recognizing that a full understanding of the landscape is only possible by linking together multiple scales of analysis that range from the local to the regional level (Balée 1998; Balée and Erickson 2006:12; Crumley 1994b:10, 2007:16–17).

Our central argument is that the deposition of shellfish fundamentally altered the ecosystem by both creating and modifying upland habitats. Specifically, we focus on small islands of upland habitat surrounded by marsh, located between the larger barrier islands and the mainland, known as marsh islands, back-barrier islands, or hammocks. These marsh islands should be characterized as "keystone structures" (Pennings et al. 2010), which are defined as "a distinct spatial structure providing resources, shelter, or 'goods and services' crucial for other species" (Tews et al. 2004:86). Thus, because humans played a critical role in the formation of many of these marsh islands, much of the coastal ecosystem of Georgia represents a distinctly anthropogenic landscape.

We argue that these marsh islands comprised a considerable component of the overall economy of Native coastal societies (Thompson and Turck 2010). Further, we argue that, at least in terms of intensity of use, the hammocks and associated marsh are comparable to the larger barrier islands. Finally, we suggest, following island biogeography theory (MacArthur and Wilson 1967), due to the size and relative isolation of some of these islands, they are more susceptible to human impacts.

To illustrate this argument, we provide a brief outline of the Native

American occupation of coastal Georgia. We then present a series of data at varying scales of analysis (e.g., regional site distributions, survey data, excavations) to illustrate the impact and scale of human alteration of islands in this environment. Finally, we discuss the relevance and implications of this study in terms of historical ecology and the long-term health of this ecosystem, emphasizing the idea that the cessation of Native American activities may have real consequences for the long-term health of dependent ecosystems.

Study Area

At around 160 kilometers in length, the Georgia coast hosts complex systems of barrier islands, marsh islands, salt marsh lagoon systems, brackish water marshes, tidal creeks, river channels, and maritime forest communities (Elliott and Sassaman 1995:7). The present-day barrier islands are actually composed of Pleistocene islands fronted by Holocene islands (Hayes et al. 1980:285). The Pleistocene islands are part of the Silver Bluff shoreline, which formed sometime between 110,000 and 25,000 BP (Howard and Frey 1985:78). Deglaciation and eustatic sea level rise led to the re-flooding of these areas during the mid-Holocene, and the formation of a salt marsh lagoon system (Brooks et al. 1989; DePratter and Howard 1981; Elliott and Sassaman 1995:7). During the mid-Holocene, the river systems gradually deposited sand and clay, forming a brackish water marsh drained by tidal creeks behind the Silver Bluff islands (Elliott and Sassaman 1995:7).

The back-barrier area of the South Carolina and Georgia coasts is about four times larger than other back-barrier areas along the Atlantic coast (Hayden and Dolan 1979:1069). In addition, the marshlands of South Carolina and Georgia boast the highest biotic values on the Atlantic Coast (Hayden and Dolan 1979:1063). These factors have combined to give the Georgia coastal ecosystem one of the highest concentrations of biomass on the Atlantic coast (see figure 5.1). While there are about 1,670 marsh islands along the Georgia coast, they only make up around 12 percent of the intertidal landscape (figure 5.2) (Alexander unpublished; Pennings et al. 2010). Despite this fact, these landforms have a significant impact on the ecosystem as a whole. Recent ecological research suggests that such isolated uplands may affect over 45 percent of the marsh environment by providing refuges for plant and animal species, as well as through the transference of materials through foraging and excretion (Pennings et al. 2010; Alexander unpublished data). Without such structures, the distribution of species and the nature of the entire ecosystem would be fundamentally altered; therefore it is useful to consider these landforms as keystone structures (Pennings et al. 2010; Whitaker et al. 2004).

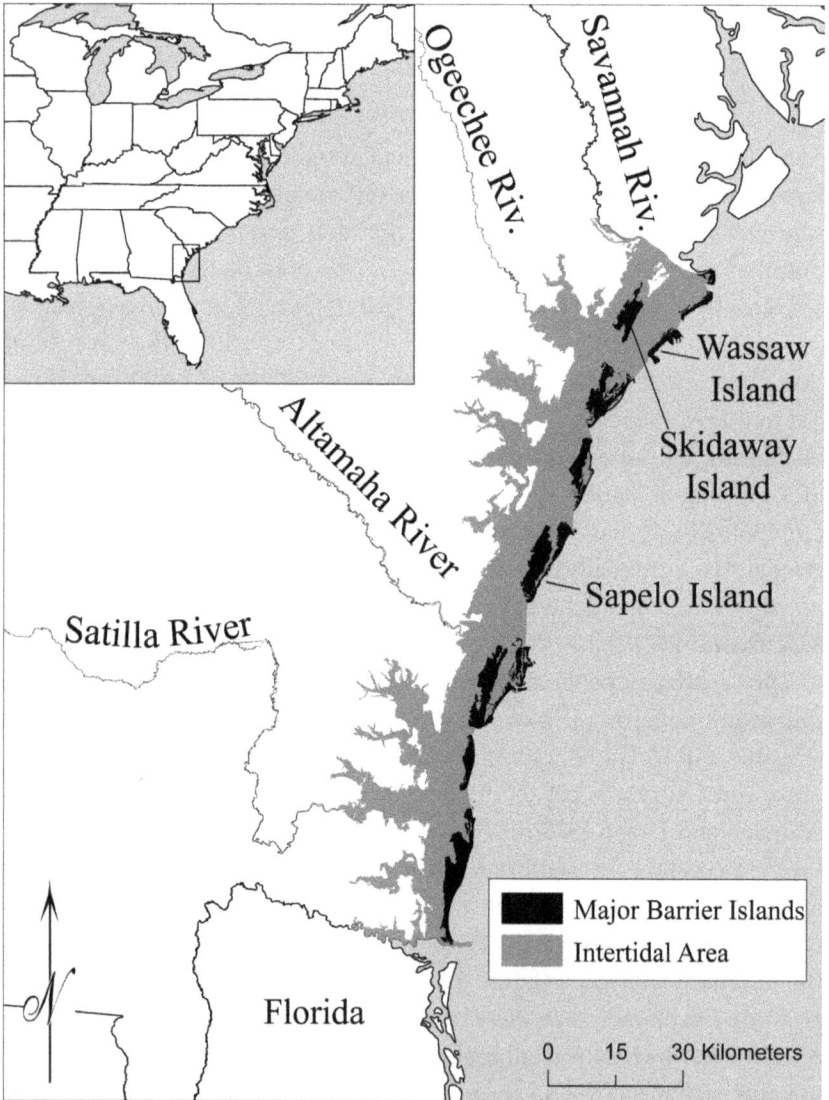

Figure 5.1. Map of the Georgia coast showing major resource zones.

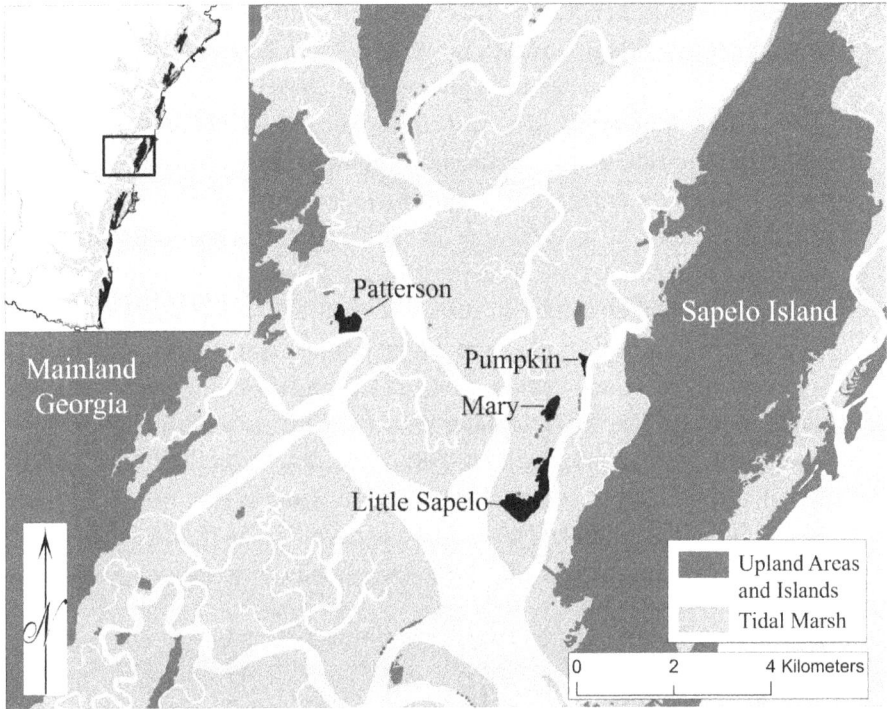

Figure 5.2. Map showing study area marsh islands along the Georgia coast.

Native American Occupation of the Coast

Before we examine the supporting evidence, a brief background regarding the major trends during the Native American occupation of the Georgia coast is necessary. While many researchers provide this basic information in numerous publications (e.g., DePratter 1991; Larsen 1982, Thomas 2008a, 2008b, 2008c; Thompson and Turck 2009, 2010), this overview will familiarize the readers with the archaeology of the study area, and allow them to better understand the context of our points regarding this landscape.

Intensive use of shellfish on the Georgia coast spans more than 4,500 years. The major subdivisions during this time frame includes what archaeologists refer to as the Late Archaic (2500 BC–1100 BC), Early Woodland (1100 BC–400 BC), Middle Woodland (400 BC–AD 500), Late Woodland (AD 500–AD 1000), Early Mississippian (AD 1000–AD 1325), Late Mississippian (AD 1325–AD 1580), and the Historic Contact (AD 1580–AD 1700) periods (DePratter 1991; Thomas 2008a).

The earliest evidence of shellfish consumption dates to the Late Archaic period. During this period, sea levels were 1.5 to 1.2 meters below present mean sea level (DePratter and Howard 1980, 1981; Colquhoun and Brooks 1986; Gayes et al. 1992). The numerous sites that evidence shellfish consumption indicate that the estuaries supported thriving shell beds at this time. Some sites during this period include the large ring complexes of shellfish remains, such as the one on Sapelo Island (Thompson 2007, 2010; Thompson et al. 2004). Such deposits reach heights of up to three meters and can be over 90 meters in diameter (figure 5.3). Archaeologists have posited several different interpretations for these ring-shaped shell deposits, including ceremonial mounding and feasting sites, village sites, or some combination of the two (DePratter 1976, 1979; Russo 2004; Saunders 2004; Thompson 2007, 2009; Trinkley 1985). Recently Thompson and Andrus (2011), through stable isotope analysis on clams and oysters from the Sapelo Island Shell Ring complex, identified a pattern of year-round collection of shellfish. Despite the fact that Late Archaic hunter-gatherers seem to be

Figure 5.3. Ring I at the Sapelo Island Shell Ring complex. Photo by Victor Thompson.

using specific sites over the course of the year, there are also many other nonring shell middens of varying sizes. This indicates that archaeological deposits are both intensive and extensive over the landscape at this time.

The intensive use of shellfish appears to have waned by the beginning of the Early Woodland period (ca. 1100 BC), possibly due to the lowering of sea levels of up to four meters. Such a drop in sea levels would have changed salinity levels in the estuaries, and thus would have impacted the ranges of oyster and clam habitat (DePratter and Howard 1980; 1981; Gayes et al. 1992; Thompson and Turck 2009). Concomitant with these environmental changes, it appears that during this time Native peoples relied more heavily on terrestrial resources (DePratter 1976, 1977, 1978:70–72; Marrinan 1975:78); and, although a small amount of shell fishing continued to be practiced, it did not match that of the Late Archaic, nor that of subsequent occupations of the Georgia coast.

By 400 BC, sea level had risen to approximately where it was prior to the drop, and the archaeological record once again indicates a reliance on shellfish by hunter-gatherer-fishers (Thompson and Turck 2009). During the Middle Woodland and Late Woodland periods, there is not only the proliferation of sites with substantial shell deposits, but also a shift in overall settlements to be located closer to the estuaries (Thompson and Turck 2009). In addition, growth band analysis on clam shells from these time frames indicates collections over multiple seasons during the year (Quitmyer et al. 1985, 1997).

Up to this point, the Native populations were primarily coastal foragers, and there is little evidence of use of cultigens. After AD 1150, (i.e., throughout the Mississippian and early Historic eras), maize was utilized to varying degrees (Hutchinson et al. 1998; Keene 2004; Larsen et al. 2001). Although there is some variation over time, the general pattern is one that indicates a gradual increase in the use of maize during this time frame (Hutchinson et al. 1998). Despite the fact that maize becomes part of the diet, populations continued to rely heavily on estuarine resources, including shellfish (Crook 1984; DePratter and Howard 1980; Hutchinson et al. 1998; Jefferies and Moore 2009; Larsen et al. 2001; Schoeninger 2009:637; Thomas and Larsen 1979).

While later-period shell-bearing sites do not reach the height of the Late Archaic rings, they do contain considerable shell deposits usually comprised of many individual household middens clustered together. Typically, these midden mounds are around four meters in diameter and can be over a meter in height. For example, the Bourbon Field site on Sapelo Island, which has both large Late Woodland and Mississippian components, is over 14 hectares and contains more than 119 individual shell middens (Crook 1984:247–48). At Kenan Field, a 60-hectare Mississippian site on Sapelo Island, there are almost 600 individual shell middens (Crook 1995:44). In terms of season of collection, stable isotope analysis on oysters from the Groove's Creek site, a Late Mississippian site on Skidaway Island, indicates that such resources were used throughout the year (Keene 2004).

The coming of Europeans and the establishment of Spanish missions along the coast severely disrupted both the overall health and diet of coastal Native Americans. In general, their diet becomes more homogenous, and use of estuarine resources declines as these groups become more reliant on maize (Hutchinson et al. 1998; Larsen et al. 2001; Schoeninger 2009). Contact with Europeans led to the decline in the health of coastal populations and eventually led to large-scale demographic collapse (Hutchinson et al. 1998; Larsen 2002; Larsen et al. 2001; Stojanowski 2005; Thompson and Worth 2011). By AD 1700, the indigenous populations that once inhabited the coastal estuaries and islands of Georgia were completely decimated.

Data Illustrating Human Impact

The brief background that we provide regarding the Native American occupation of the Georgia coast illustrates some of the general patterns that are important regarding the past use of the coastal landscape. In addition, we stress that for the better part of 4,500 years, the coastal ecosystem functioned in concert with human predation of numerous species as well as modifications to the landscape in the form of trash disposal, village occupation, etc. In order to explore the impact that such cumulative activities might have had regarding the landscape, we examine several data sets, including regional survey data, intensive island survey, and site-specific information.

Regional Data and the Shoreline Survey

DePratter's initial survey of the back-barrier environment in the 1970s and 1980s involved a rapid assessment of islands. This involved traveling by boat to marsh islands and determining the extent of shell deposits by walking over islands and recording the locations of visible shell, while also using a metal probe to record belowground shell deposits. Chronological information was recovered by making surface collections of ceramics along exposed shorelines and other exposed surfaces. This survey encompassed most of the coastline of Georgia and documented more than 200 archaeological sites. Based on this survey data, an estimated greater than 50 percent of back-barrier islands contain evidence of Native American use and/or occupation.

As an example of site density, we present data of the Holocene back-barrier area between Skidaway and Wassaw islands (figure 5.4). DePratter (1978, unpublished data) recorded many of the sites in this area as part of his initial survey. The area is comprised of 48.1 km² of marsh and 1.6 km² of upland area, made up of marsh islands. There are 53 sites located on these landforms, resulting in a site density of 33.1 sites per square kilometer of upland area. This is a high density of sites for such a small area. While only 11 of the 53 sites here have more than one component, this is most likely due to a lack of diagnostic artifacts found during surface surveys. The landscape

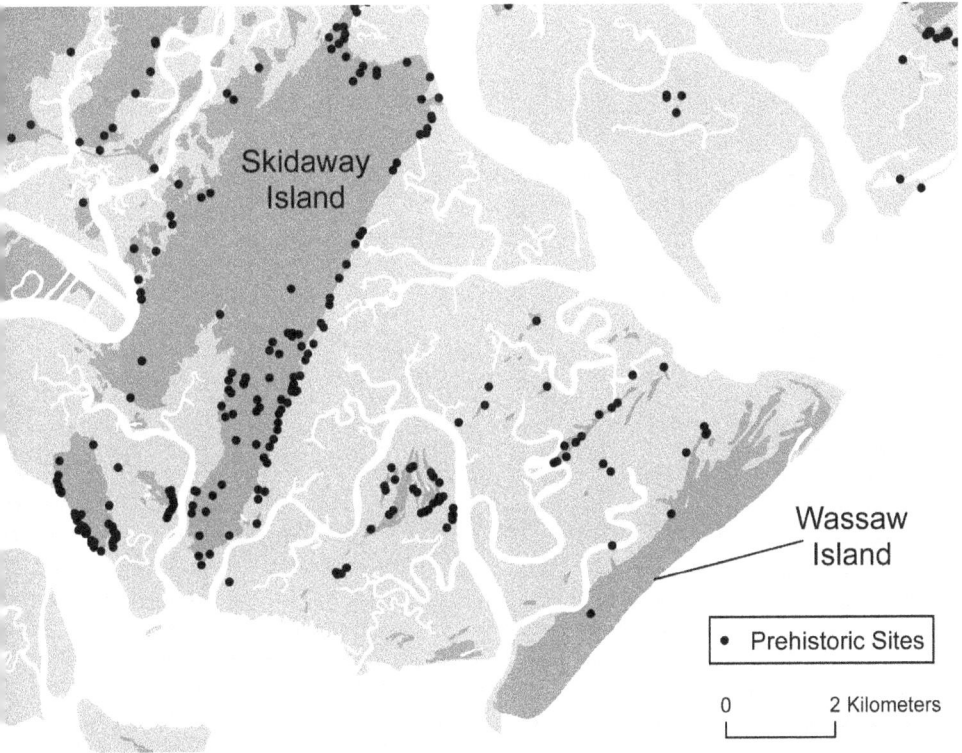

Figure 5.4. Site frequency in the Holocene back-barrier area between Skidaway and Wassaw islands.

here formed progradationally over the last 4,500 years, meaning that sediment was deposited laterally over time, in a seaward direction. When site chronology is taken into consideration, it appears that people utilized new upland areas almost as soon as they formed (see DePratter and Howard 1977; DePratter and Thompson in press; Turck and Alexander in press). This example indicates that during the past 4,500 years, people utilized much of the available upland landscape.

When data for the entire coast of Georgia are analyzed using the Georgia Archaeological Site File database, (which includes all of the information that DePratter has collected in his surveys), it reveals that high site density is characteristic of much of the coast. As seen in table 5.1, the number (and percentage) of sites in the back-barrier area is less than on the major barrier islands. However, when the densities of sites are looked at, the focus is turned to the back-barrier area (table 5.2). Although the total back-barrier area is about 2,296.3 km^2 (including rivers, streams, and other water bodies), the total habitable upland area (i.e., marsh islands) is only

Table. 5.1. Number and percentage of sites over time within the barrier and back barrier island areas of the Georgia coast

Period	Total sites	Back-barrier area		Barrier islands	
		# of sites	% of sites	# of sites	% of sites
Archaic	90	31	34.40%	59	65.60%
Woodland	485	164	33.80%	321	66.20%
Mississippian	407	125	30.70%	282	69.30%
Historic Contact	65	17	26.20%	48	73.80%
Total	1,047	337	32.20%	710	67.80%

Table 5.2. Number of sites and site density within the back-barrier and barrier island areas

Habitat	Area (km^2)	Sites	Site density
Barrier islands	344.9	710	2.1
Back-barrier areas	2,296.3	337	
Marsh	2,222.9	0	
Marsh islands	73.5	337	4.6
Total	2,641.2	1,047	

73.5 km^2. This includes areas designated as palustrine, which are intermittently flooded (as designated in the NWI wetlands data set produced by the U.S. Fish and Wildlife Service). This results in a site density of 4.6 sites per square kilometer, which is over two times greater than that on the barrier islands.

It is important to note that some of the sites included here are actually found within the marsh, on former landscapes. Unfortunately, sites in the marsh cannot be readily differentiated from those on marsh islands, due to even slight discrepancies with site coordinates and/or with borders of the wetland data set. On the other hand, only a handful of marsh sites have been recorded in the site file database, and the former landscapes those sites are on include drowned marsh islands. Thus, it is appropriate to include the few marsh sites as sites on marsh islands. With that in mind, we believe this shows that for marsh islands on the entire Georgia coast, site density is relatively high.

The Island Survey

In order to present a picture of how intensively people utilized these landforms, we now turn to our intensive survey data. Unlike the rapid island assessment, the intensive survey is comprised of a systematic shovel test survey at 20-meter intervals over entire islands. To date we have data from four marsh islands: Little Sapelo Island, Pumpkin Hammock, Mary Hammock, and Patterson Island. These islands range in size from 44.9 ha to 3.3 ha. (table 5.3).

In all four cases, evidence of Native American activity in the form of ceramics and shell deposits covers the majority of the island (figure 5.5). This is commensurate with what DePratter found in the shoreline survey. However, while the shoreline survey showed that marsh islands, in general, were used from the Late Archaic through the Historic periods, our intensive shovel test survey revealed that use waxed and waned differentially

Table 5.3. Marsh island sizes and total number of shovel tests

Marsh island name	Area (m^2)	Area (km^2)	Hectares	Total shovel tests
Little Sapelo Island	448,567.30	0.47	44.9	769
Pumpkin Hammock	33,386.30	0.03	3.3	57
Mary Hammock	104,002.30	0.1	10.4	222
Patterson Island	182,171.00	0.18	18.2	393

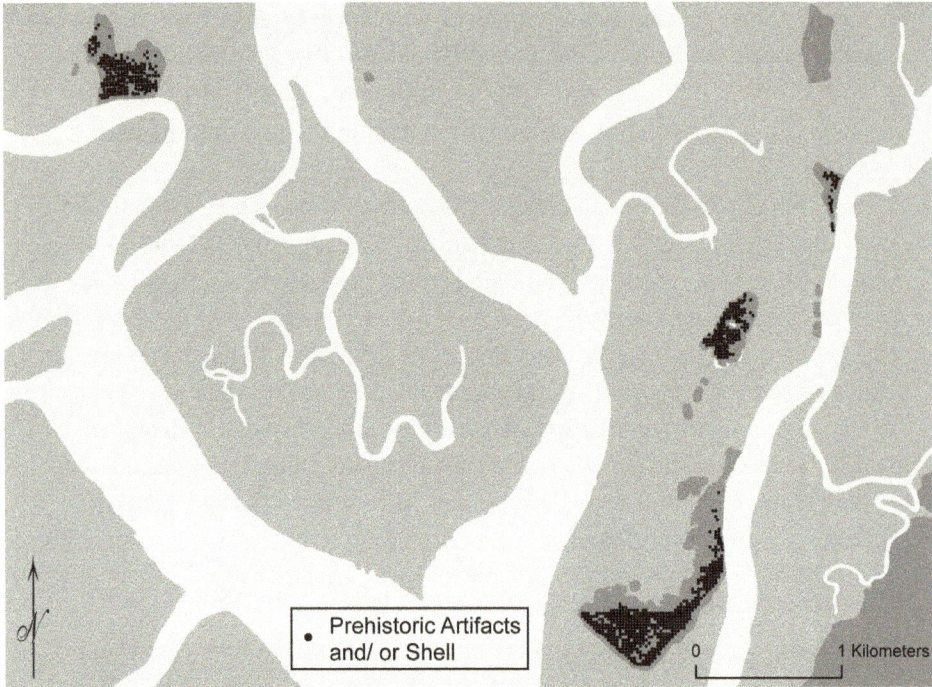

Figure 5.5. Artifact and shell distributions over the marsh island survey area.

from island to island. Table 5.4 shows the percentage of shovel tests with ceramics from the various time periods. One interesting observation is the periods of nonuse during the Late Archaic on Mary Hammock and the Early and Middle Woodland periods on Pumpkin Hammock. In addition, Late Mississippian period ceramics were found in the highest percentages of shovel tests for all islands except one—Pumpkin Hammock. Ceramics from the Historic period were found in higher frequencies on Pumpkin Hammock than on any other marsh island.

Human-deposited shell is a major part of the data we collected, especially subsurface deposits. In general, shell was found over the majority of the islands. Large shell deposits forming shell middens can typically be found along the edge of the islands, especially along tidal creeks, but they are by no means relegated to such areas (see Thompson and Turck 2010). In some cases, the deposition of shell on the surface added enough height to keep these landforms as uplands in the face of sea-level rise and marsh accretion. This is illustrated in our probe study of the southwestern projection of Mary Hammock that shows large accumulations of shell added to the landform, some of which continue under the marsh (figure 5.6). Another

Table 5.4. Number and percentage of shovel tests with ceramics from each period, for each marsh island

	Little Sapelo Island		Pumpkin Hammock		Mary Hammock		Patterson Island	
	# of STs	% of STs	# of STs	% of STs	# of STs	% of STs	# of STs	% of STs
Late Archaic	11	1.4	2	3.5	0		20	5.1
Early Woodland	4	0.5	0		3	1.4	3	0.8
Early/Middle Woodland	11	1.4	0		0		2	0.5
Middle Woodland	17	2.2	0		4	1.8	13	3.3
Late Woodland	7	0.9	5	8.8	5	2.3	7	1.8
Late Woodland/Early Miss.	14	1.8	2	3.5	10	4.5	32	8.1
Early Mississippian	2	0.3	0		0		1	0.3
Middle Mississippian	27	3.5	3	5.3	2	0.9	4	1
Middle/Late Mississippian	35	4.6	0		4	1.8	19	4.8
Late Mississippian	127	16.5	3	5.3	53	23.9	37	9.4
Late Miss./Historic Indian	27	3.5	2	3.5	2	0.9	6	1.5
Historic Indian	12	1.6	7	12.3	3	1.4	4	1
Unknown (Total)	147	19.1	14	24.6	26	11.7	85	21.6
None	467		36		143		245	
Total STs	769		57		222		393	

example of this effect is from Pumpkin Hammock, where shell deposits add almost a meter of elevation over high tide to the island (figure 5.7). The addition of shell to these areas makes them, in part, anthropogenic, and increases the overall amount of upland of these islands.

Marsh and Island Excavations

Excavations also attest to the intensive use of marsh islands. Our research on Pumpkin Hammock identified at least seven shell midden piles on the north end of the island, with some over one meter high. Based on the ceramics and the radiocarbon dates, these midden pile deposits date to the Late Woodland and Late Mississippian periods. Based on the shovel test and shoreline collections, the hammock also saw human use during the Late Archaic and the Historic Contact periods.

The midden piles on Pumpkin Hammock are comparable in form and structure to ones found at large habitation sites, such as those of the north of the Shell Ring Drain Mission Period site and the Late Mississippian site

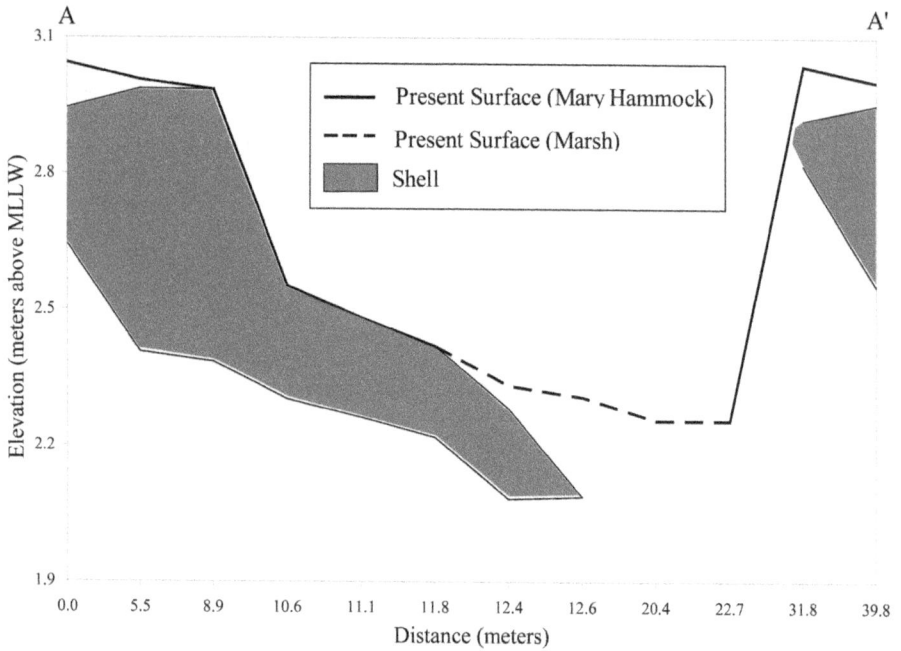

Figure 5.6. Probe study of the southwestern projection of Mary Hammock.

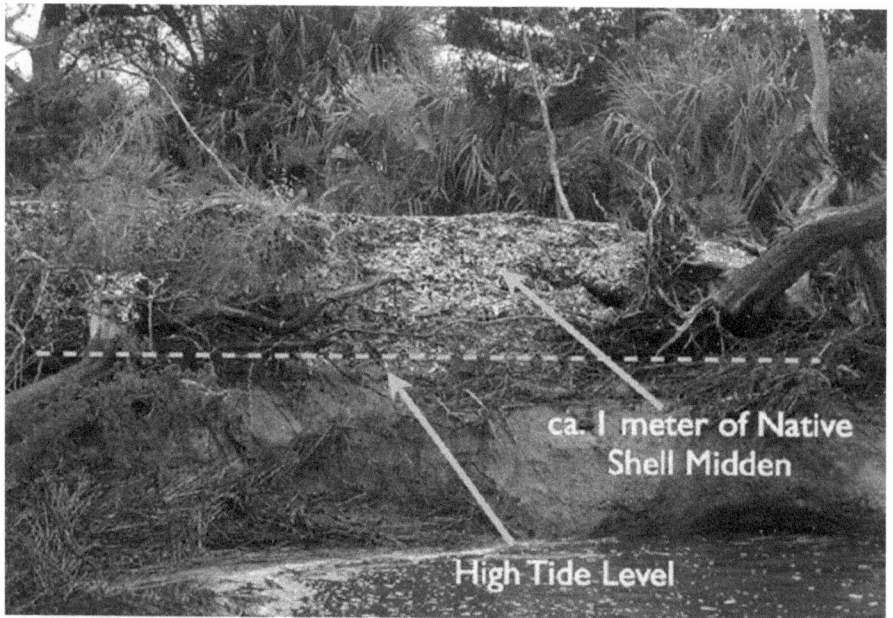

Figure 5.7. Pumpkin Hammock showing shell midden deposits in relation to high tide line. Photo by Victor D. Thompson.

of Bourbon Field on Sapelo Island (see Crook 1984; Jefferies and Moore 2009). There is considerable debate over how mobile coastal populations were prior to Spanish contact (e.g., Andrus and Thompson 2012; Jones 1978; Thomas 2008; Thompson and Andrus 2011). While we defined no formal structures in our excavations, we did identify several posts and associated pit features. Following Kent's (1991) ideas regarding anticipated mobility, we suggest that these features, coupled with dense ceramic deposits, indicate that groups were either returning to and/or re-occupying these places. Thus, the overall picture is that Native groups utilized these marsh island environments to a considerable degree over time.

While our examples given previously have shown that human deposition of shellfish helped to create or maintain upland environments in light of Holocene sea-level fluctuations, not all archaeological deposits rise above the marsh surface. Shellfish deposits have been found buried under marsh sediment, indicating the potential for more sites to be found in this intertidal environment. Further, despite being covered by marsh sediments, sites located in these environments can potentially influence the distribution of plant species in the marsh.

Summary

In sum, there are multiple lines of evidence supporting the claim that humans modified the marsh environment to a considerable degree. The number and density of sites in back-barrier areas, the large number of positive shovel tests on marsh islands, the large amount of Native American ceramics, and the wide extent and sometimes extremely deep shell deposits, all indicate the intensive use of this area by people. That shell midden deposits were noted up to one meter deep, and the fact that vegetation and salinity within the marsh are intimately tied to elevation, indicates the great effect that humans have had on this environment.

Keystone Structures and Socio-Ecological Systems

The marsh islands discussed here represent keystone structures of Georgia's coastal ecosystem. We hypothesize that without their presence the coastal environment would be a distinctly different place in terms of its biodiversity and distribution of plants and animals in the marsh. Anthropologists and ecologists affiliated with the Georgia Coastal Ecosystem Long-Term Ecological Research project are currently attempting to qualitatively and quantitatively address this very issue in their current research. Regardless, our overview of marsh island archaeology points to humans as significant actors in the maintenance of these structures in that humans have contributed to maintaining above-marsh topographic relief. Thus, such actions provided refuges for species, including humans, in the marsh ecosystem. Moreover, hunter-gatherer-fishers may have, to some extent, intentionally modified the environment through their depositional practices, such as throwing detritus into the wetland areas to attract economically important fishes (i.e., catfish), as Reitz et al. (2009:28) suggest. It is likely that each island had a different historical trajectory contributing to overall landscape of the coast. Such histories and events would have been important to the overarching interaction between humans and their environment. At this point in our research, we view these socio-ecological interactions and modifications to the Georgia coast as intentional on the small scale; however, their overall cumulative effect was *most likely* unintentional. Taken together these observations support the view that much of the intertidal area of the Georgia coast is rightfully thought of as anthropogenic in character. Further investigations into the historically contingent use and abandonment of these islands will allow us to more fully understand the role these landforms played among Native American populations.

Finally, yet another key point of this study is that one part of a small-scale economy (shellfishing) transformed this landscape over time. To be sure, other modifications most likely have impacted the Georgia coast; however, we do not have the data to address other human impacts (e.g., the use of fire, but see Reitz et al. 2009 for estuarine fishing) as of yet. The point here is that the production, consumption, and deposition of this particular resource had a cumulative effect and was an integral part of the development of the Georgia coast as a socio-ecological system.

Long-Term Health of the Ecosystem

Recently, archaeologists are increasingly concerned with the historical ecology of marine environments and what these long-term histories say about the current trajectories of these ecosystems and their relationship to human populations. The publication of Rick and Erlandson's (2008) book *Human Impacts on Ancient Marine Ecosystems,* and the founding of the *Journal of Island and Coastal Archaeology* underscore this concern. For the Georgia coast, our study has implications for the long-term health of this ecosystem. For 4,000 years, the Georgia coast developed in concert with human use of the landscape. These actions, we argue, created a symbiotic system and contributed to the overall productivity and resilience of this ecosystem. Beginning in the sixteenth century, coastal Native populations were eventually wiped out (Thompson and Worth 2011; Worth 1995). During the nineteenth century, industrialized harvesting and dredging decimated oyster populations (Thomas 2008a), and natural wave action as well as increased boat traffic has led to the erosion of some of the marsh islands. The makers and maintainers of these keystone structures no longer dwell along the coast. In order to understand how such systems will be affected and/or managed in the future, we must look now to the archaeological record before it too has vanished.

Acknowledgments

This research was supported, in part, by a grant in association with the Georgia Coastal Ecosystems LTER project, National Science Foundation Grant (NSF grant OCE-0620959). The Georgia Department of Natural Resources (GDNR) and the Sapelo Island National Estuarine Research Reserve provided additional support. Several individuals were instrumental in supporting our fieldwork, and they include David Crass, Dorset Hurley, Fred Hay, and Buddy Sullivan. Finally, the authors would like to thank Steven Pennings, Merryl Alber, and Clark Alexander of the Georgia Coastal LTER project for their support of our past and ongoing research. As always, the authors are responsible for all errors, omissions, mistakes, and gaffes.

6

A Historical Ecological Perspective on Early
Agriculture in the North American Southwest
and Northwest Mexico

PATRICIA A. GILMAN, ELIZABETH M. TONEY,
AND NICHOLAS H. BEALE

In the North American Southwest, a lengthy discussion continues regarding the extent to which agriculture produced dramatic changes in land use
during the Late Archaic period (2000 BC–AD 150). Specifically, researchers
debate to what degree Late Archaic societies were structured around maize
cultivation, and the extent to which people may have altered their land-use
patterns as a result of maize adoption. From the perspective of historical
ecology, the debate is interesting because Late Archaic early agriculturalists likely modified their landscapes in ways that affected later farmers, just
as they were working with the dynamics of the landscapes inherited from
Middle Archaic hunter-gatherers. In contributing to the discussion about
changes in social and economic organization during the Late Archaic period, we suggest that an historical-ecology framework can help address
these issues by focusing on anthropogenic changes in biotic communities.
While we know that every human group modifies the landscape, the impacts of the Late Archaic period modifications are more subtle and nuanced than we might have expected.

We examine the historical ecology of hunter-gatherers who had begun
to incorporate farming into their small-scale foraging economies. Such an
investigation is in contrast to many other historical-ecology studies that
focus on large-scale agriculturalists (Balée 2006; Crumley 1994a; Fish 2000;
Hastorf 2006), and it is useful because archaeologists might expect that
Late Archaic groups who had embarked on a more intensive relationship

with cultigens to have made a significant impact on their environment. Our research and that of others suggest that hunter-gatherers who incorporated maize into their subsistence economies did not impact the environment in the same ways as farmers later in time, even though they extensively and intensively modified parts of the landscape.

Following Dean's (2003, 2005) model, we use the proportions of disturbance species (certain species of rodents and perching birds) (Bye and Linares 2000; Linares 1976; Mellink 1985; Rea 1983; Stahl 2000) and the proportions of prey species (lagomorphs and artiodactyls) as measures of anthropogenic change in three study areas. Human behaviors, such as land clearing, irrigation, and the creation of storage facilities and human refuse areas, allow disturbance species to take hold in these newly formed niches (Diehl and Waters 2006; Fish 2000; Stahl 2000). Finally, we compare the disturbance rodent species and prey species from the Late Archaic period to those of subsequent periods, when such data are available, to assess the degree to which Late Archaic groups altered their environments in ways that impacted future generations on the land.

Three Case Studies

The debate about the role of early agriculture in people's lives has focused on two regions that have much evidence for maize cultivation—the Tucson Basin of southern Arizona and northern Chihuahua in northwestern Mexico (figure 6.1). Diehl and Waters (2006) have suggested, based on recent Late Archaic site excavations in the Tucson Basin and subsequent diet breadth studies, that cultigens were only one part of a very intricate foraging economy and that people continued to use low-ranked wild plant and animal resources despite the presence of cultigens. Alternatively, Hard and Roney (2005) have argued that, at the site of Cerro Juanaqueña in northern Chihuahua, maize very quickly became a major part of the diet. We note here that most archaeologists working in the Tucson Basin and at Cerro Juanaqueña have renamed the Late Archaic period as the Early Agricultural period to highlight the incorporation of cultigens into the subsistence regimes of groups inhabiting these areas.

We investigate anthropogenic changes to the environment in both regions, and we compare them to those in the San Simon Basin in southeastern Arizona (figure 6.1), an area in which there is less evidence for the incorporation of maize cultivation during the Late Archaic period. There are

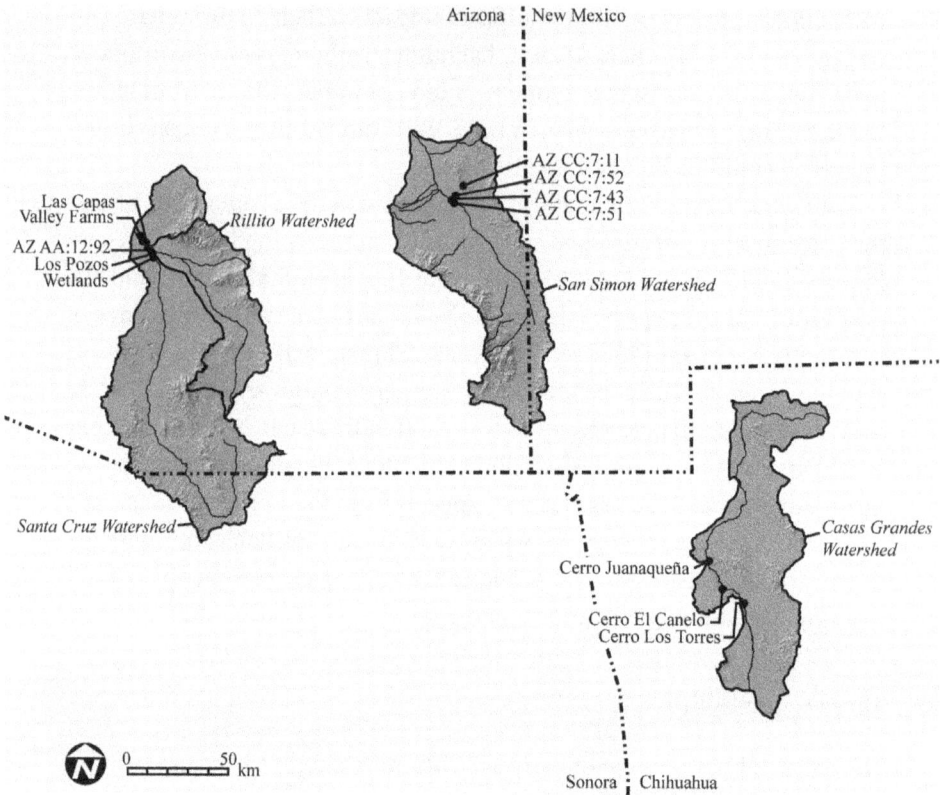

Figure 6.1. Late Archaic sites used in this study from the Tucson Basin, the San Simon Basin, and northern Chihuahua.

many recorded Late Archaic sites in the San Simon Basin (Dew 2007; Gilman 1995, 1997; Gilman et al. 1996; Rapp 2006; Thurtle and Roth 2008), a region that never was a population center like the Tucson Basin and northern Chihuahua and a place that had one of the earliest permanent abandonments in the Southwest at about AD 1050. In fact, there are almost as many Late Archaic sites in the basin as there are later Pit Structure period sites (Dew 2007). Limited excavations at a few Late Archaic sites (Gilman 1995; Gilman et al. 1996; Rapp 2006:205; Thurtle and Roth 2008:7.1–7.3) have produced faunal remains (Schmidt 1998) but almost no paleoethnobotanical remains. There is a possible early Late Archaic corn cupule at one of the excavated sites (Schmidt 1998:41–42), but at present there is little evidence for Late Archaic agriculture.

Human Impacts, History of Landscape Use, and Early Agriculture

Historical ecology would have us consider the consequences of past activities and landscape modifications for the people who lived on the same land later and how those activities and modifications affected the ecosystem. The historical-ecology themes of human impacts and the importance of those to subsequent people on the landscape are especially applicable to our research, and indeed the early agriculture debate in the Southwest revolves around human impacts. Southwestern archaeologists have been concerned with understanding how people affected their environments (Briggs et al. 2006, 2007; Fredrickson et al. 2006; Minnis 1985a; Redman 1999). What we have not often considered, although there are exceptions (Briggs et al. 2007; Dean 2003, 2005; Redman 1999; Schmidt 2011; Stahl 1996), is how people used or dealt with previous landscape modifications. In order to address these questions, some background into the land-use strategies of groups occupying the Tucson Basin, Cerro Juanaqueña, and the San Simon Basin during the Late Archaic period is necessary.

Northern Chihuahua and the San Simon Basin are both in the Chihuahuan Desert, while the Tucson Basin is in the Sonoran Desert. Although the Sonoran Desert is lower in elevation and hotter, it has higher plant diversity than the Chihuahuan Desert, due in part to the presence of both summer and winter showers in the Sonoran Desert compared to predominately summer rainfall in the Chihuahuan Desert. These three study areas, however, are all in desert environments in the southern Southwest, and as our analyses will show, the environmental impacts of people living during the Late Archaic period are quite similar. While there are certainly environmental differences between the two deserts, they do not seem to have affected people's environmental impacts at the time of the earliest agriculture, although we will note that the Tucson Basin has somewhat more artiodactyls and cottontails than the other two areas. The comparison of the two deserts, in terms of human responses, uses, and modifications, however, is a fertile topic for future study.

Middle Archaic Land Use in the Tucson Basin, Northern Chihuahua, and the San Simon Basin

People living during the Middle Archaic period (3500–1500 BC) (Huckell 1996) presumably provided an anthropogenically changed environment for later people, perhaps especially in terms of the numbers, distribution, and kinds of wild plants and animals available. Unfortunately, the Middle Archaic period in the Southwest is poorly known, and Freeman (1999:77–78) notes that this is because of difficulties with preservation, identification, and discovery. This is especially true in northern Chihuahua, where archaeologists have recovered some Middle Archaic points from Late Archaic sites, but have found very few true Middle Archaic sites (Justice 2002).

Middle Archaic sites, such as Las Capas and Los Pozos in the Tucson Basin, have yielded some of the earliest maize dates (Mabry 2005; Whittlesey et al. 2007) in the Southwest. In excavations of the Middle Archaic components at Los Pozos (Gregory 1999) and Las Capas (Whittlesey et al. 2007), archaeologists found remnants of Middle Archaic houses and a few storage pits, but they did not note large-scale effects on the landscape, such as canals or ritual sites, until the early Late Archaic (Freeman 1999). Evidence from Los Pozos and Las Capas indicates continuity from the Middle Archaic through the terminal Late Archaic periods.

In the San Simon Basin, Middle Archaic projectile points are not uncommon (Dew 2007; Gilman 1997), but there are no recorded sites that date solely to the Middle Archaic period. Middle Archaic points occur as isolated artifacts and on later sites, both with and without ceramics. Just north of the San Simon Basin in the Gila Mountains, Huckell et al. (1999) have excavated Middle Archaic materials in McEuen Cave. Tucker and Ezzo (2006) report on several excavated Middle Archaic sites in Tollgate and Tollhouse canyons just northeast of the San Simon Basin. The use of McEuen Cave and Tollhouse and Tollgate canyons in the mountainous areas above and away from the river valleys implies that Middle Archaic land use in the San Simon region was considerably different than any later time when sites were instead located along large and small drainages in the basin. It is possible, though, that people during the Middle Archaic period used or occupied those later sites with Middle Archaic points in the basin. If, however, the Middle Archaic points on later sites are just part of the scatter of "isolated" points across the landscape that were perhaps lost during hunting, then people had a very light footprint on the drainages during the Middle Archaic period.

Roth and Freeman's (2008) recent argument about a shift from upland logistical and residential sites to areas along the floodplain in the Tucson Basin between the Middle and Late Archaic periods parallels the settlement pattern in the San Simon region. They argue that environmental changes during the Middle Holocene were a major factor that led Middle Archaic groups to move to the floodplain, which are rich in nutrients for plants. With increasing aridity during the Altithermal, reliable floodplain sites became more attractive for seasonal rounds.

Late Archaic Land Use in the Tucson Basin, Northern Chihuahua, and the San Simon Basin

Recently, archaeologists have suggested numerous models concerning the land use and mobility strategies of people during the Late Archaic/Early Agricultural period in the Tucson Basin. These debates center on issues regarding the intensity of agricultural pursuits (Diehl and Waters 2006), the type of mobility practiced by people inhabiting the area (Roth 1989, 1992), and the number of cultural groups in the Tucson Basin during this time period (Fish et al. 1990, 1992; Huckell 1995). Late Archaic landscape use in the Tucson Basin has generally been conceptualized as a bimodal pattern based on the identification of sites dating to this period in both riverine and upper *bajada* zones (Mabry 2005). However, excavation has centered on sites in the floodplain along the margins of extinct river channels below 3,000 ft (Diehl and Waters 2006; Mabry 2005).

Despite the lack of excavation in the upper *bajada*, archaeologists have proposed different models to explain mobility and land use within the floodplain itself and within the two landscape settings. As an example of the former, Diehl (2001), Gregory and Diehl (2002), and Diehl and Waters (2006) all argue for a residentially mobile strategy where residential sites on the floodplain represent small populations. Gregory and Diehl (2002) have suggested that only small groups of no more than 10 to 80 people inhabited the floodplain landscape. They also propose that people used houses on the floodplain intermittently, most likely seasonally, and that the floodplain sites were occupied no more than a year or two at a time and most likely by extended family members. The residentially mobile model for the Tucson Basin has some interesting supporting arguments. One argument for residential movement across the landscape is that the river often flooded into residential and storage areas during these periods, which likely caused a 100 percent loss in stored food sources (Gregory and Diehl 2002; Schurr and Gregory 2002), which in turn caused people to move their houses and sites.

Considering movement and land use between the floodplain and the upper *bajada*, Roth (1992, 1995) suggests that maize was part of a seasonally repetitive and logistical pattern of movement that used resources in different environmental zones. Fish et al. (1990, 1992) propose that the bimodal pattern indicates two independent settlement and agricultural systems. One group focused on floodwater farming on the floodplain and alluvial fans, while the group focused on the upper *bajada* practiced dry farming. In contrast, Huckell (1995) has suggested that during the Late Archaic there were groups that had strictly foraging adaptations and other groups that practiced a mixed farming-foraging economy, particularly in certain areas of the Tucson Basin.

Interestingly, Roth and Freeman (2008) show that a repetitive pattern of land use emerges during the Middle Archaic period, suggesting continuity in land use from the Middle Archaic to the Late Archaic. All of the proposed models suggest many people and the potential for much impact in the Tucson Basin during the Late Archaic period. Because of the impressive Late Archaic field and irrigation systems, sets of roasting pits, concentrations of houses, and presence of field houses in the Tucson Basin, as well as the massive walls that may date to the Late Archaic period encircling the top of Tumamoc Hill in the basin (Wallace et al. 2007), there was also clear continuity with the post-Archaic period, and so the impact of previous landscape use between the Late Archaic and post-Archaic in the Tucson Basin is also a critical issue.

Much less is known about human impacts and land-use patterns in northwestern Mexico and the San Simon Basin, although according to Schmidt (1998, 2008), people in both regions used logistical mobility. Furthermore, there is a lack of evidence that people occupied northern Chihuahua intensively until the Medio period (AD 1250–1450; Whalen and Minnis 2001), although Schmidt (2008) delves into the land-use strategies for the few Late Archaic sites in this region. Therefore, we have relied on Schmidt's (2008) dissertation for much of the northern Chihuahua data and ideas for the Late Archaic land use in this area. Schmidt argues that the faunal remains in conjunction with the macrobotanical and pollen data suggest that groups of people who employed both logistical and residential mobility depending on the season occupied the *cerros de trincheras* sites in Chihuahua. Schmidt states that during the summer and fall seasons, Late Archaic groups would use the *cerros de trincheras* sites for agriculture but would be more mobile during other seasons. Besides the impact from agriculture, the Late Archaic groups heavily affected the landscape with the construction of large terraces.

Dew (2007) has pointed out that, in the San Simon Basin, there were almost as many Late Archaic sites (1500 BC–AD 100) as Pit Structure period sites (AD 100–1050). This suggests that for about 2,000 years there may have been relatively many people in the region, compared to before and after these periods. As we noted earlier, these are the only two time periods during which people used the basin to any extent at all, and so human impacts were likely to have been heaviest then.

Our Research Question, Expectations, and Measures

Assuming that humans have affected all environments in some way, and addressing the current debate in the Southwest about the long-term impact of Late Archaic agriculture, our research question is whether early southwestern agriculture changed the interaction between people and the environment during the Late Archaic period and impacted the relationship of people with that environment later in time. We use disturbance and prey species to measure the intensity with which Late Archaic societies were altering their landscapes and creating new niches. That is, disturbance and prey species are measures of anthropogenic change. Our analyses suggest that various Late Archaic groups impacted their landscapes in different ways, but that none of them impacted their environments to the same degree as later agriculturalists.

Recent literature shows that fluctuations in human residential mobility and economic strategies affect the impact that people have on plant and therefore animal habitats (Dean 2003, 2005; Grayson 1991; Linares 1976; Minnis 1985a; Stahl 2000). Faunal remains recovered from archaeological sites can help measure site-use intensity. Fauna not only show differences in site-use intensity because of changes in human diet that result from hunting pressure or increased cultivation but also changes in the ubiquity of nonprey species (Dean 2003). This is especially true if the plants and animals are attracted to habitats that human disturbance or alteration have created or enhanced (Dean 2003, 2005; Fish 2000; Grayson 1991; Mellink 1985; Minnis 1985b; Stahl 2000). Thus, disturbance flora encourages disturbance fauna and vice versa (Dean 2003). Much of the data in this chapter therefore explores what the proportions of disturbance species in our study areas suggest.

Our expectations for measurable effects of agriculture during the Late Archaic period are that there would be increases in disturbance rodents, perching birds, and jackrabbits, and decreases in cottontails and artiodactyls (deer and antelopes). Some rodents and perching birds are drawn to the large number of seeds produced by weedy annuals (Doolittle 2000; Rindos 1984) that spread into the newly formed habitat. The prey species entering people's diets also can reflect anthropogenic changes in the landscape. In general, lagomorph populations, which in this study include species of jack-rabbits and cottontails, can indicate intensity and duration of occupation. Sites with more intensive, long-term occupations should contain fewer cottontail and more jackrabbit remains, while sites with minimal site-use intensity should have a higher proportion of cottontails. Cottontails favor habitats that provide vegetative cover, while jackrabbits prefer open habitat and occur in greater numbers away from the floodplain (Badenhorst and Driver 2009; Dean 2003; Driver 2002; Driver and Woiderski 2008; Gillespie 1994; Szuter and Bayham 1996). Cottontails may have experienced a more marked population decline compared to jackrabbits with land clearing because their primary brushy habitat near the floodplain would have been diminished.

Low indices of artiodactyls are indicative of the growing size of human settlements, where increased human presence in areas of repeated use along with continuous predation can alter local game populations (Badenhorst and Driver 2009; Nelson and Schollmeyer 2003). Sources of water, forage, and cover are important factors for habitat selection in deer (Marshal et al. 2005). Interestingly, under harsh weather conditions, thermal cover is more important than food availability when drinking water is available (Krausman et al. 1997). Studies of deer in desert environments (e.g., Jason et al. 2005) have shown that seasonally available water in the absence of forage and cover will not as often create a deer habitat as will forage and cover in the absence of water. Further, in the Sonoran Desert of Arizona, mule deer remain inactive during diurnal hours of the summer season to reduce water loss and conserve energy, and female mule deer typically drink during hours around sunset (Hervert and Krausman 1986; O'Brien et al. 2006). Therefore, while it is possible that the increased use of cultigens and clearing areas for fields may create some new food choices for deer, cover would become diminished. Deer may have chosen habitats with better cover farther away from more populated human settlements. Additionally, wildlife management evaluations of deer (Masters and Stewart 1995) have shown that deer prefer native plant communities over non-native ones because of the diversity needed in the diet. It is possible that more agriculture would increase the productive habitats—that is, croplands, for artiodactyls, thereby increasing their numbers—but our analyses and those of others

(Badenhorst and Driver 2009; Eder 1978; Hames and Vickers 1982; Milton 1984; Nelson and Schollmeyer 2003) suggest otherwise.

The artiodactyl index records the relative abundance of artiodactyls in relationship to lagomorphs (Badenhorst and Driver 2009; Dean 2003; Diehl and Waters 2006; Schmidt 2008; Szuter and Bayham 1989:90), and archaeologists have used variation in the artiodactyl index to signal changes in the environment, hunting strategies, and large-game resources. Research involving modern horticulturalists has shown that horticultural activity can degrade large-mammal habitat as well as reduce large-animal presence around cultivated fields. As a result, low indices can be indicative of the growing size of human settlements where increased human disturbance altered the habitat and food choices for artiodactyls.

We also use a lagomorph index (LI) to measure the ratio of cottontails to jackrabbits. The index is the number of identified specimens (NISP) of cottontail (*Sylvilagus sp.*) divided by the combined NISP of cottontails and jackrabbits (*Lepus sp.*). The resulting formula is S/(S+L), and it provides a measure of the relative frequencies of cottontails/jackrabbits in an assemblage (Bayham and Hatch 1985; Driver 2002; Driver and Woiderski 2008; Schmidt 1998, 2008). Lower lagomorph indices could be the result of the removal of cottontail habitat near sites because of the need to clear land for fields or more village space (Bayham and Hatch 1985; Szuter and Bayham 1996:69).

We also expect that if people in the Late Archaic period were becoming more residentially sedentary, using the floodplains more intensively, and investing more in maize cultivation, then the relative abundance of disturbance species in the environment would be greater in comparison to those areas that were not as intensively used and altered. Most agriculture would occur on or near floodplains, and so if there was an increase in the land use around floodplains as a result of increasing agriculture, then disturbance species, especially weedy annuals, would spring up along the margins of or within the floodplains. This in turn would alter the proportions of disturbance rodents and perching birds in these areas. Along similar lines, we suggest that if people were altering their subsistence regimes, then the number of prey species entering their diet should likewise reflect changes in the anthropogenic landscape. Under these circumstances there would be a substantial decrease in large-bodied taxa and an increase in small-bodied prey, especially jackrabbits.

The rodents we analyze are those whose diet focuses on seeds from colonizing weedy annuals that take root in areas where building, planting, irrigation, trash disposal, and other human activities have caused ground disturbance (Dean 2003, 2005; Rindos 1984; Szuter 1991). Rodents such as kangaroo rats, white-footed mice, deer mice, pocket mice, and antelope ground squirrels are attracted to these weedy annuals, and as a result, they are quick to respond to anthropogenic changes in the environment (Aguilar 2002; Dean 2003; Szuter 1991).

Kangaroo rats, which strictly depend on seeds for food (Dean 2003, 2005; Parmenter and Van Devender 1995:216), are some of the more aggressive colonizers of disturbed anthropogenic environments. Similarly, deer mice are attracted to brushy areas bordering agricultural lands where they can forage on both seeds and insect larvae (Aguilar 2002; Wilson and Reeder 1993). Antelope ground squirrels prefer disturbed environments created by both agricultural clearing and human refuse practices. Ground squirrel species in general have a diet of seeds, insects, and plants, as well as suet or smaller animals (Dean 2003, 2005).

Because of their small size (30–40 g), these rodents are not likely to have been prey animals, or at least people did not seek them beyond the immediate boundaries of a site or a set of agricultural fields (Dean 2003, 2005; Szuter 1991). Ethnographically, rodents that are eaten tend to be the larger species, such as pocket gophers, cotton rats, and wood rats (Rea 1998). These larger rodents are not good indicators of increasing agricultural clearing and anthropogenic change since they are attracted to cacti or tuberous plants that are not so commonly cultivated or enticed to grow in ancient southwestern villages or agricultural fields. Rather, these rodents would be found in areas where large yucca and other succulent stands prosper—on the *bajada* slopes rather than the floodplains of the study areas. The small rodents discussed previously are therefore appropriate measures of human-disturbed environments in that they were probably not encouraged for their food value.

Perching birds are attracted to villages or fields where insects and seeds are readily available. These birds are divided into two categories—the granivores, attracted to agricultural foods, and the insectivores that eat the bugs on crops. Common granivores are geese, ducks, quails, cranes, mourning doves, horned larks, flickers, corvids (crows and jays), shrikes, and icterids (meadowlarks, cowbirds, blackbirds, grackles, and orioles). Insectivores include kestrels, nighthawks, swallows, robins, bluebirds, warblers, and corvids.

Because much of the case we make here assumes that there was less Late Archaic agriculture in the San Simon Basin than in the Tucson Basin or at

Cerro Juanaqueña, and because the paleoethnobotanical remains are so sparse in the San Simon Basin, we use Late Archaic projectile points from the three regions to support our contention that there really was less agriculture, or at least more mobility, in the San Simon Basin. Projectile-point morphology may be an indirect indicator of how Late Archaic peoples interacted with their landscape in that groups employing different hunting strategies and different kinds of mobility would require different technologies (Nelson 1991), and the projectile-point morphology would reflect technological needs. Curation technologies are optimal for a subsistence strategy that relied heavily on hunting large game in that people would anticipate the lack of raw material availability during times of mobility (Bamforth 1986; Binford 1973, 1979).

San Simon Late Archaic San Pedro points (a prolific type of Late Archaic point in the southern Southwest) should therefore have evidence for more curation than the San Pedro points from the other two regions. Specifically, the San Simon points should have more re-sharpening than those from the Tucson Basin or northern Chihuahua, because this indicates maintainability during these Late Archaic groups' movements when raw material availability was uncertain (Bleed 1986; Hayden et al. 1996; Thacker 1996; Torrence 1983). Re-sharpening the projectile points would affect the overall width and length of the point as well as the length and width of the blade. Hence, San Pedro points from the San Simon should be statistically smaller in total length, weight, blade length, total width, and blade width in comparison with points from the Tucson Basin and Cerro Juanaqueña in northern Chihuahua.

Conversely, less hunting practiced by the early agriculturalists in the Tucson Basin and at Cerro Juanaqueña would have had different effects on the morphology of the San Pedro points from those regions where there would be less evidence of curation technologies (Odell 1996; Shott 1986). The need to have maintainable points in the Tucson Basin and at Cerro Juanaqueña would not have been as important as in the San Simon drainage. Projectile points from these regions should have less evidence of re-sharpening than those from the San Simon drainage.

We note that chipped-stone raw materials are easily available in all three study areas in the Quaternary gravels and cobbles that cover the desert basins and are present in washes, and so material availability should not affect projectile-point morphology. While a specific kind of raw material may not be available in every locale, one that meets specific hardness and fracture mechanic requirements likely will be. In most places, people literally could have stepped off their site into the nearest wash and found the kind of raw material they were seeking. For example, in the Tucson Basin, Sliva (2005:50) has suggested that at Late Archaic sites, such as Las Capas, most of the raw materials selected for tool manufacture were made from fine-grained to cryptocrystalline materials, which mostly occur as river cobbles along the Santa Cruz River next to the site. Likewise, Vierra (2005:193) has noted that the majority of raw materials worked on the Cerro Juanaqueña site in northern Chihuahua were made from locally available river gravel sources. Finally, Keleher (1997:109–15) has shown that cryptocrystalline materials, such as chert and chalcedony, were locally available in the San Simon River cobbles and gravels, as were basalt and rhyolite, and all were used in chipped-stone manufacture.

Results from an analysis of variance demonstrate that the San Pedro points from the Tucson Basin are the largest compared to the points from Cerro Juanaqueña and the San Simon Basin in terms of the morphological variables and ratios (table 6.1). San Pedro points from the San Simon Basin

Table 6.1. Projectile-point morphological variables from the three study areas

Variable	Cerro Juanaqueña	San Simon	Tucson Basin
Weight	overlaps SS; smaller than TB	overlaps CJ; less than TB	greater than CJ and SS
Total length	less than SS and TB	greater than CJ; less than TB	greater than SS; overlaps CJ
Blade length	not measured	less than TB	greater than
Blade width	greater than SS; overlaps TB	less than CJ and TB	greater than SS; overlaps CJ
Stem length	not measured	overlaps TB	overlaps SS
Base width	less than SS and TB	greater than CJ; less than TB	greater than CJ and SS
Thickness	less than TB; overlaps SS	less than TB; overlaps CJ	greater than CJ and SS
Length/width	less than SS and TB	greater than CJ; less than TB	greater than CJ and SS
Base width/ maximum width	less than SS and TB	greater than CJ; overlaps TB	greater than CJ; overlaps SS
Total length/stem length	not measured	overlaps TB	overlaps SS

Note: CJ=Cerro Juanaqueña, SS=San Simon Valley, TB=Tucson Basin.

overall are larger or overlap the point sizes from Cerro Juanaqueña. The Cerro Juanaqueña San Pedro points are the smallest compared to the other two regions.

Re-sharpening may be the reason that the San Pedro points in the San Simon Valley have a smaller total length and in turn a smaller blade length (which would affect the length/width ratio) than Tucson Basin points (figure 6.2). Re-sharpening the distal portion of the projectile point would decrease the total length and the blade length of the point. This supports the contention that the people in the San Simon Valley maximized the use-life of existing projectile points versus spending time creating new points. In essence, this would indicate more curation and thus more mobility and hunting.

Overall, much variation is evident among San Pedro points from Cerro Juanaqueña, the San Simon Valley, and the Tucson Basin in terms of their morphological measurements. The Late Archaic points in the San Simon Basin had smaller blades than those at Cerro Juanaqueña and had smaller overall projectile-point size in comparison to the San Pedro points in the Tucson Basin. The smaller total length, blade length, and maximum width between the San Simon and Tucson Basin San Pedro points are likely due

Figure 6.2. San Pedro points from the San Simon Basin (*left*) and the Tucson Basin (*right*) (actual size). This figure simply shows a rather extreme example of re-sharpening of the San Simon point for illustration purposes. Photo by Nicholas Beale.

to the difference in re-sharpening in the San Simon Valley to maximize the use-life of their points. In contrast, the Cerro Juanaqueña San Pedro points are smaller than the other two areas, but this may have to do with raw material type in that the unworked raw material cobbles tend to be smaller in this region, which limits the overall size (Beale 2007). But, the larger blade width of the Cerro Juanaqueña San Pedro points compared to those from the San Simon Valley conforms to the expectation that the San Simon Late Archaic peoples were practicing more re-sharpening than those groups from northern Chihuahua. Because of different curation strategies, the analysis of the San Pedro points suggests that the groups from the San Simon Valley practiced a more mobile lifeway with more hunting than Late Archaic groups from Cerro Juanaqueña and the Tucson Basin (Beale 2007). Therefore, in relation to our expectations, the evidence from the projectile points suggests that both the inhabitants of Cerro Juanaqueña and the Tucson Basin would have affected their landscape differently because of a higher reliance on sedentism and agriculture than those Late Archaic groups who lived in the San Simon Basin (for complete statistical results and in-depth discussion, see Beale 2007).

Comparison of the Late Archaic Faunal Assemblages in the Three Regions

For the following analyses, we compiled faunal data from published reports analyzing Late Archaic sites from all three regions (figure 6.1, table 6.2). From the faunal assemblages at each site, we used the reported number of identified specimens (NISP) of disturbance rodents, artiodactyls, lagomorphs, and perching birds. Our analyses use the relationship of these species to the proportion of total faunal NISP reported for each assemblage.

The relatively low artiodactyl indices (table 6.3) suggest that artiodactyls were not recovered from the archaeological sites in our study areas in anywhere near the quantities as lagomorphs during the Late Archaic period. The region with the highest average index is the Tucson Basin (.13), while the other two areas are lower, at .05 for the San Simon and .04 for northern Chihuahua. Despite the fact that artiodactyls were the highest-ranked resources during the Late Archaic, lagomorphs overwhelmingly outnumbered them in Late Archaic assemblages in all three regions. According to Bayham (1979), the use of small, lower-ranked resources is likely dependent on the availability of larger game. Schmidt (1999, 2008) has argued, based

Table 6.2. Sites used for the analysis of Late Archaic fauna in the three study areas

Region	Site	Reference
Northern Chihuahua	Cerro Juanaqueña	Schmidt 2008
	Cerro El Canelo	Schmidt 2008
	Cerro Los Torres	Schmidt 2008
Tucson Basin	AZ AA:12:92	Dean 2003
	Las Capas	Dean 2003; Schmidt 2008
	Los Pozos	Waters 2001
	Valley Farms	Schmidt 2008
	Wetlands	Schmidt 2008
San Simon	AZ CC:7:11	Schmidt 1998
	AZ CC:7:43	Schmidt 1998
	AZ CC:7:51	Schmidt 1998
	AZ CC:7:52	Schmidt 1998

Table 6.3. Artiodactyl indices for the Tucson Basin, the San Simon Basin, and northern Chihuahua during the Late Archaic period

Region	Artiodactyl index
Northern Chihuahua	0.04
Tucson Basin	0.13
San Simon	0.05

Table 6.4. Lagomorph indices for the Tucson Basin, the San Simon Basin, and northern Chihuahua during the Late Archaic period

Region	Lagomorph index
Northern Chihuahua	0.16
Tucson Basin	0.35
San Simon	0.04

on generating similar values for each of our study areas, that in terms of dietary significance, artiodactyl exploitation was not as important as small game, which is easier to capture. The low artiodactyl indices may also be due to overhunting artiodactyls during the previous Middle Archaic period, although we currently have no evidence to support or refute this. We suggest that if agriculture was affecting the artiodactyl populations, then it was affecting them similarly in all three regions.

For the lagomorph index, a value greater than 0.50 denotes more cottontails in the site area, while a value less than 0.50 indicates more jackrabbits. The lagomorph indices for the three regions were all low (table 6.4), suggesting either that people had cleared extensive areas for fields or that the vegetation was naturally sparse, providing little cover for cottontails. The area with the highest average lagomorph index value (.35) is the Tucson Basin, having more cottontails and therefore more ground cover than in the other two regions. While the Tucson Basin inhabitants were altering their environment, it may have not been as significant as in the other two areas. Also, the environments of the San Simon and northern Chihuahua, being in the Chihuahuan Desert rather than the lusher Sonoran Desert, may have naturally had more jackrabbits than cottontails.

All three regions show similar patterns at a gross level in that there were always many lagomorphs and few artiodactyls (figure 6.3). Even though the proportions were low, however, the Tucson Basin had more artiodactyls and cottontails than either northern Chihuahua or the San Simon Basin, suggesting less impact in the Tucson Basin from agriculture than in the other regions. Again, however, this could be because of the higher biomass in the Sonoran Desert.

Interestingly, the proportions of disturbance rodents and perching birds in the Late Archaic Tucson Basin and northern Chihuahua faunal assemblages are similar to those of the San Simon Basin (figure 6.3). In all three regions, there were surprisingly few disturbance rodents and very small proportions of perching birds, although the proportions of disturbance rodents are higher at one northern Chihuahua site (Cerro Los Torres) and at a Tucson Basin site (Valley Farms). Perhaps, though, the perching birds are not present in faunal assemblages from sites because they are field birds.

Contrary to our expectations, the Late Archaic faunal assemblages from the Tucson Basin and northern Chihuahua did not show high proportions of these creatures, as would have been the case if people were heavily modifying and clearing the land for farming. In fact, the proportions of both are quite low. This hints that the impacts of this early agriculture were not as heavy as the built environment of canals, fields, and houses might suggest.

Human Impact through Time in the Three Regions

The proportions of disturbance rodents were surprisingly low in all three regions during the Late Archaic, regardless of the amount of agriculture that people might have practiced and regardless of the fact that there was

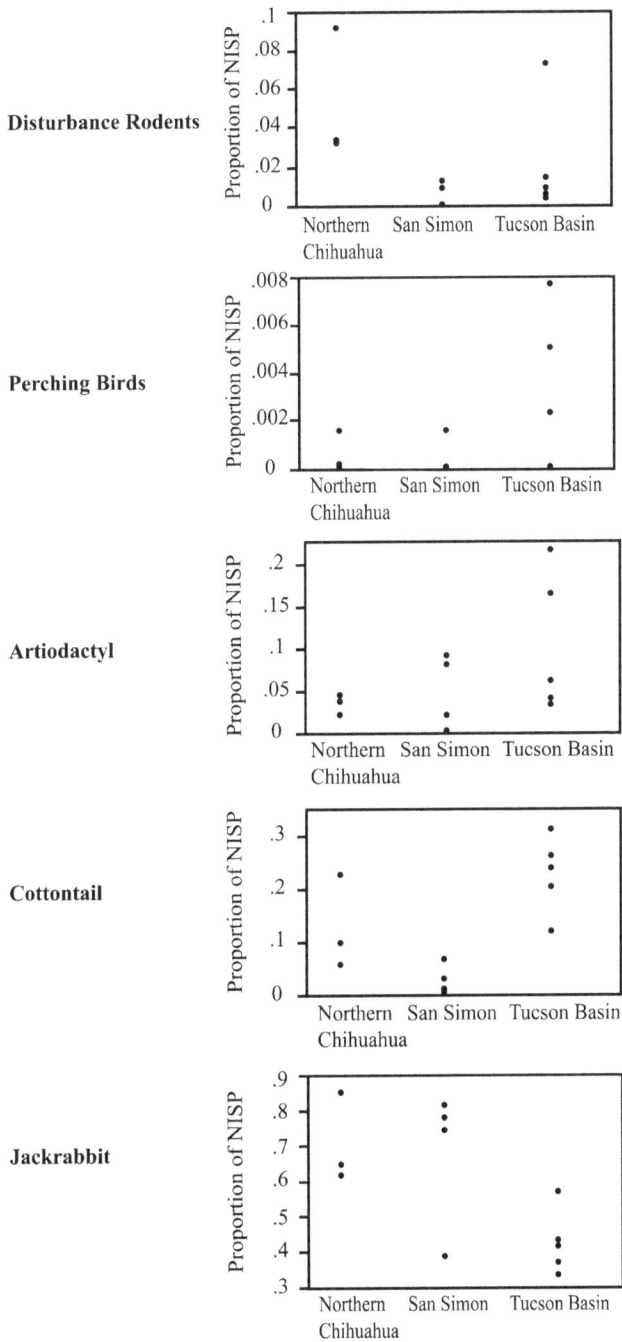

Figure 6.3. Faunal categories represented as a proportion of total NISP for each Late Archaic study area.

quite a bit of land disturbance in terms of fields, irrigation, storage, and houses in the Tucson Basin and disturbance of the steep hill on which Cerro Juanaqueña is located. The telling comparison, then, is between the Late Archaic faunal remains and those from post-Archaic deposits.

The Tucson Basin

Data for our analysis of the Tucson Basin post-Archaic faunal assemblages are derived from Dean's (2003) extensive examination of faunal remains at both Late Archaic and later Hohokam period sites in the Tucson Basin. Subsequent Colonial, Sedentary, and Classic period Hohokam sites in the Tucson Basin have higher proportions of disturbance rodents than Late Archaic sites. Dean's (2003, 2005) research revealed that during the Late Archaic period an average of three percent of the features contained kangaroo rats compared with 19 percent during the Hohokam periods. Our data from a smaller sample of later Hohokam sites similarly reflect an increase in the amount of disturbance rodents and perching birds through time (figure 6.4). These data suggest that heavy human impact and landscape modification happened later in time than the early presence of agriculture and relatively large numbers of people during the Late Archaic might suggest. Given that there were no indications of heavy agricultural impact in the Late Archaic, it is not surprising that there was much more impact later in time.

Northern Chihuahua

A similar pattern is apparent for the Late Archaic sites in northern Chihuahua. Using the three sites that compose the Late Archaic sample, which is considerably smaller than the Tucson Basin sample, the proportion of disturbance rodents in relation to the total faunal assemblage is the greatest of the three regions (figure 6.3). Although equivalent data are not available for the post-Archaic periods because recent publications do not have the rodent faunal data separated into subtype, there could be a drastic increase in the kangaroo rat population later in time. For the Medio period (AD 1250–1450) at the very large nearby site of Casas Grandes, there was an MNI of 45 kangaroo rats (Di Peso et al. 1974:242–43), which is far more than reported for all three of the Late Archaic sites. Although this is only a single data point at a very large site, the excavation material was not screened according to current standards, and the presence of any rodent

Disturbance Rodents

Time Period (number of assemblages)

Perching Birds

Time Period (number of assemblages)

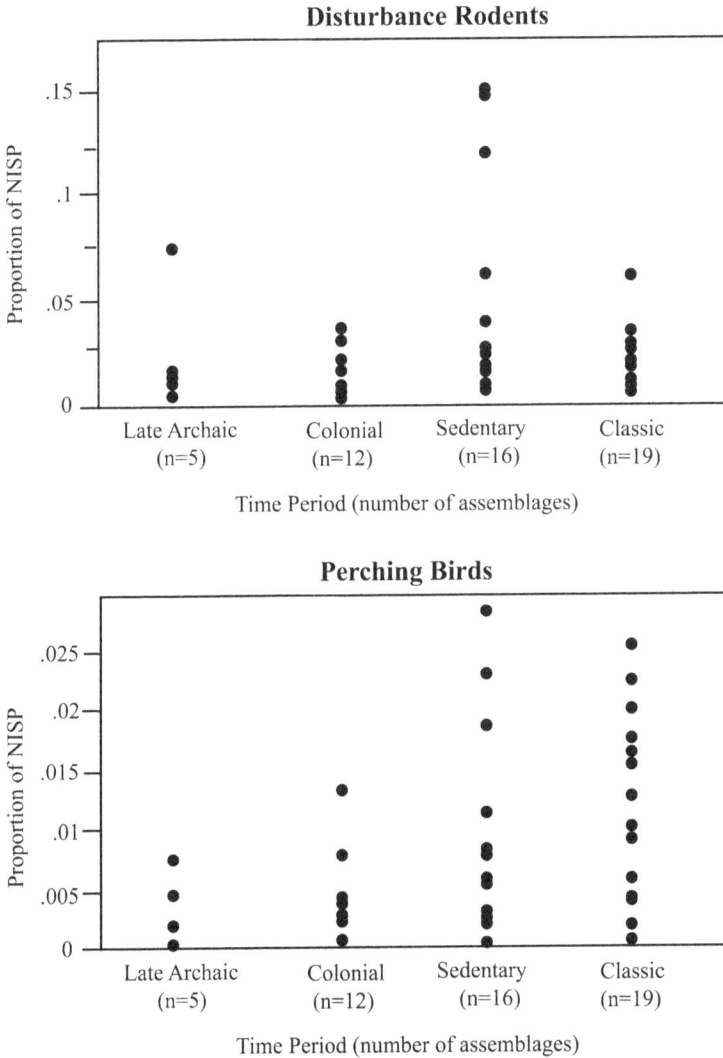

Figure 6.4. Disturbance rodents and perching birds as a proportion of total NISP for the Late Archaic and later Hohokam periods in the Tucson Basin. Later-period NISP data from Dean (2003:415–534).

bones in the analyzed assemblage is surprising. Regardless of this intriguing hint, the low proportion of disturbance rodents in the Late Archaic data from northern Chihuahua suggests that inhabitants of the earlier sites were not anthropogenically altering their environments in an intensive manner, as the people in the Tucson Basin also were not doing.

The San Simon Basin

The San Simon Basin presents a similar pattern to those in the Tucson Basin and northern Chihuahua (figure 6.5). During the Late Archaic period, there were low proportions of disturbance rodents and perching birds. Interestingly, those low proportions continued into the Pit Structure period

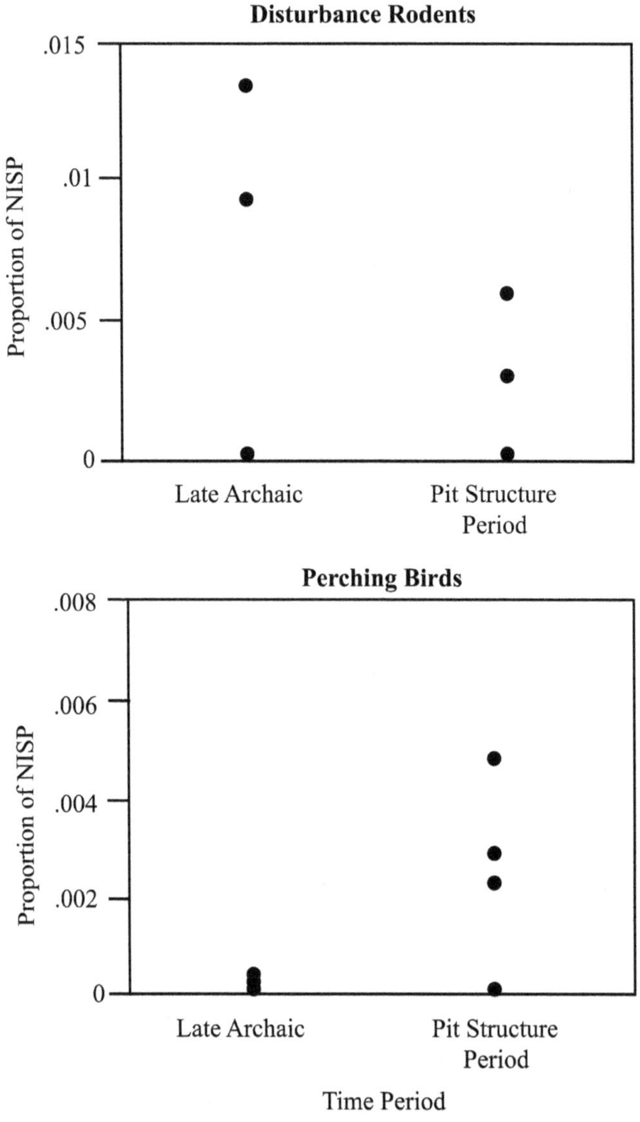

Figure 6.5. Disturbance rodents and perching birds as a proportion of total NISP for the Late Archaic and later Pit Structure periods in the San Simon Basin.

(AD 100–1050), after which the basin was essentially abandoned for habitation purposes through to the present time. This analysis could certainly be affected by the limited data from a small sample of excavated sites, but it does appear to be the same Late Archaic pattern of low proportions of disturbance rodents and perching birds as in the Tucson Basin and northern Chihuahua.

The low proportions of these disturbance species during the subsequent Pit Structure periods are interesting. Given the early abandonment of the basin, it could suggest that the landscape was not suitable for any sort of intensive agriculture, and at the point when people intensified their agricultural practices (about AD 1000), the inhabitants of the San Simon area opted to move out of the drainage instead. Coupled with the few artiodactyls in either period, the faunal assemblages suggest that people in the San Simon were farmers making little impact on their environment for 1,000–2,000 years from the Late Archaic through the Pit Structure periods (Schmidt 2011). Unlike the pattern in the Tucson Basin where there are marked changes through time, people in the San Simon region appear to have had a smaller anthropogenic footprint.

Conclusions

Perhaps our most important conclusion is that the disturbance rodents and perching birds provide no evidence that the earliest relatively intensive agriculturalists in the Southwest—those in the Tucson Basin and northern Chihuahua—altered their environments as much as people did in later periods. Although at least some Late Archaic farmers modified their landscapes with land clearing, irrigation ditches, large field systems, domesticated plants, storage pits, and field houses, our analyses suggest that the subsistence practices and land-use behaviors did not drastically affect disturbance-animal populations. Had the greater numbers of people and the possible decrease in residential mobility during these early periods of agriculture incurred more intensive transformations, the archaeological record would yield more disturbance-faunal signatures of heavy site-use intensity, which in turn would suggest major transformations in the agricultural field areas beyond the sites themselves. Perhaps the weedy annuals that are often encouraged to grow in and near agricultural fields were not substantial enough to attract disturbance rodents to these areas, in turn possibly because the human population during the

Late Archaic was not great enough to encourage heavy growth of these colonizing species.

Importantly, the San Simon rodent and bird data are similar to the data from the other two regions, and there is no evidence, at least not yet, that people in the San Simon during the Late Archaic were practicing the same kind of relatively intensive agriculture as people in the other two regions. In fact, projectile-point evidence hints that people in the San Simon were more mobile and perhaps doing more hunting (Beale 2007). All of this suggests that, although the agriculture in the Tucson Basin and northern Chihuahua appears intensive because of large sites and the presence of fields and irrigation, in fact it was minimal in terms of land modification compared to what would come later, though it did set the stage for land-use practices, arguably irreversible ones, later in time. Therefore, we propose that early agriculturalists, even with the presence of large sites, fields, and irrigation, will not necessarily heavily modify their environments in ways that impact wild animal populations.

This is not necessarily the expected result of our analyses, although Dean (2003, 2005) and Diehl and Waters (2006) have proposed something similar for the Tucson Basin. In fact, the results of our analyses show that all distur-bance species proportions are low in the Late Archaic, although the three regions have different proportions of those species. While the actual agri-cultural-built environment may have impacted later people using the same land, the low proportions of disturbance species suggest that people had not yet significantly changed the natural environment. We agree with Schmidt (2008) that the major landscape transformations incurred by agriculture may have been both more nuanced and later in time than previously imagined.

Further, some people, like those in the San Simon, never practiced the kind of agriculture that would cause extensive and intensive landscape modification. Not only were there low proportions of disturbance rodents, and perching birds during the Late Archaic period, but they continued that way until the drainage was abandoned about AD 1050. In other words, peo-ple in the San Simon apparently never participated in agricultural practices that would cause extensive and intensive landscape modification, although as we argue below, they likely impacted the environment in negative ways. Likewise, the artiodactyl remains suggest that the inhabitants of the San Simon area did not participate in much large-game hunting either during any time period, and the projectile points indicate that the people were more mobile and perhaps doing more hunting than their contemporaries.

Once people in the San Simon started practicing agriculture, it was a small-scale endeavor with low environmental modification for at least a thousand years, if not longer.

Relevance of Ancient Human Impacts to the Past and the Present

Did the actions of people on the land in the ancient past affect their descendants' and our use of that land today? The San Simon Basin presents perhaps the clearest indication that the past human impacts affected the landscape there in the past and even now. Evidence suggests that the San Simon Basin today is an anthropogenic environment from the Late Archaic and post-Archaic periods. That is, although the basin was never a "center" in the ancient Southwest, it did have a relatively large number of Late Archaic and Pit Structure period sites. At about AD 1050—the end of the Pit Structure period—people almost completely abandoned the basin. There were occasional seasonal and habitational uses of the drainage after that time, but none of them lasted more than a few decades (Gilman 1997). In the late 1800s and early 1900s, a few families homesteaded this land, but it is clear from the sparseness of trash on these sites that those families soon left the basin (Gilman 1996). No one has lived in the northern part of the basin since. While it is quite plausible that people left the basin at about AD 1050 for social reasons that had nothing to do with the impacts they had had on the landscape, it is surprising that almost no one has since lived in this place that supported people for at least 2,000 years.

We suggested earlier in this chapter that even post-Archaic agriculturalists in the San Simon caused minimal anthropogenic change of the natural landscape compared to contemporary people in the Tucson Basin. It is therefore possible that what people did in the San Simon during the Pit Structure period was all that the land would hold. Indeed, they may well have affected the land in such an adverse manner that no one could make a living farming there for the next thousand years. Although we do not yet have data to support this contention, it remains interesting that the San Simon Basin was perhaps the earliest abandoned region in the Southwest, and that, unlike many other such regions, once it was abandoned, it remained that way. If this scenario is correct, then past activities and impacts certainly did have consequences in this drainage.

7

Monumental Shell Mounds as Persistent Places in Southern Coastal Brazil

PAUL R. FISH, SUZANNE K. FISH, PAULO DEBLASIS,
AND MARIA DULCE GASPAR

Long-favored locales on ancient landscapes enfold the remains of repetitious or continuous occupations over extended periods. When such locales are marked by monuments that served substantial and sustained populations, they are typically associated with middle-range to complex agricultural societies. However, fishers and foragers also built monuments of this sort that anchored persistent places in coastal southern Brazil. They constructed massive sambaquis, or shell mounds (figure 7.1), often in active use for more than a millennium. These monumental shell mounds appear to have exerted "inanimate agency" in the sense that, once established, they

Figure 7.1. Sambaqui da Figuierinha, Santa Catarina, Brazil (adapted from Fish and Fish 2010:232).

continued to mediate relationships between culture and environment, reflecting remarkable stability through time. We focus on sambaquis in the state of Santa Catarina, Brazil, and consider their mid-Holocene record of long-term locational, cultural, and demographic persistence in the dynamic lagoonal setting of this lowland coastal region.

A Historical-Ecology Perspective on Monuments and Persistent Places

Theoretical approaches informed by historical ecology attempt to comprehend temporal and spatial relationships of human societies to their local and global environments and to situate human behavior and agency within a landscape perspective (Balée 2006:75). The methodology of historical ecology is commonly articulated as an interdisciplinary research program that examines interactions between societies and environments through time, along with the consequences of these interactions, in order to understand the formation of contemporary and past cultures and landscapes. We believe that persistent places in archaeological landscapes are particularly useful locations from which to examine these processes.

Sarah Schlanger (1992:92) used the term "persistent place" to describe those elements of southwestern U.S. puebloan landscapes that were the focus of repeated activity through time. She describes two general types of persistent places: (1) features of natural environment that attract repeated human occupation, and (2) man-made features and resources that draw people to a particular location. For hunters and gatherers, persistent places are typically discussed in terms of activities, practices, and behaviors organized around interaction with the natural environment and seasonal mobility (e.g., Littleton and Allen 2007; Shiner 2009). Concepts of persistent place emanating from the built environment, on the other hand, are most frequently applied to the archaeology of fully agricultural peoples. Furthermore, a prominent role for monumentality in creating and perpetuating persistent places tends to be linked with the more politically and socially complex of these societies (see, for example, Ashmore 2002; Bowser and Zedeno 2009; Tilley 1993, 1994).

Our firmly grounded interpretation of huge Brazilian shell mounds as symbolically charged and highly visible monuments in a context of persistent places challenges previous interpretations of them as primarily giant middens or as platforms for dry, elevated residence and other domestic activities (e.g., Beck 1972; Hurt 1974; Kneip 1977; Prous 1992; Rauth 1986). Although sambaquis are of variable scale overall, massive shell mounds are characteristic of Brazil's southern coast and particularly the state of Santa Catarina. The largest rise tens of meters (after historic mining of shell, the maximum height today is approximately 30 m) and cover as much as several hundred thousand m². They are monumental in their great size and visual obtrusiveness in their flat coastal settings and are noteworthy for pervasive burials.

The effort to create the Santa Catarina shell mounds is unlikely to have been incidental or without compelling purpose (Gaspar et al. 2008). To emphasize this point and to justify our designation of these sambaquis as monumental, we compare the present-day volume of the largest shell mound (Garopaba) and a medium-sized one (Jabuticabeira II) in our Santa Catarina, Brazil, study area with a series of other well-known New World monuments (table 7.1), which were constructed by unequivocally complex, agricultural societies in all but one case (Poverty Point). The two sambaquis fit respectably within the range of mound volumes in this comparison. The active duration of these monumental shell mounds—individually for more than a millennium and collectively more than 5,000 years—is also impressive. During this lengthy interval, the role of sambaquis in mortuary ritual created and perpetuated persistent places on the productive coastal landscapes inhabited by their builders.

Table 7.1. Comparison of two Santa Catarina sambaqui volumes with volumes of other New World monuments

	Archaeological affiliation	Volume	Citation
La Venta–Great Pyramid	Olmec, Mexico	99,000 m³	Heizer 1968:17
Tikal–Temple 4	Maya, Guatemala	260,000 m³	Carr and Hazard 1969
Jabuticabeira II	Sambaqui, Brazil	320,000 m³	Fish et al. 2000:70
Garopaba	Sambaqui, Brazil	>700,000 m³	Fish et al. 2000:70
Poverty Point–All Earthworks	Southeast Archaic, U.S.	670,000 m³	Gibson 2004: 265
Cahokia–Monks Mound	Mississippian, U.S.	730,000 m³	Pauketat 2004:69
Moxeke–Huaca A	Initial Period, Peru	750,000 m³	Pozorski and Pozorski 1986:384
Temple of the Sun	Teotihuacan, Mexico	1,200,000 m³	Blanton et al. 1981:158

Sambaquis of the Brazilian Coast

Sambaquis (the Brazilian term for shell mounds, derived from the Tupi language) are widely distributed along the shoreline of Brazil and were noted in European accounts as early as the sixteenth century. Sambaquis typically occur in highly productive bay and lagoon ecotones where the mingling of salt and freshwaters supports mangrove vegetation and abundant shellfish, fish, and aquatic birds. More than 1,000 sambaquis' locations are officially recorded, but they represent a fraction of the original number because colonial through modern settlements coincide with these favorable environments (Gaspar et al. 2008).

The term "sambaqui" is applied to cultural deposits of varying size and stratigraphy in which shell is a major constituent, undoubtedly encompassing accumulations representing a range of functions and origins. Small sambaquis often consist of shell layers over sandy substrates or sequences of shell and sand. The larger shell mounds tend to have horizontally and vertically complex stratigraphy, including many alternating sequences of shell deposits, narrower and darker layers with charcoal and burned bone that mark occupation surfaces, and clusters of burials, hearths, and postholes descending from these surfaces.

Despite abundant food refuse in sambaquis and the presence of several feature types that would be commonplace in residential occupations, recognizable dwellings have not been encountered, nor do distributions and arrangements of features indicate sustained domestic activity, with very few exceptions (e.g., around lakes in the state of Rio de Janeiro: Barbosa et al. 1994; Kneip 1992). In some cases, small sambaquis with simpler stratigraphy and minimal features or artifacts may represent campsites or processing stations. Most others serve mortuary functions, particularly the massive mounds with complex stratigraphy (Gaspar et al. 2008).

It is clear that sambaquis do not represent ordinary habitation, but rather are specialized elements of settlement systems in which very little is known about the other kinds of sites. The current lack of a well-defined settlement context that includes habitation sites is due to the very limited amount of survey or subsurface sampling techniques in the damp, heavily vegetated, and depositionally active Brazilian coastal zones. The lack of large-scale, systematic inventory is compounded by the pronounced difficulty of finding and identifying other contemporary site types. Residential sites would not be similarly marked by heaped shell and they would have no ceramics, little chronologically diagnostic chipped or ground stone, nondurable shell and bone tools, and perishable structures. The location of other site types related to the sambaquis is an ongoing goal of study area projects and activities.

The earliest dates of 9200 BP for sambaquis are inland along the Ribeira de Iguape in the state of São Paulo. Here, small mounds of edible land snails, rather than bivalves, display stratigraphic sequences resembling those of coastal locations and already hold numerous burials (Neves et al. 2005). Although intervening ages are well documented, the bulk of radiocarbon determinations on ensuing and largely coastal shell mounds are concentrated between approximately 5000 and 2000 BP.

Because shells of mostly edible species are by far the most abundant constituents of sambaquis, along with fish bone and other faunal remains, they have been strongly associated with hunting and gathering economies heavily dependent on mollusk collection. The absence of pottery in most cases, or its restriction to the uppermost layers, strengthens the impression that sambaquis are not components of primarily agricultural settlement systems. Artifacts are almost exclusively confined to burials. Grinding stones are seldom formally shaped. Other common items in artifact assemblages are consistent with a marine and lagoon orientation. Largely expedient chipped stone, ground stone objects ranging from informal pebble and cobble forms to well-shaped and polished axes, and shell and bone implements (such as hooks, points, and needles), are typical (e.g., Bryan 1993). Important sculpted and polished stone items that are technologically sophisticated include decorated plates, vessels, staffs or maces, and ornaments (Prous 1977, 1992). The most distinctive of these polished stone objects, however, are fish, bird, and mammal effigies, termed zooliths, and similarly well-sculpted geometric shapes. These are always rare, but occur throughout most of the area containing sambaquis.

Traditionally seen as remains of successive camping episodes by mobile mollusk-gathering and fishing bands, sambaquis have yielded increasing evidence in recent studies to suggest more complex communities in terms of demography, social organization, and long-term territorial stability based on highly productive estuarine and lagoonal environments (DeBlasis et al. 1998; Gaspar et al. 2008). Zooarchaeological studies (Figuti and Klökler 1996; Klökler 2008) as well as isotopic analyses of human bone (De Masi 2001) show that fishing was predominant in dietary input, supplanting the idea of a simple nomadic shellfish-gathering economy and pointing toward a more territorially stable regime of occupation and subsistence—a view reinforced by the few available settlement studies of regional scope (Gaspar 1991; DeBlasis et al. 2007). Bone artifacts from sambaquis are compatible with net- and hook-fishing technologies (Figuti and Klökler 1996). Skeletal and botanical studies reveal evidence for canoeing and diving, as well as the importance of vegetal contributions to the sambaqui economy, also implied by the variety of stone grinding tools frequently accompanying burials (Okumura and Eggers 2005; Boyadjian et al. 2007; Scheel-Ybert 2000; Scheel-Ybert et al. 2009).

Sambaquis have been most intensively studied along the Brazilian coast from the states of Rio de Janeiro to Santa Catarina, including Paraná and São Paulo (e.g., Prous 1992; Gaspar 1998, 2000; Lima and Mazz 2000). The numerous shell mounds further north have only occasionally been described (e.g., Calderón 1964; Simões and Correa 1971; Roosevelt et al. 1991). To the south, in the state of Rio Grande do Sul and on into Uruguay, shell mounds become smaller and infrequent, and are replaced by earthen mounds (*cerritos*) that exhibit significant parallels. The huge sambaquis of Santa Catarina are among the best-preserved and -reported (e.g., Beck 1972; Prous 1992; Rohr 1984).

A Sambaqui Settlement System

Since 1996, the authors and colleagues have pursued a long-term program of inventory and excavation encompassing 420 km^2 in the southeastern part of the state of Santa Catarina (figure 7.2). The research area consists of flat lagoonal expanses among elongated hilly promontories and isolated mountain outcrops that often formed islands in the more open coastal bays of Middle to Late Holocene times. Holocene sea-level fluctuations, peaking at approximately 5700 BP (Martin et al. 1988; Angulo et al. 1999 and 2006), strongly influenced a changing coastal landscape. Although the area still offers a rich and predictable abundance of fish and waterbirds with nearby forest resources, both the archaeological and environmental records (Scheel-Ybert et al. 2009) indicate enhanced aquatic resources in the past, when bays were more open to the sea. Shellfish in particular should have been more abundantly available; continuous, heavy exploitation over the centuries of the sambaqui era suggests little impact from human predation (Klökler 2008).

The predominant species in the earliest shell mounds is oyster (*Os-*

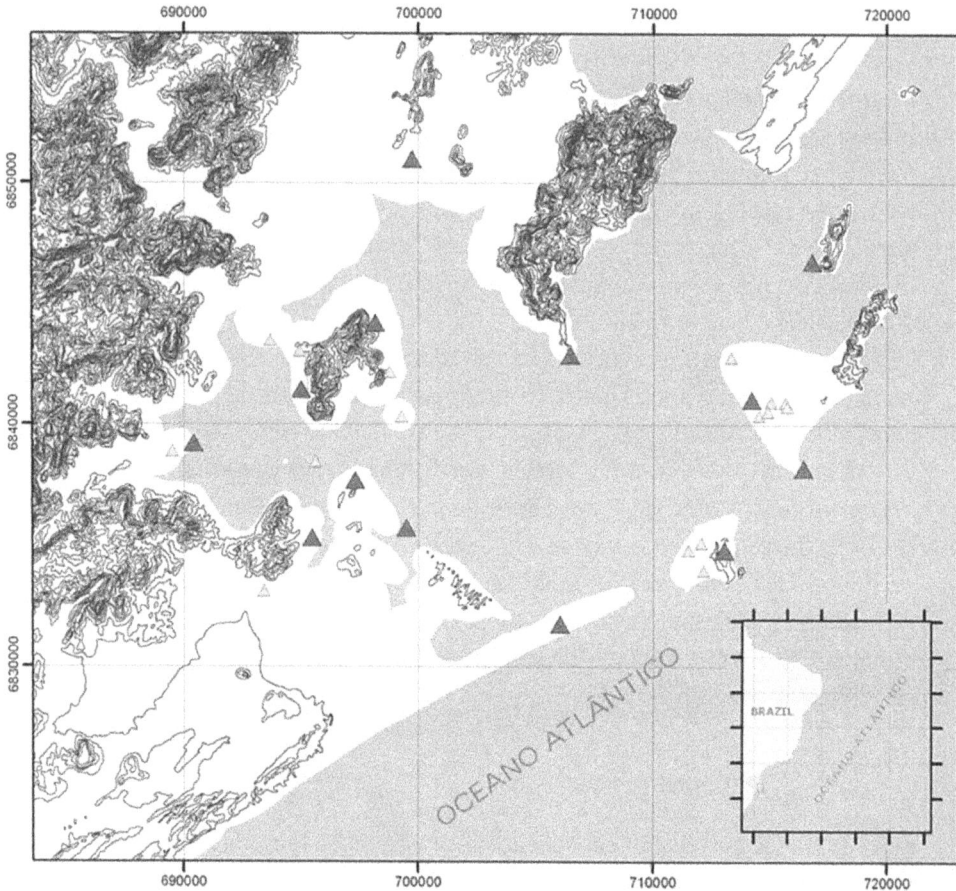

Figure 7.2. Large sambaquis in Santa Catarina study area.

trea)—consistent with bay environments more open to the sea than in later occupations. Subsequently, the evolution of barrier islands progressively changed bays toward more enclosed lagoons (Kneip 2004; DeBlasis et al. 2007). Mangrove vegetation, indicative of warm climate and extinct in the area today, has been detected by 5400 BP (Scheel-Ybert et al. 2009).

Our research has outlined a sambaqui settlement system encompassing more than 90 shell mounds, yielding 165 radiocarbon dates between 6500 and 1300 BP (figures 7.2 and 7.3: DeBlasis et al. 2007; Eastoe et al. 2002; Fish et al. 2000). The numbers include small, single-layered heaps of shell in the vicinity of the monumental mounds. Shell sites appeared by at least 6500 BP, beginning continuous occupation of the study area by sambaqui-builders for more than 5,000 years. (DeBlasis et al. 2007). Loose clusters of sambaquis containing one or two exceptionally large (maximum basal axis >200 m and current height >5 m) mounds are associated with a series of resource-rich lagoons providing fish, shrimp, shellfish, and water-birds (DeBlasis et al. 2007:37). Although there are differing models of sea-level trends and concurrent lagoonal configurations, all depict significant change during the sambaqui time span, with generally modern shorelines and closed lagoons emerging only during the last 2,000 years (e.g., Angulo et al. 1999, 2006; Kneip 2004).

Initial shell mounds were present in many of the loose clusters by 5000 BP and mound building in all of them appears to have ceased around 1300–1500 BP (figure 7.4). Mounds in the same cluster produce variable dates, but the overall patterning in the periodicity and duration of mound use and the cultural significance of these chronological sequences is not yet clear. An intensively dated sambaqui, Jabuticabeira II (figure 7.3), in one cluster was built more or less continuously for close to 2,000 years (Fish et al. 2000). Mounds in other clusters likewise have yielded dates suggesting generally sustained use for 1,000 years or more (DeBlasis et al. 2007; Hurt 1974). Many older mounds fell out of use before the end of the sambaqui

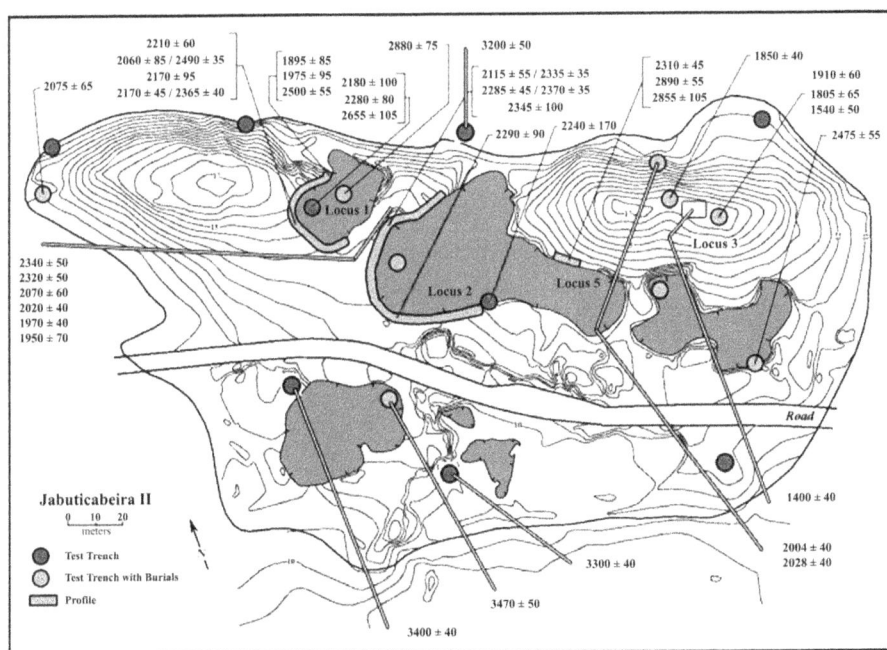

Figure 7.3. Jabuticabeira II map showing profiles and test trenches. C14 dates are uncalibrated.

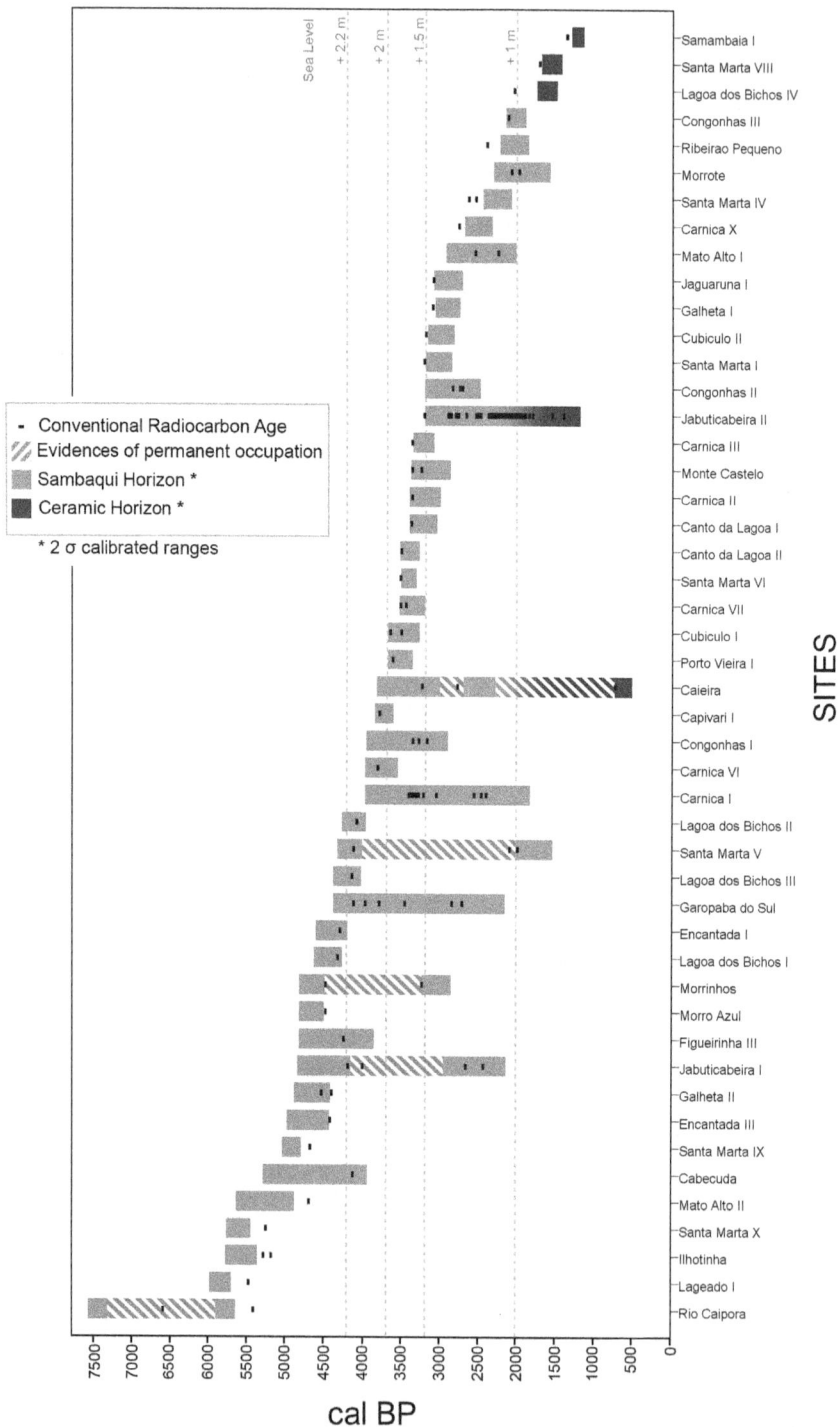

Figure 7.4. Radiocarbon dates from Santa Catarina study area sambaquis. In cases where stratigraphic continuity could be confirmed between earlier and later dates for a sambaqui, permanent occupation is graphed for that interval.

era. Available dates show that in multiple instances new shell mounds were added to existing clusters after 4500 BP and that more than one of these later mounds sometimes were simultaneously active in the same cluster.

With few exceptions, study area sambaquis are marked by abundant burials. Similar practices of interring the dead in towering monuments in the same set of circumscribed locales over almost five millennia implies a notably enduring social system. These practices also imply relative sedentism in the sense of persistent occupation of the same districts of the highly productive littoral zones.

Insights from Jabuticabeira II

Our extensive excavations at Jabuticabeira II in the vicinity of the Camacho lagoon near the city of Jaguaruna clarify and add critical details to previous research on monumental sambaquis and their mortuary contents in our Santa Catarina study area and elsewhere in Brazil (Fish et al. 2000; DeBlasis 2005). A mid-sized mound among the exceptionally large sambaquis, Jabuticabeira II appears to have risen over 10 m in maximum original height, covered 90,000 sq m at the base, and substantially exceeded today's remnant volume of approximately 320,000 cu m. As with most huge sambaquis, prior to legal protection, it was heavily mined for shell to use as modern construction fill and as raw material for cement (figure 7.5), leaving behind cavities with near-vertical walls throughout the mound (figure 7.3). Long profiles documenting 125 linear meters of these cuts from the edges to the center of the mound and totaling 373 m² reveal the repetition of many smaller, internally mounded stratigraphic sequences (figures 7.6 and 7.7). Thin, dark organic layers containing plentiful charcoal and burned fish bone are widely interspersed and are covered over by thicker and lighter-colored deposits of relatively clean shell. Burials, hearths, and postholes originate on these thin, dark occupation surfaces. In addition to the lengthy profiles, further careful testing (figure 7.3) confirmed the presence of burials throughout and demonstrated that the repetition of the basic two-part stratigraphic sequence accounts for the eventual mass of the mound as a whole.

We originally assumed that the postholes and hearths were the remnants of dwellings and that the dark organic occupation surfaces reflected the incorporation of domestic refuse. Postholes and hearths correlate strongly with concentrations of burials, however, and do not exhibit outlines corresponding to houses. Potentially domestic features other than a standard-

Figure 7.5. Shell mining at Pernambuco II in 1953 is typical of the destruction affecting most large sambaquis on the southern coast of Brazil during the twentieth century. The photograph is adapted from Bigarella, Tiburtius, and Sobanski 1954, estampa 15.

ized type of hearth are virtually absent. Most of these hearths are immediately adjacent to graves or directly overlie them. Artifacts are infrequent outside of burials, and we rarely encountered debris associated with their manufacture. Only by observing the horizontally and vertically recurring combinations of features in hundreds of square meters of profiles did we come to understand that the sambaqui stratigraphy registers a repetition of mortuary events at successive funerary loci rather than ongoing residence.

The great preponderance of burials are grouped into discrete funerary areas that recur throughout the height and breadth of Jabuticabeira II. We believe these funerary areas were dedicated to specific affinity groups, whose membership was based on kinship, territorial affiliation, or other social principles. More than one affinity group likely used separate funerary areas in different mound sectors at any given time. Horizontal exposure of 32 m^2 within one of the funerary areas (figure 7.8) strengthens our interpretation of the thin, dark layers as occupation surfaces on which burial, feasting, and mortuary ceremonies were performed. Posts often encircle burial pits and similarly demarcate edges of the funerary area. The many additional posts may have supported miniature structures over graves (a practice among Brazilian indigenous peoples), marked the locations of burials, suspended offerings, or served still other purposes.

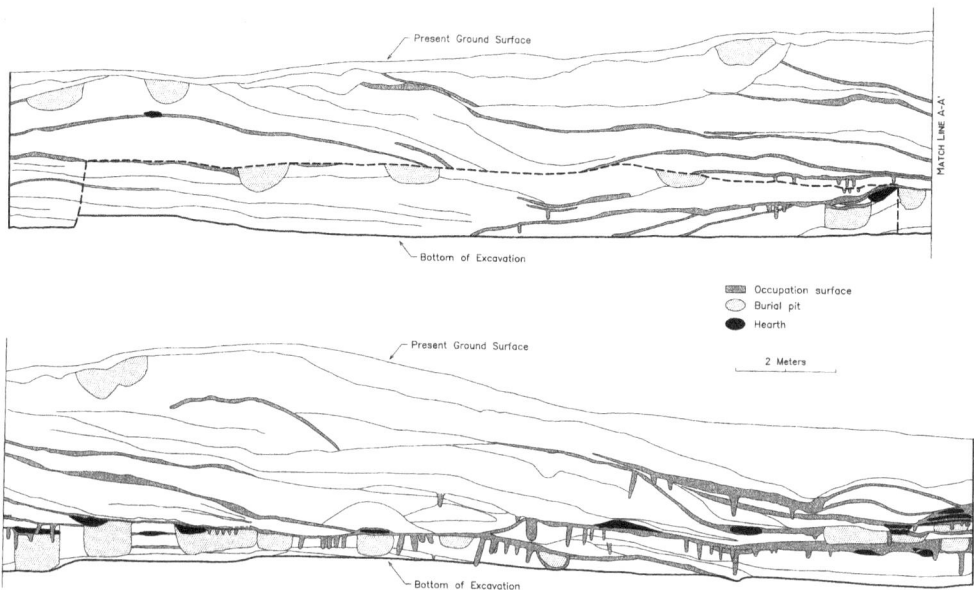

Figure 7.6. An extended section of the Jabuticabeira II Locus 1 profile.

Jabuticabeira II

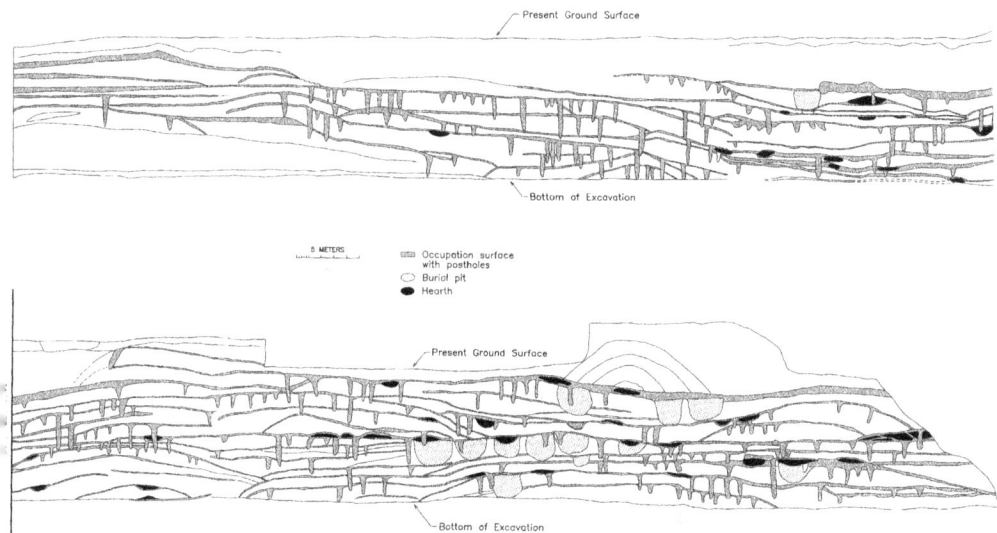

Figure 7.7. An extended section of the Jabuticabeira II Locus 2 profile.

Figure 7.8. Horizontal exposure of 32 m² within one Jabuticabeira II funerary area encompassing 12 burial pits and associated postholes and hearths.

The dead were interred in pits closely accommodating tightly flexed bodies and offerings, but extended burials occur too in the uppermost of Jabuticabeira II layers. Multiple burials in a single pit—sometimes a combination of adult and child—are not uncommon. Secondary burials are the rule, with bodies apparently prepared elsewhere by desiccation or other methods and wrapped before transport to the sambaqui (Fish et al. 2000; Okumura and Eggers 2005). Affinity groups may have transported all of their members who died during a specified interval to their currently active funerary area at a prescribed time, to be interred with communal ceremonies. Typical accompaniments, when present, are utilitarian items of bone and stone, shell jewelry, and small sets of rounded pebbles; large stone objects such as grinding stones often were placed near the head.

During the interment ceremonies, and also during subsequent visits to the funerary area, mourners lit commemorative fires in hearths at the sides of graves and overlying the burial pits, paralleling widespread practices of post-contact groups (e.g., Metraux 1946a, 1946b). Again, following the mortuary customs of many later indigenous peoples, numerous participants consumed large quantities of food on these occasions. Charcoal from fires and refuse from feasting are responsible for the dark color and organic composition of the surfaces of funerary areas. The character of these feasting surfaces, and the predominantly consumed fish, catfish, and whitemouth croaker, remain essentially constant from the beginning of the Jabuticabeira II sequence to the end, despite ongoing lagoonal enclosure and continuing intense exploitation of these resources (Klökler 2008).

Many small lenses and discrete depositional episodes can be distinguished within the thin, dark occupation layers. These have varying proportions of constituents, including burned and unburned fish bone, crushed mussel (Mytilidae) shells, other bivalves, charcoal, sand, and clay. Occasional pebbles and fire-cracked rock also occur. All these materials tend to be compressed and fragmented by occupational activities.

After some specified interval, an affinity group ceased to use its funerary area and then "closed" it by covering it with heaped shell. These loose, sandy shell layers contrast sharply with the dark occupation surfaces as they are overwhelmingly composed of light-colored *Anomalocardia brasiliana,* the bivalve that replaced oysters as the major component of all but the earliest shell mounds. More minor inclusions in the covering deposits include fish bone, other shells, and rare tools or fire-cracked rock. The quantities of shell mounded over an occupation surface would have required procurement elsewhere and transport to the sambaquis, as was the case with the bodies of the deceased and the generous provisions for feasting.

Ensuing funerary areas were established on new surfaces atop previously mounded shell deposits in an extended process of both horizontal and vertical accretion. The ritual program of burial, feasting, and mounding of shell over a current funerary area was re-enacted over centuries, incrementally giving rise to the final huge volume and monumental quality of the sambaqui (Fish et al. 2000). Repetitions of such events also appear to account for the core stratigraphy of the various other confirmed burial mounds in the study area.

The western part of Jabuticabeira II is capped by a dark earthen layer of varying depth that covers many other study area sambaquis in the same manner. In this dark cap, those burying the dead substituted a redeposited anthropogenic soil rich in burned fish bone and charcoal instead of shell as a construction material and shell is only a minor and localized component (Klökler 2008; Villagrán et al. 2009). Interment continued and burials are even more concentrated (Nishida 2007). This final dark earthen phase of construction has been dated approximately between 2000 and 1300 BP at Jabuticabeira II and yielded a similar beginning date at a second sambaqui in another cluster. Because of the continuity in mortuary function throughout, we consider the whole of Jabuticabeira II to be a long-standing communal cemetery and funerary structure (Fish et al. 2000).

Burial Rates and Demographic Reconstructions

The impressive numbers of bodies and their distribution throughout the vertical and horizontal limits of Jabuticabeira II leaves little doubt that its foremost function was funerary (Fish et al. 2000). The sample of burials is small in terms of overall sambaqui volume, but it is spatially comprehensive. Our combined view into stratigraphic deposits and their contents from long profiles (figures 7.6 and 7.7), dispersed test trenches (figure 7.3), and the horizontal exposure of an occupation surface (figure 7.8) allows us to make inferences about the long-term implications of burial and the incremental growth of the sambaqui.

Profiles of 373 m² in Locus 1 and Locus 2 contained a minimum of 51 separate locations of burials, a conservative tabulation that excludes imprecisely located human remains recovered during profile cleaning. Again in a conservative mode, we count each of these burial locations as the grave of a single person despite the demonstrated occurrence of multiple interments in a single pit. Our confidence that projections of burial totals from profile observations are not overblown is further strengthened by the discovery of 12 burials in the partial horizontal exposure (32 m²) of a funerary area, even though no burial pits could be seen extending from this surface in the adjacent profile cut.

Assuming that each square meter of exposed profile was a representative sample of the surrounding cubic meter, we use 51 burials in 373 m³ to derive an estimated ratio of .137 burials per cubic meter (table 7.2). This estimate produces a total of nearly 44,000 people placed in the 320,000 m³ mound over approximately 2,000 years (table 7.3). This projection to the sambaqui as a whole is justified by the confirmed presence of burials in widely spaced locations and the repetition of funerary areas in conjunction with the same stratigraphic sequences throughout. The total calculated for burials at Jabuticabeira II is surprisingly large, and calls for quantified comparison. One such comparison is provided by 1950 and 1951 investigations at Cabeçuda (Castro Faria 1959:99–102), a larger sambaqui approximately 17 km to the northeast near the city of Laguna. Here, 191 burials were recovered in an excavated block measuring 10 by 14 by 8.5 m (table 7.2). These figures produce a ratio of 0.16 burials per m^3, quite similar to the conservative estimate of 0.137 burials per m^3 derived for Jabuticabeira II. If the Cabeçuda ratio were applied to the volume of Jabuticabeira II, the projected total would rise from 43,840 to 51,200 burials (table 7.3). Alan Bryan's (1993:3, 89) excavations at Forte Marechal Luz, in Santa Catarina near its border with Paraná to the north, provide yet another indication of the realistic nature of our estimates. Bryan encountered 79 burials in an excavated area approximately 240 m^3, yielding a higher estimate of 0.329 burials per m^3 (table 7.2) and a correspondingly greater total (table 7.3).

At first glance, these totals might intuitively seem excessive for a foraging population in even the most favorable of environments and under conditions of the greatest social complexity for such groups. Assuming an even rate of burial over the 2,000-year period of active mound use, however, only 22 persons would have been buried per year at Jabuticabeira II (table 7.4). The 550 persons buried over a generational span of 25 years should approximate the size of the population using the mound as a cemetery at any given time. Our estimate of burials in Jabuticabeira II is undoubtedly low as a momentary representation of local population in light of the fact that radiocarbon dates (figure 7.4) from nearby Jabuticabeira I indicate this second mortuary mound in the same cluster was also active at least part of the time. These demographic figures, even if very rough estimates, are indicative of relatively sizable and stable populations rather than "nomadic shellfish collectors." Furthermore, because the massive sambaquis in the region encapsulate continuous and increasing mortuary functions over five millennia, we believe that demographic conditions should have been conducive to sedentism and population growth.

Each active shell mound in a cluster must have represented the cemetery for a prescribed hinterland population and its territory (perhaps analogous to the named *bairros*, or fishing communities, of the Santa Catarina coast today that correlate well with the locations of prehistoric shell-mound clusters). Such population "catchments" for burials in large sambaquis dated between 3500 and 2000 BP in the study area are roughly modeled using Thiessen polygons (figure 7.9). More than one contemporary sambaqui in the same cluster after 3000 BP suggests increasing territorial circumscription and economic intensification based on rich lagoon resources and the possible addition of cultivation.

Table 7.2. Burial density comparison of Jabuticabeira II, Cabeçuda (Castro Faria 1959), and Forte Marechal Luz (Bryan 1993)

Sambaqui	# of burials	m^3 sampled	Burials/m^3
Jabuticabeira II	51	373	.137
Cabeçuda	191	1190	.160
Forte Marechal Luz	79	240	.329

Table 7.3. Total burial estimates for Jabuticabeira II based on burial/m^3 indices from Jabuticabeira II, Cabeçuda (Castro Faria 1959), and Forte Marechal Luz (Bryan 1993)

Burial/m^3 Rate	Total m^3	Estimated # of burials
Jabuticabeira II	320,000	43,840
Cabeçuda	320,000	51,200
Forte Marechal Luz	320,000	105,280

Table 7.4. Estimated burial rates for Jabuticabeira II

Number of burials	43,840
Number of years	2,000
Burials/year	22
Burials/generation (25 years)	550

The presumption of maximal population densities commensurate with occupationally stable hunting and fishing societies in rich coastal settings is borne out by a ballpark estimate derived from the average 60 km² average area of the Thiessen polygons centered on mound clusters. Using these approximations of territory size for the Santa Catarina clusters, Jabuticabeira II's 550 persons per generation produces a density of about 9 persons/km². This admittedly broad-brush figure is close to the most populous (Chumash at 8.4 persons/km²) of the North American coastal hunting and gathering groups compiled by Robert Kelly (1995:Table 6–4, pp. 232–36).

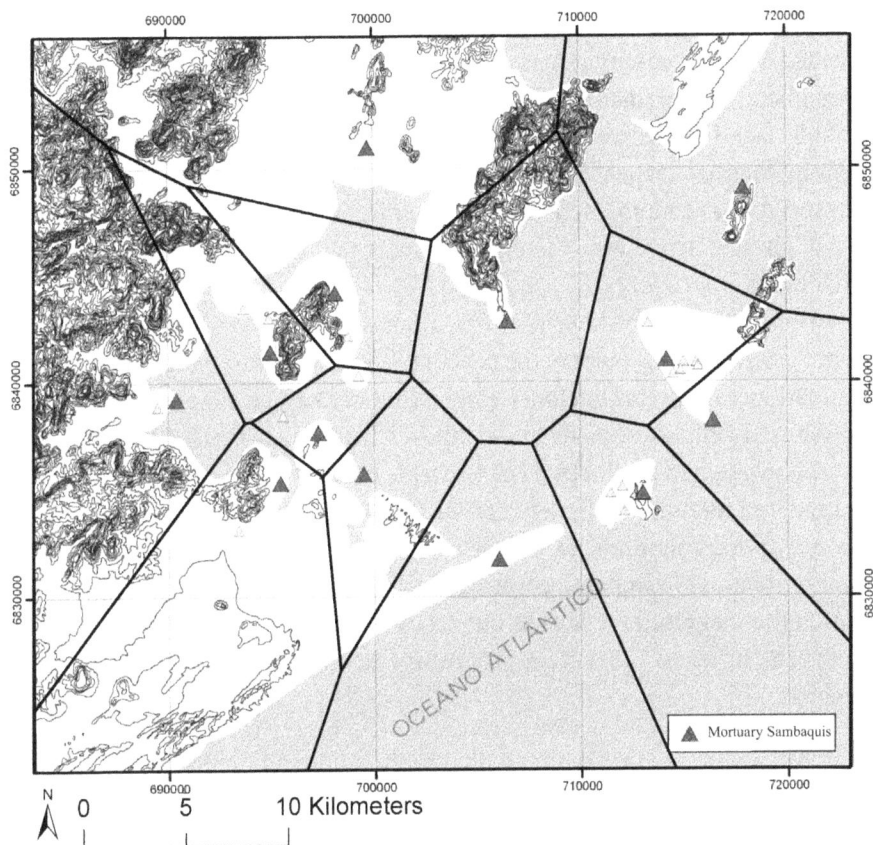

Figure 7.9. Theissen polygons approximate territories and population "catchments" for burials incorporated in large mortuary sambaquis dated between 3500 and 2000 BP in the Santa Catarina study area. Shoreline and topography correspond to reconstructed sea level during this interval (Kneip 2004).

Demography and Territory

The long sequence of mortuary mounds reveals some important features of the enduring sambaqui tradition. First is the circum-lagoonal pattern of mound clusters around these productive bodies of water. Settlement changes during the long occupational time span appear primarily linked to the progressive enclosure of the lagoons and their borders, rather than fundamental economic or social transformations (Kneip 2004). The nature of settlement evolution reinforces the centrality of the lagoons both for subsistence and social networking. Throughout the occupational history of the area, the lagoon was the center of the sambaqui social sphere; it represented a vital, communal space for economic and social interaction among members of a permanent, largely sedentary population, with long-term stable, face-to-face relationships. The distribution of sambaquis around lagoons suggests that each of the mound clusters represents a nuclear focus of social and economic territory and identity, but that each cluster was also strongly interactive with the others sharing that communal aquatic space (DeBlasis et al. 2007).

The availability of high resource biomass and diversity, together with cooperative management of the productive infrastructure, would have promoted increasing productivity, population density, and intensification of territorial control, perhaps in conjunction with environmental trends toward heightened productivity of estuarine environments as the postglacial rise of sea levels slowed after 7000 BP (Yesner 1980, 1987). The number of contemporary mounds, as well as mound size, increased throughout the earlier phases of sambaqui construction (figure 7.4). Taking into consideration the magnitude of burials per mound, it is difficult to interpret these patterns in terms other than progressive demographic expansion in the region.

Conclusions

Beyond the existence of affinity groups that are inferred from the shared space and observances of funerary areas, and their probable corporate nature, there is little direct evidence for the institutions and organization of the societies that built sambaquis. Social differentiation is not well delineated by burial offerings or treatment. An exception is the highly restricted accompaniment of zooliths—effigies of fish, birds, mammals, and a few other forms. Zooliths are skillfully executed in polished stone and hint of craft and ritual specialization. Occasional mounded shell over an individual burial and unusually large shell deposits over a few funerary areas may also indicate elevated standing for these persons and groups. Other markers of political, religious, or economic leadership and power were not expressed in an archaeologically detectable manner.

How are we to understand the prolonged repetition of ritual and construction events that required increasing effort as the sambaquis grew to monumental size? How are we to understand the chronological periodicity among shell mounds in the same cluster and among the various regional clusters? What are the implications for the societal configurations of their builders?

A primary contrast between sambaquis and the monuments of more complex societies is the duration of the cultural system that generated distinctive forms of collective construction. Sambaquis and the sustained mortuary rituals that generated them persisted much longer than the typical chronological divisions of complex societies and their corresponding monument styles. The striking persistence of the material and behavioral correlates of the ideological tradition embodied in the mortuary program over several millennia is a hallmark of the sambaqui era.

For sambaquis, the labor requirements and the duration of each building event were of limited scope compared to the comparably sized monuments of middle range and complex societies, which often were constructed in fewer stages and through broader recruitment of workers. Even the largest volume of shell mounded over a specific funerary area was of relatively modest scale. Although the participants in sambaqui mortuary activities may well have extended beyond the individual affinity group, demands for coordination likewise were modest. Sambaqui funerary events and feasting undoubtedly offered opportunities for leadership, social negotiation, generosity, and other interchanges conducive to the exercise of agency but, individually, also were of limited scale. The repetitive planning, provisioning, and orchestration of feasts characterizes the enduring and essentially unchanged mortuary ritual throughout the 2,000-year sequence at Jabuticabeira II. Such feasts were equally grounded in rights to rich lagoonal resources and the social networks that maintained position and identity through reenacting those rituals.

Especially after 3000 BP, we know that some shell mounds became inactive and others were added, within single clusters and across the region as a whole. More than one contemporary sambaqui in the same cluster and regionally growing numbers indicate demographic and social conditions likely to foster social differentiation and competition. Similarly, the notably greater massiveness of a few sambaquis may signal some degree of hierarchical relations among the associated populations and territories. Current information provides little insight into the factors that might have ended the active status of a mortuary monument after centuries of use or that might have initiated construction of a new one. The persistence of individual sambaquis for nearly 2,000 years and possibly more seems overly long, however, to reflect dynamics akin to chiefly or even dynastic succession and related societal processes.

The fact that the sambaqui builders were fisher-foragers lowers our expectations for the role of agency and power in monumentality, no matter how impressive the ultimate mass and magnitude. Archaeological evidence bears out these theoretical biases in several respects. Although their final size rivals that of the monuments of many complex societies in the Americas, the huge sambaquis are the outcome of repeated incremental events that do not individually contradict our perceptions of the capabilities of populous complex hunter-gatherers in rich coastal environs. Truly packed with ancestors and founders, the giant shell mounds were highly visible reminders of deeply rooted claims to prime territories.

At the same time, sambaqui rituals may have offered the means for adjusting and integrating local populations as they shifted and expanded, accommodating cooperation in the shared use of lagoons as well as competition. By adding their dead to the monuments, successive generations and social groups legitimated their rights to share the abundant aquatic resources. Sambaquis provided highly visible cues to landscape structure and anchored its cultural and territorial partitions. The enduring ideology and ritual program that produced the giant shell mounds likely signaled belonging and territorial rights while promoting the exploitation of abundant resources in a manner that conserved their viability across expanding generations. The shell mounds define persistent places in an ecological sense but also in a fundamentally social sense wherein the built environment was as vital as the "natural" setting to interlinked and ongoing occupations.

Acknowledgments

Our sambaqui investigations in Santa Catarina have been supported by FAPESP (Fundação de Amparo a Pesquisa do Estado de São Paulo), the Heinz Foundation, Wenner Gren Foundation, Office of the Vice President for Research at the University of Arizona, and Pró Reitoria de Pesquisa da Universidade de São Paulo. We also wish to acknowledge the numerous contributions of colleagues and students at Universidade de São Paulo, Universidade Federal do Rio de Janeiro, University of Arizona, and Instituto do Patrimônio Histôrico e Artistíco National.

8

To Become a Mountain Hunter

Flexible Core Values and Subsistence Hunting among Reservation-Era Blackfeet

MARÍA NIEVES ZEDEÑO

When anthropologist John Ewers entitled his landmark ethnography "The Blackfeet: Raiders on the Northwestern Plains" (1958), he cemented the tribe's reputation as fierce equestrian warriors and bison hunters. Ewers, as well as many other scholars before and after him, assumed that, without bison, hunting would no longer define Blackfeet identity, society, and culture. In his study of the horse in Blackfeet culture, Ewers (2001:320) further remarked that the disappearance of the bison in the late nineteenth century eliminated one of the horse's most important functions: hunting. But the Blackfeet have been big-game hunters since time immemorial, or, in archaeological time, since their ancestors arrived to this continent. So it is a small wonder that today nearly 4,000 or approximately 50 percent of reservation residents exercise their treaty right to hunt, own hunting horses, and train small children in the pursuit of elk and other big and small game. Historically, wild game constituted an important nutritional complement to commodities in reservation households (Johnston 2001), and it continues to provide economic respite in times of unemployment.

Granted, hunters, prey, and hunting ground have changed variously in the past century, but native subsistence hunting, both as concept and as practice, remains strong among the Blackfeet, having left a distinctive material signature on the landscape. Twentieth-century hunting in the reservation, particularly that associated with migrating elk herds, has been examined almost exclusively from the perspective of ideological and practical conflicts between the Blackfeet Tribe and its neighbor Glacier National Park—conflicts fueled by President Theodore Roosevelt's legacy and conservation goals pursued by the National Park Service in the early 1900s (Warren 1997). However, the cultural and ecological significance of this practice, and particularly its role in the evolution of modern Blackfeet identity, has been largely ignored.

In this chapter, I discuss the transition from bison and elk hunting in the prairie to elk hunting in the Rocky Mountains among the reservation-era Blackfeet (1873–present) and its ecological, social, cultural, and political implications. Following one of Carole Crumley's (1994:8) directives for historical ecology, the chapter's conceptual framework and case study center on the long-term role of *core values* in the development of flexible human adaptations to changed or unstable natural and social conditions. The framework has three components. First, I develop the proposition that core

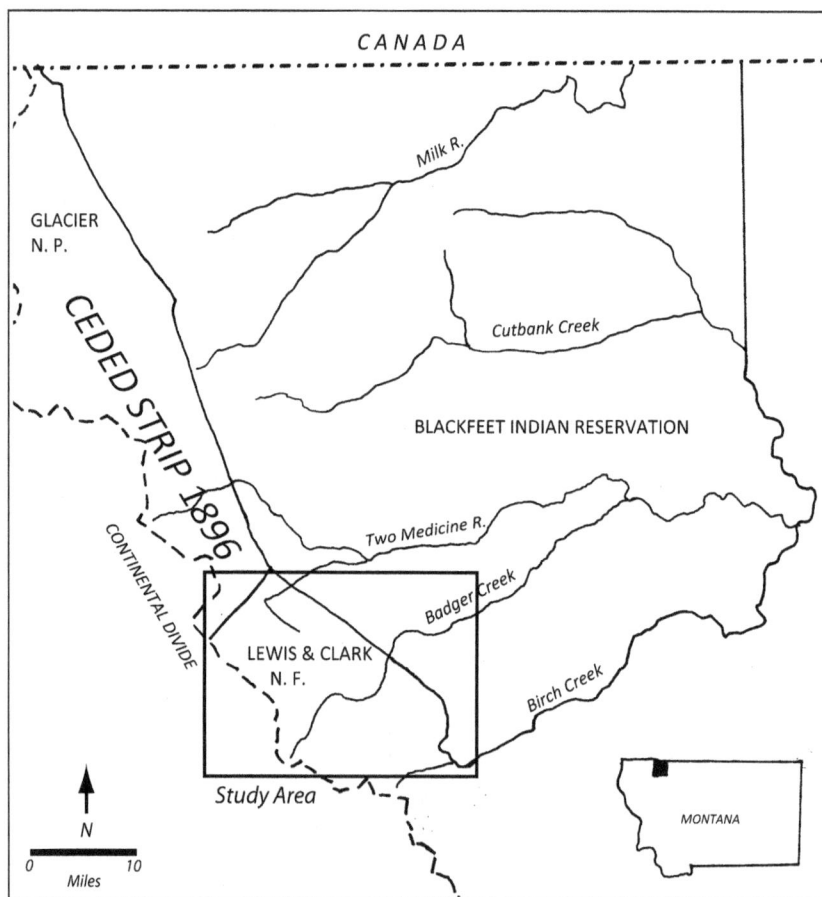

Figure 8.1. Location of the Blackfeet Indian Reservation and study area, Montana.

values may be found in the *hunting ethos*, which is defined as a set of shared principles, dispositions, and practices deployed by hunters in response to predictable and unpredictable conditions affecting prey and place. Second, I discuss how the survival of hunting in the twentieth century was possible both because the Blackfeet preserved core values from their age-old hunting ethos, and because they applied strategies of accommodation, resistance, and negotiation of a middle ground in order to adjust to new ecological and geopolitical conditions. Last, I utilize a data subset from a collaborative land-use study on ceded lands managed by the Lewis and Clark National Forest, Montana (Zedeño 2007; Zedeño et al. 2006, 2007, 2008) (figure 8.1) to illustrate how changes in the focus, context, and social structure of hunting have helped the Blackfeet cope with revolutionary changes brought about by the elimination of the bison and establishment of the reservation system. Finally, I argue that these changes led to the emergence of a tradition and an identity that is uniquely situated in the context of reservation life.

Temporality, Identity, and the Hunting Ethos

Among the most intractable problems to resolve in the reconstruction of hunters' historical trajectories is the apparent juxtaposition of an instantaneous present made of singular events in restricted spatio-temporal frameworks and a lengthy past. Writing about the images of subarctic hunters that populate anthropological imagery, Harvey Feit (1994:421) observed that this juxtaposition is a product of anthropological models of hunter-gatherer lifeways, which tend to project snapshot observations of hunters' daily lives onto long-term evolutionary trends, thus obviating the existence of an enduring present oriented toward a future shaped by human agency. Such models perpetuate the classic image of hunters as "inhabiting a special world, connected yet other; people with a short vision and a long history" (Feit 1994:425). Yet, as David Turner (1979:206) once pointed out, hunters across time and space have confronted the need to plan for the future by creating conditions for group permanence and preserving knowledge even in the midst of high mobility and uncertainty, and have found diverse solutions to problems ranging from the retention of hunting ground ownership rights to the averaging of environmental stresses affecting staple prey. In other cases, populations have optimized their environment by introducing exotic species that not only satisfied subsistence needs but also supported belief systems and ritual practices (Rick, this volume).

A dearth of multiscalar frameworks for the study of terrestrial big-game hunters, in particular, has retarded our understanding of the role of agency in planning for the future by creating predictable human-environment relations, as well as in structuring deliberate responses to unstable or changed ecological and sociopolitical conditions (Milner, this volume; Thompson et al., this volume). While research on the rise of complex forager societies has found an answer to the scalar conundrum in Fernand Braudel's (1980) *longue durée* approach of the Annales school (e.g., Ames 1991; see Balée 2006; Habu and Hall, this volume), studies of prehistoric and historic big-game hunters lag well behind in the adoption of models that reconcile past, present, and future from landscape, agency, and practice perspectives. Of the many reasons for this lag, the one that most prominently stands out to me is the conventional conceptualization of hunting as a subsistence activity with narrow technological, ecological, and economic objectives and end results—one that is dictated by prey and place rather than chosen or negotiated by people (e.g., Oliver 1962; Sahlins 2003; Steward 1997; cf. Ingold 2003). This convention has been largely perpetuated in cultural- , behavioral- , and evolutionary-ecological models of forager societies (e.g., Bettinger 1991; Winterhalder and Smith 1981; see Binford 2001 and Kelly 1995 for comprehensive reviews of these models).

Alternatively, there is the notion that hunting (or foraging, Fish et al., this volume) is not simply an activity but a worldview that permeates every realm of life and thought (e.g., Gillespie 2008; Oetelaar and Meyer 2006; Oetelaar and Oetelaar 2006; Potter 2004; Sassaman 2001; Zvelebil 1997). The hunting ethos, as defined in this chapter, subsumes timeless ontological and epistemological postulates shared and transferred intergenerationally as well as strategies for updating and tailoring such principles to the peculiarities of the prey, the hunting ground, and the historical contingencies surrounding hunter groups at any given time. The hunting ethos thus shapes decisions about social investment in the short, middle, and long ranges (Anderson and Zedeño 2009; Ballenger and Zedeño 2009; Nunley 1991). When engaged in the act of hunting, individuals and groups simultaneously recapitulate timeless principles and past experiences and transform them according to present conditions and future decisions. Through time, this "structured agency" (after Joyce and Lopiparo 2005:365) manifests itself in long-enduring human landscapes and materially distinctive hunting traditions that are "neither passive nor benign ways of doing things, but malleable, subject to politicization, and always negotiated between persons and among peoples at multiple scales" (Pauketat 2001:3).

As a millenary tradition, *hunting is just not what people do but who they are*—this intricate and intimate human-prey-place relationship defines individual and group identity regardless of age, gender, and social standing. Among the contemporary Blackfeet, hunting is indeed a right-of-being, even among men and women who have never hunted or who no longer do. It is recounted in storytelling and relived in corporate religious rituals that once aimed at promoting the reproduction and capture of bison but that may still be adapted to the demands of reservation life and hunting practices governed by modern rules and regulations. To explain the emergence of the twentieth-century reservation-era hunting tradition and identity, it is necessary, therefore, to identify the domains of stability and change in core values associated with the Blackfeet's relationships with prey and place.

Core Values: Domains of Stability and Change

Romanticized portrayals of the North American Plains, where long-gone, mounted warrior-hunters reigned, have obscured the fact that ancestral Blackfoot speakers were mobile pedestrian big-game hunters uniquely adapted to the mountain-prairie ecotone, having access to both the forested slopes of the Rocky Mountains and the short-grass prairie. The deceivingly monotonous northwestern Plains landscape offered abundant and diverse resources on river bottoms, spring-fed coulees, rich grasslands, and sand formations that the ancestral Blackfoot-speaking bands utilized in a territory defined by the upper Saskatchewan River, the Continental Divide, and the north bank of the Yellowstone River, from its northern headwaters to its mouth (Jackson 2000:xii). Core values upheld by the Montana Blackfeet reflect this prairie-mountain continuum and are evident in their cosmology and traditional practices aimed at maintaining and regenerating their relationships with prey and place as well as in the material record of their presence in the aboriginal territory (Zedeño and Murray 2008).

The prehistoric origin and territorial extent of the Blackfoot speakers have been a matter of debate since their first contact with European fur traders in the eighteenth century (Dempsey 2001; Ewers 1958; Tyrrell 1916; cf. Jackson 2000). Only recently have Canadian and North American archaeologists reconciled their views on the cultural history of the group, particularly regarding the connection between massive archaeological evidence of habitation and hunting practices dating at least to 200 BC (and perhaps much earlier) and the ancestral Blackfoot (Greiser 1994; Kehoe 1978; Peck and Hudecek-Cuffe 2003; Reeves 1993). While a detailed review of the contentious archaeological record of the group is beyond the scope of this chapter, it is nonetheless important to note that the social investment placed upon hunting clearly reaches far in time, encompassing ritual, technological, and ecological bodies of knowledge as well as regulatory institutions, such as esoteric societies whose membership crosscut kin and band and whose liturgy, landscape associations, and ritual paraphernalia included both prairie and mountain elements (McClintock 1999; Wissler 1916).

At the time of contact, these bodies of knowledge were upheld and mediated by powerful societies that regulated bison hunting practices of four Blackfoot ethnic subgroups—Siksika, or Blackfoot proper; Kainaa, or Blood; North Peigan; and South Peigan, or Pikaani. The South Peigan, or Pikaani, were the largest subgroup and the ancestors of the Blackfeet Tribe of Montana.

The horse preceded the European fur traders who first encountered Blackfoot speakers in the late eighteenth century (e.g., Peter Fidler in Molenaar 2000; David Thompson and Alexander Henry in Tyrrell 1916); consequently, the line separating pre- and post-equestrian lifeways became increasingly blurred in the influential writings of traders, travelers, and ethnographers that came into contact with the mounted Blackfoot speakers and particularly the Pikaani (e.g., Prince Maximilian de Wied, in Thwaites 1906). Partly because the Pikaani allowed very few, if any, Europeans into their territorial home at the foot of the Rockies until the mid-1800s, historical accounts of their lifeways are strongly biased toward equestrian life on the plains, with comparatively little documentary information on their relationship with foothills and mountain environments and particularly with elk, which is their most valued prey today. The temporal depth of this relationship, on the other hand, is demonstrated in oral tradition and ritual (Zedeño and Murray 2008).

The Prey

The connection between Blackfeet and elk has profound ontological and epistemological roots. As a primordial animal, elk figures in origin stories, group ceremonies, bundles, and individual visions (McClintock 1999;

Wissler 1910). Both ecologically and culturally, elk stands at the transition between the mountains and the prairie. Elk is the Wind Maker; its emergence from the waters of upper St. Mary's Lake at the foot of East Glacier symbolically connects both environments (Schultz 2002:187). Elk also has associations with the bear and water birds and animals (Schaeffer 1934). One of the most important associations of elk is found in the origin story of the Natoas headdress, which is worn by the Holy Woman during the ceremony of the Okan Medicine Lodge, also known as the Blackfoot Sun Dance. Wissler and Duvall (1995:84) recorded a Peigan version of this origin story as follows:

> There was once an Elk who was deserted by his wife. When he found that she was gone, he went out to look for her, and finally saw her in the thick woods. He was very angry and wished to kill her: so he walked toward her singing a song. Now this was a medicine-song, and he intended that its power should kill his wife. He had great power. The ground was very hard; but at every step his feet sank deeper into it. Now his wife was frightened; but she had some power also. She began to sing a song, and as she did so she turned into a woman. In her new form she wore a medicine-bonnet, a robe of elk-hide over her shoulders, and elk-teeth on her wrists. The song that she sang when she became a woman was:
>
> "My wristlets are elk-teeth;
> They are powerful."
>
> Then the woman moved toward a tree, moved her head as if hooking at the tree, and it almost fell. Now when the Elk saw what she was doing, he stopped in great surprise at her power. He did not kill her as he had intended. This was Elk-Woman. In the sun-dance a tree or post is put up in the centre of the sun-lodge and the woman who wears the bonnet makes hooking motions at the pole, as did the Elk-Woman in the first part of the story.

This narrative illustrates not only the centrality of elk in the most significant of Blackfoot rituals, the Okan, but also it shows how core values that mediate hunting practices, which are shaped by engendered rules of engagement between hunter and prey, are internalized through origin stories and ritual. Among traditional Blackfeet men, elk is thought to be a magical animal with male sexual power and thus it is prized for his proclivity to transfer this power to those hunters who spare his life but take cows and juveniles instead (Zedeño et al. 2006). Female religious practitioners continue to honor the power of Elk Woman by wearing elk teeth jewelry. Female shirts embroidered with elk teeth are further associated with star stories. Designs on the elk tipi and the elk medicine were originally obtained in a dream and then transferred from person to person (Schaeffer 1934).

Oral accounts and sparse archaeological evidence (Lapinsky 1998:36; McCabe 2002:132) suggest that drives were once used to harvest elk—a hunting strategy most commonly used for bison. The first elk jump was done by the Creator, or Old Man Napi (Bullchild 1985:203). Thereafter, drive lanes that connected elk grazing grounds or mineral licks to a cliff were presumably built by placing large rock cairns and tree branches at regular intervals. Lanes followed the contour of the terrain and habitual elk paths; hunters would herd elk toward the drive lanes and jump them over the cliff, finishing them off at the base of the jump. Unfortunately, except for passing references to elk bones found intermingled with bison bone beds (Lapinsky 1998:36), remains of elk hunting are poorly represented archaeologically in prehistoric, historic, and modern hunting sites in Montana and southern Alberta (Frison 2004:182; McCabe 2002:122).

Although the northwestern Rockies were reportedly elk-poor throughout the late prehistoric and colonial periods (Lyman and Wolverton 2002; Kay 2002), in the early nineteenth century elk were abundant across the Plains, second in numbers to bison (Szuter and Martin 1999). Small herds also ranged along the Rocky Mountain Front. Historical records indicate that the Blackfeet hunted elk and other ungulates opportunistically and incidentally, either on foot or on horse, and more for the utilitarian, social, and economic value of the ivory tusks and hides than for its meat (Ewers 2001:170; McCabe 2002). Evidence of historic elk hunting comes primarily from manufactured goods, although there is the occasional journal entry describing a hunting episode. Elk and ungulates in general were not the food of choice among the Blackfeet, so long as bison was available; according to Schultz (1962:30), the Pikaani considered bison meat to be the only "real food." Narratives of pre-reservation life recorded by Claude Schaeffer (1934) suggest that regular capture and consumption of elk for its meat was limited to one Pikaani band whose members were horse-poor and therefore reduced to stalking elk and other game on foot, remaining close to the foothills.

Elk byproducts were used in a variety of ways; most notably, teeth were used in the manufacture of female dresses, which were considered a sign of high status and wealth (Ewers 1958:130) as well as a means to harness elk power. A woman's shirt could have as many as 100 pairs of tusks sewn to it or equal the number of elk needed to adorn it; these were valuable items that were often obtained from the Kootenai in exchange for bison hides and parfleches (Schaeffer 1934).

As long as bison were abundant, commercial trade in elk hides did not figure prominently in the Native economy, but by the mid-1870s, bison herds were rapidly diminishing and other sources of profit were being sought. Wholesale killing of elk by White hunters and, presumably, Native hunters dealt a blow to the once teeming elk populations and, by the 1880s, only remnant herds could be found along the Rocky Mountain Front (McCabe 2002:165; O'Gara and Dundas 2002:99; Picton and Picton 1975:7). Although elk herd populations were fast to recover in this region, the introduction of cattle and sheep by White ranchers placed a serious stress upon elk and wildlife in general, as livestock competed for grazing range with wild game. Ranching and settlement also brought about the near-extermination of elk's natural predators, the coyote and wolf. Without predators, elk herds grew rapidly in the first decade of the twentieth century, but a reduced winter range negatively affected calf crops. Given that wildlife management strategies were still in their infancy, the "elk problem" became a highly contested issue in the public domain, prompting the Montana state legislature to create game preserves in 1913 in order to protect elk's winter range along the Front (Picton and Picton 1975:14).

Without bison, subsistence elk hunting on the foothills and intermountain valleys, where the remnant herds had taken refuge, radically increased in frequency and intensity. The Blackfeet, whose reservation at first included portions of prime elk range from the Milk River to the Sun River, were ideally positioned to point their sights on this prey. The intermountain forests and valleys that became the modern Blackfeet hunting grounds could not be better for elk. Migration corridors, vast sedge meadows in protected forest clearings, aspen groves in transition zones, numerous mineral licks scattered across the forest, and the absence of competing cattle and sheep in the remote intermountain valleys facilitated the expansion of native and implanted elk. Logging and fire further opened these remote elk ranges far beyond the foothills. With the creation of game preserves and the institution of elk restocking programs and hunting quotas by the U.S. Forest Service and U.S. Fish and Wildlife Service, herds expanded their migration routes to the west of the Continental Divide. By 1920, there were three mature and very large elk herds whose calving and wintering grounds were established immediately to the south and southwest of the reservation on both sides of the Continental Divide (Smith 1978; West 1941), as well as one large herd and a handful of small ones scattered along the eastern foothills (Picton and Picton 1975).

The Hunting Ground

The Blackfeet relationship with the Rocky Mountains is as old as the Blackfeet–elk relationship. The mountains figure prominently in Blackfeet origin stories, and their use of mountain resources presumably dates to the prehistoric period (Vest 1988), although the archaeological record of their presence is not well defined and analyzed. Classic and contemporary renditions of Blackfoot cosmology agree that this connection began with the creation of the Rocky Mountains by Old Man Napi (Bastien 2004; Grinnell 1962; McClintock 1999; Schultz 2002). The mountain cosmology focuses on forces such as thunder, wind, and snow, which inhabit the high peaks and control the renewal of the natural world. People establish alliances with these forces, which in turn give them power and allow them to find ways to live well and be prosperous. Thunder, in particular, is known to have bestowed many gifts upon the people, notably the Blue Thunder Medicine Pipe, which is also strongly associated with grizzly bears and black bears (Zedeño 2008).

A number of sacred bundles (particularly beaver bundles) and painted tipis originate from mountain lakes and rivers, and the liturgical order associated with the former further links the prairie to the mountains. For example, beaver bundle songs are sung to call the medicine buffalo, which, upon hearing this calling, descends from the mountains onto the plains, leaving behind it a trail of sacred ground (McClintock 1999:81). The mountains contain resources that are critical to the practice of Blackfeet ceremonies, including springs, paints of various colors, medicinal, smudging, and hallucinogenic roots, and a variety of birds and mammals whose bodies are sought for making and replenishing bundles (Beidl 1992; Deaver 1988; Greiser and Greiser 1993; Reeves and Peacock 2001; Vest 1988; Zedeño 2008; Zedeño et al. 2006, 2007, 2008). Creation stories, ritual resources, magical animals, and practices such as vision quests, are in turn associated with particular landmarks along the Rocky Mountain Front.

Evidence of prehistoric hunting on the Front comes primarily from a few hunting stations and campsites along the foothills dating to the Paleoindian–Archaic transition or approximately 8,000 years ago and from isolated surface findings elsewhere in the uplands (Campbell and Foor 2002; Kehoe 2001; Reeves and Peacock 2001). The historic record is not particularly illustrative of the Blackfeet presence in the mountains, but available documentation suggests that, beginning in the 1750s, parties of warrior-hunters and horse raiders were endemic along the north–south mountain trails to and from the Crow and Shoshone territories. These warpaths were used to conceal people and horses from enemy pursuers (Ewers 2001:188; Jackson 2000:68–70; McClintock 1999:16, 40).

Ethnographic data collected by Claude Schaeffer (1934) indicates that in the pre-reservation era the Blackfeet did not frequent the mountains in pursuit of game even though they routinely harvested subalpine forest resources, such as lodgepole pine for tipi and travois construction. Elk hunting took place on the foothills, where many Pikaani and Blood bands set up their winter camps. There is also indication that individuals and families who maintained kin and trade networks with mountain tribes, particularly the Kootenai, spent the summer hunting in the intermountain regions and western ranges (Schaeffer 1934). From the Kootenai, in fact, the Pikaani obtained the Blacktail Dance (Duvall 1909:85)—a game-charming ceremony still used by contemporary elk hunters. But for the most part, until the 1880s life revolved around bison, which they hunted year-round (Kehoe 1993). The large-scale communal hunts took place throughout the late fall and winter, involving complex ritual preparation, planning, and community-wide involvement in its execution (Ballenger and Zedeño 2009). Each band would winter on the upper valleys from the Milk River to the three forks of the Missouri, and used nearby bison drives, jumps, and corrals (Schaeffer 1934). Hunting of secondary game species for meat specifically took place in the late winter and early spring when the bison cows had exhausted their fat reserves or were calving.

Beginning with the Lame Bull Treaty of 1855, the Blackfeet suffered a series of staggering losses of their hunting ground. The Executive Order of 1873, which established their first reservation, excluded most of the Sun River elk range and a vast area from the Judith River to the mouth of the Yellowstone River. The Agreement of 1888 took away the Sweetgrass Hills, where the last bison herds were sighted, and the Agreement of 1895 terminated their settlement and mineral rights on the Rocky Mountain Front but preserved the rights to hunt, fish, timber, collect, and worship along what became known as the Ceded Strip (see figure 8.1). Thus the year of 1900 found the Blackfeet at the climax of their misfortunes: it had been more than 10 years since the last bison hunt; they had lost more than half of their people to massacre, famine, and disease, and they had been forced to give up most of their hunting grounds and sacred sites along the Front (Ewers 1958; Farr 1984). This loss had incredibly important implications because it forced the Blackfeet to redefine the geography of their cultural practices in ways that only recently have come to light.

In 1900, the newly reduced Blackfeet Indian Reservation extended across 1.3 million acres of prairie now populated by free-ranging cattle and sheep to which they had no access except through astringent Indian Agency rationing rules (Foley 1986). Reluctant trappers and marginal farmers, and chastised by the Indian agent for illegally hunting agency cattle, the Blackfeet took to the Rocky Mountains to hunt in order to supplement their meager government rations. Although familiar with this environment, the Blackfeet never before had depended on mountain game to the extent that they did now and they took the exercise of hunting rights to heart. It was not to be an easy transition, however. Although the Ceded Strip was spared from the mining rush that permanently changed the landscape in other regions, stock-raising, logging, railroad construction, and fire suppression impacted aspen and subalpine forest habitats at different rates and in varying degrees. Alarmed by the impact of settlement on the pristine Rocky Mountains, in 1910 the federal government withdrew the northern portion of the Ceded Strip from the Blackfeet hunting range to create Glacier National Park. This permanent hunting ban was fought hard by the Blackfeet, but it eventually forced them to turn to the forest reserve (Lewis and Clark National Forest) located to the south and west of the reservation. Rich in game and accessible, the forest became their primary hunting ground (Warren 1997).

For the next five decades the Blackfeet struggled to assert their hunting rights on the forest, even though it was clear that hunting was important to the management of expanding elk herds on public lands. When certain areas along the front became crowded and denuded, the Blackfeet moved farther into the range, to the west of the Continental Divide where large elk herds ranged, where they established hunting and outfitting camps, thus solidifying the Blackfeet presence there. As a 65-year-old Blackfeet hunter explained: "At the beginning of the reservation the people went to visit Two Medicine and out there they were so hungry that they only ate porcupine for Thanksgiving. At Old Agency the rations were not enough so people began hunting in the mountains. As time went on rations got upgraded but hunting was still strong. Badger [Creek] was quickly over hunted and so they moved to Birch [Creek] and the Bob Marshall [Wilderness]" (Zedeño et al. 2007:43). It is at this juncture that a culture of mountain hunting emerged as the marker of modern Blackfeet identity.

Mountain Hunters

I have pointed out that the Blackfeet as a people maintain ancient and stable connections to elk and the Rockies; ecological and ritual knowledge in particular embody long-term and stable but flexible core values that made adaptation to twentieth-century conditions possible. The collaborative research project I undertook in 2004–8 among Blackfeet mountain hunters, ages 25 to 95, demonstrates that the most dramatic changes to hunting practices were in the structure of the hunting group, the organization of the hunt, and the management of hunting space (Zedeño 2007; Zedeño et al. 2006, 2007, 2008) (figure 8.2). On the basis of findings from

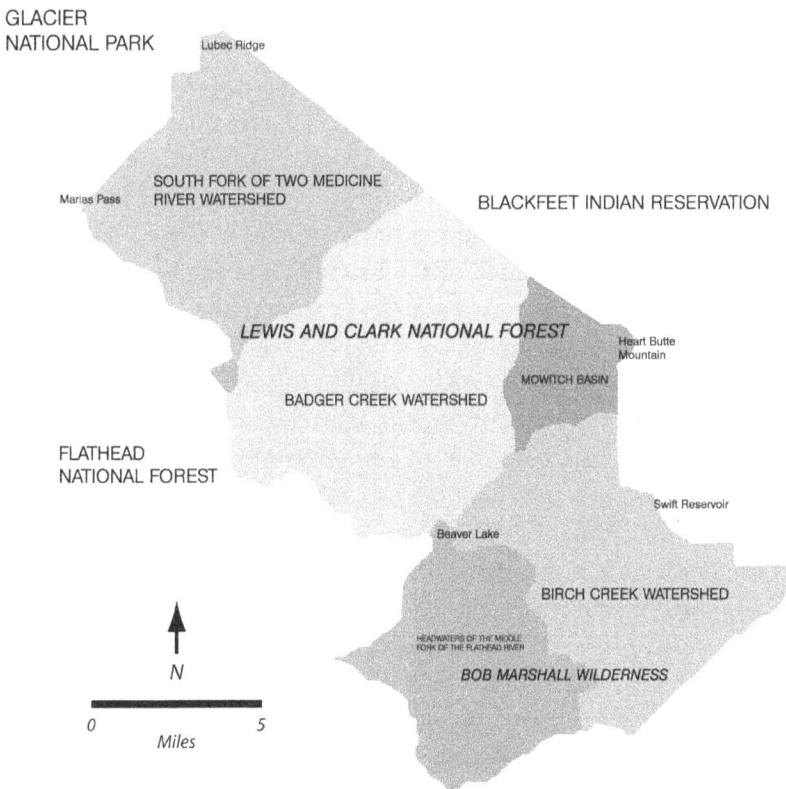

GLACIER
NATIONAL PARK   Lubec Ridge

SOUTH FORK OF TWO MEDICINE
Marias Pass   RIVER WATERSHED   BLACKFEET INDIAN RESERVATION

LEWIS AND CLARK NATIONAL FOREST   Heart Butte
Mountain

MOWITCH BASIN

BADGER CREEK WATERSHED

FLATHEAD
NATIONAL FOREST

Swift Reservoir

Beaver Lake

BIRCH CREEK WATERSHED

N

HEADWATERS OF THE MIDDLE
FORK OF THE FLATHEAD RIVER

BOB MARSHALL WILDERNESS

0   5
Miles

Figure 8.2. Watersheds included in the Collaborative Blackfeet Land Use Study 2004–8.

hunters' oral histories and archaeological surveys of the upper reaches of five watersheds on both sides of the Continental Divide, I argue that these changes were necessary *politically,* to assert a clear and rightful presence on ceded land by creating a sense of physical permanence through resistance and negotiation of a middle ground; *economically,* to secure subsistence hunting returns and increase predictability by delimiting informal hunting territories and establishing hunting etiquette; *socially,* to develop networks that best fit sedentary reservation life; and *ritually,* to transpose sacred sites from areas no longer accessible onto the peaks and lakes of the modern hunting ground.

The Hunting Group

Although in pre-reservation times elk and other ungulates were some-times hunted using the drive, jump and corral, which required a group effort to plan and execute, this activity did not attract the kind of long-, mid-, and short-range social investment of bands and supra-band aggregations that communal bison hunting did (Ballenger and Zedeño 2009; Reitze and Zedeño 2009; Verbicky-Todd 1984). Ostensibly, the elimination of bison terminated community-wide investment in the hunt, even though bison remains central to Blackfeet ceremonialism. Communal hunting was replaced by the hunting group as a community of practice (*sensu* Wenger 1998) with hands-on investment of mostly male hunters organized in pairs or small groups of relatives and friends—community participation became limited to food sharing and feasting. In principle, this was by no means a novel social arrangement: the mountain hunting group resembled the composition of the old raiding party that traversed the secluded Continental Divide trails: five to eight hunters representing four or five generations, each 15 years apart. However, the social and political makeup of the mountain hunter group differed from the raiding party in important ways: it not only suited the habits of the prey and the ruggedness of the new hunting ground but also responded to the character of twentieth-century reservation settlement, where the old bands were now splintered in nuclear families living in allotments loosely clustered around isolated rural communities, such as Heart Butte, on the south side of the reservation (Farr 1984:109). Initially, women and children accompanied the hunting parties, particularly in the warm months. But school and employment obligations later kept families away from the men's hunting ground.

The dynamics of this transition also combined tradition and transformation. Historic records and oral histories show that, in the early reservation years, there were a handful of great lone hunters of warrior and raider vintage (Schaeffer 1934; Warren 1997) who established permanent campsites deep in the intermountain elk ranges and trained younger men in navigating the uplands, training mountain horses, and hunting in the forest. Tree-ring dating of structural wood and camp-ownership genealogies confirmed that "pioneer" campsites range from 77 to 120 years in age (Zedeño et al. 2008). Lone hunters and their apprentices kept various campsites at different locations and elevations, which were used according to the season and the movement of elk herds. Hunting groups were somewhat stable, but through time individuals changed hunting partners as their needs, physical fitness, or hunting ground preferences changed. Older and accomplished hunters trained and hunted with numerous younger partners, who in turn passed on this knowledge and stories that their contemporary descendants are eager to acknowledge.

Organization of the Hunt

Until the 1960s, the Blackfeet hunted elk year-round, beginning in the spring along the remote intermountain ranges of the Bob Marshall Wilderness to the south of the reservation and moving closer to the foothills and the reservation as the snow accumulated on the higher elevations (figure 8.3). A few hunters also engaged in trapping and in outfitting businesses that they ran independently of their more traditional hunting expeditions. According to a 55-year-old Blackfeet hunter, a traditional mountain hunting expedition went as follows:

> In the old days people hunted from here to Schafer Meadows, sometimes as many as eight or nine of them. They hunted along the creeks all the time and would dress and dry meat in the camp for the winter. They worked their way out. They went in early spring, with the snowmelt, and in late May and June. Then in late September and October they would take a long hunt for the winter. We hunted when we needed it. The elders were very wise in a lot of ways; they would keep the location of the [mineral] licks secret, would not tell anyone about them, even if more than one group knew about them no one would talk. In the Forest now you get permanent campsites, they are in Blind, Steep, Killem Horse, but in the old days we had specific

camping places for different times of the year when the grass was good. For example, at Beaver Lake we camped on the southeast side and took the horses to the meadows. Camps would be moved every few days, to Blue Lake. The location of the licks was also important for camping.

The hunters sang Blacktail songs. Blacktail is a very important ceremony to us—it is a deer ceremony and they would sing these songs before getting started. There was a big feed the day before the hunt, and non-hunters also participated, songs were for safety and success. The lead hunter would go out and pray to the mountains and animals, so they would know we were coming. When I was growing up you showed dignity and thankfulness to animals. We would stage on this side of the mountains, so that others could use the cabin for staging too, and then went up the ridge. Sometimes we stayed at Pete Eagle's camp in Hungry Man—I saw them dance and pray there before going out. Nobody uses that camp now, they [the old ones] will blow your tent right off the side of the hill.

The Old People, they all hunted. I went with them once or twice. When we came out of the mountains we would see people gathered around my dad's cabin. Then the old hunters started singing thank you songs to let people know they were successful. Then the women would lay blankets out to unpack the meat until all they got was laid on blankets. As they did this they would tell a story about the hunt, the excitement, and things special that happened—many stories would be told. The women divided up the meat among the hunters, then the rest of non-hunters would get some share of the meat. Everyone shared in the hunt. I was fortunate to see this and the modern world too (consultant in Zedeño et al. 2007:53).

The passage of the Wilderness Act in 1964, along with a catastrophic flood that destroyed the upper creek beds and killed many Birch Creek residents, hit reservation hunters hard, and the hunting ways of the "Old People" began to wane. But even within the regulatory hunting seasons, contemporary Blackfeet hunters who were trained in the traditional ways have kept alive a number of important traditions: singing ceremonial songs on the hunting trail, leaving offerings, planning the camping arrangements according to the amount of feed they will need for their horses, and preserving the fundamentals of camp use etiquette, to name a few.

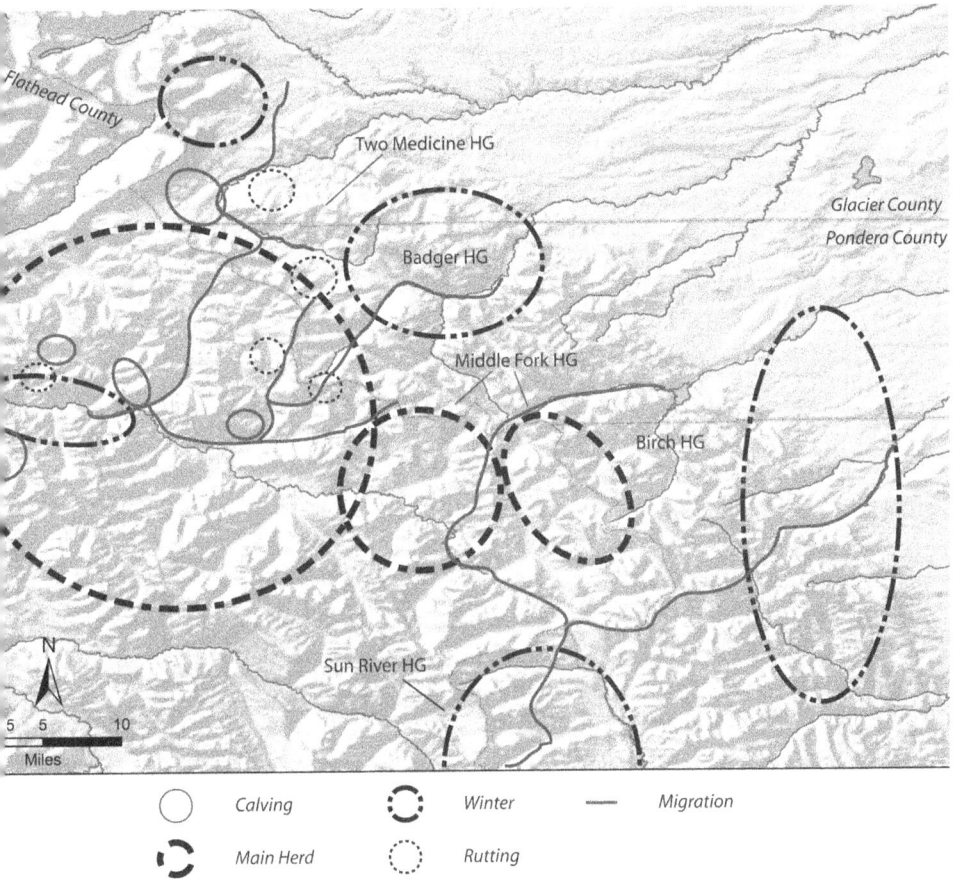

Figure 8.3. Elk herds and hunting areas.

The Hunting Space

Hunting territories, loosely defined by major upper watersheds on both sides of the Continental Divide, were claimed by hunting groups whose allotments were located on the lower reaches of the watersheds, and whose social networks were largely defined by the new allotment system. Field surveys and oral histories indicate that, throughout the first half of the twentieth century, hunters established and maintained functionally different campsites, each with its own rules of ownership and use etiquette, in one or more territories to which they had access through their hunting partners and groups (figure 8.4). This is illustrated in the following account:

On the first night we would set up a spike camp for staging. It was laid out in the open, and then we set out. We would go either from Birch to Beaver over the Divide, or from Badger to the forks and Lodgepole [Mountain], and then to Strawberry or as far as Elbow Mountain and Spotted Eagle Pass. Many Springs on Elbow Creek and Davis Lick were good places, with lots of hay for the horses. We hunted on the forks, Elbow Creek, and also behind the Ranger Station. Spotted Eagle Pass was one of the most important areas for us.

There was a network among us and we would share food and campsites. Philip Comes-at-Night would leave his camp up in season so his friends could use it until the end of season. At Winter Camp, for example, there was a cellar where people left coffee, a can to make coffee, sugar, and flour. So if you came there, you knew where to look but had to refill it. The old people had stoves, pots and pans, some left smoking tobacco for the passerby, but cigarettes were the only thing we did not share much. Old timers left tobacco offerings but young ones didn't want to waste cigarettes. They took Drum, 24 bags and paper. The Old People rationed cigarettes, one a day. We shared meat if anybody killed something. Some bones were discarded and teeth used, antler sometimes. The animal was cut up with the hide, as the younger generation did not have a use for the hide. Old people thought of each other and word of mouth helped build the network (consultant in Zedeño et al. 2007:54).

While many of the remote summer camps are no longer used for hunting, as the regulated hunting season is limited to the fall and early winter months, the fall and winter hunting camps continue to be actively used and maintained by descendants of the original hunting groups. There are at least five types of hunting camps still in active use:

1. *Staging camps* are located on the reservation or in the forest at or near the mountain trailheads. Staging camps are used as meeting places where hunters ready the equipment for the trip and pack; they are also used to distribute meat. Often, individual hunters who outfit for cash own these camps and thus they own extra packing and camping equipment as well as mountain horses and mules.
2. *Drop-off camps* are overnight camping and meeting places located at crossroads or at the base of mountain passes. More than one hunting group generally uses them at once. At key locations, there are two or three drop-off camps located near one another.

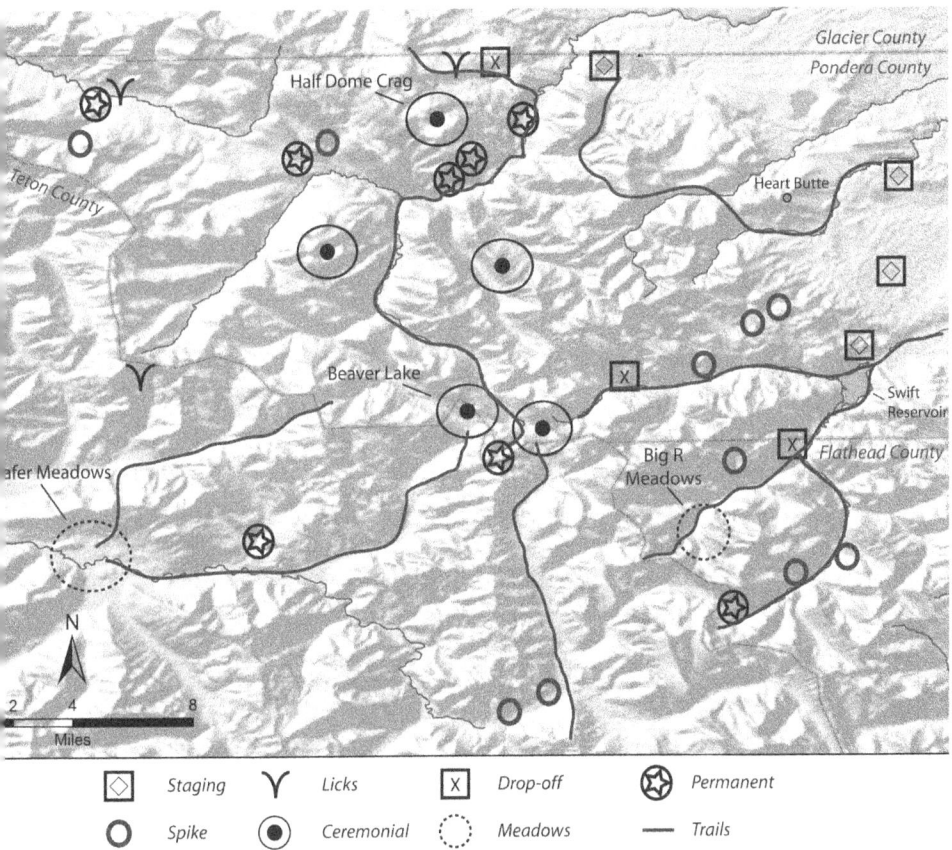

Figure 8.4. The hunting space.

3. *Base camps* are large, permanent camps located next to a major water source and next to meadows large enough to feed up to a dozen
   pack animals, although hay bales may be packed, too. Base camps
   may contain stashes of tipi poles, wood railings, corrals, cooking
   equipment and meat storage areas, waterworks, latrines, and other
   amenities that were once an important aspect of the social network. Waterworks, including spring dams, water-freeze storage
   pools, meat-smoking platforms, and makeshift spouts and drains
   are common, particularly in old camps that were once used for
   weeks at a time. Although very subtle, these features play a role in
   transforming the immediate habitat by creating pools and bogs that
   fill with small fish and attract beaver. Many of the base camps located in the survey have been continuously used for more than 100
   years and bear the scars of old beaver dams and regenerated sedge

meadows. Unfortunately, National Forest and Wilderness policies outlawing storage in campsites, and game wardens who implement these policies, have destroyed a great deal of material evidence by cleaning up historical trash and dismantling tack and camp equipment caches built high above the ground on tree branches.

4. *Spike camps* are used for stalking and still-hunting; one or two hunters set them up overnight. These are generally located on densely forested slopes near clearings, water sources, and licks where elk gather and bed. They may also be located along migration paths. Spike camps contain few features—a stone hearth and spring dam are common.

5. *Central camping areas* are located in the heart of the elk range, and are accessible from all directions. Three such camping and horse-grazing areas were documented: Big River Meadows at the foot of the Front, and Beaver Lake and Schafer Meadows, both west of the Continental Divide. Beaver Lake is the oldest and most important cultural area in the hunting ground. The great lone hunters used it for ceremonial purposes; the old hunters organized pilgrimages to Beaver Lake to gather plants used in sweat lodges and vision quests that are thought to grow only in that location, and to collect rare paints. Different hunting groups use it extensively nowadays.

Although in principle everyone may camp on National Forest land, and many hunters say that there is no attachment to any camp, ownership of a hunting camp developed after repeated use and is still expressed in subtle yet consistent gentlemen's agreements. There are certain hunting areas that are recognized as used most frequently by specific hunting groups and hunters, who feel proprietary about their grounds: "it is a learned process to know where everyone's camp is; individuals have their own camp areas and others respect it" (consultant in Zedeño et al. 2007:67). There are camps associated with the men who established and used them most; however, in the old days owners expected to share their camps as part of the hunters' social network and even made sure that enough equipment and emergency foods were cached on camp for those in need, as long as the supplies were replenished after each use. "One time we were camped at Muskrat and BF says to me, 'Go and get me a frying pan from CA's.' I got on my horse and rode all the way back and sure enough, there was a frying pan hanging high up a tree. On our way back BF said: 'Go take that pan back.' And I took the pan back to where I found it. CA always left things at his camp to help others. BF told us that things on Muskrat and Winter Camp had been there when he was a child—old stuff" (consultant in Zedeño et al. 2007:56). The right of use of certain camps dictates that users must move on when the camp owners arrive. Hunting camps at key locations are passed from father to son, from grandfather to grandson, or from master to apprentice. Camps were passed on to younger hunters either through family lines or through partnerships.

6. *Ritual Spaces.* Base camps and central camping areas were used for group ceremonies during the years of religious persecution: hunters relish the memory of how their ancestors would frustrate Indian agents and priests alike by crossing the reservation boundary at Birch Creek and holding a Sun Dance on its south bank, which is in the Lewis and Clark National Forest. Sweat lodges were also kept at base camps; hunters could use these as stages for their vision quests on the high peaks. Although it is no longer necessary to hide religious activities in the depth of the forest, the ritual space of contemporary mountain hunters is largely defined by the peaks and passes of the Continental Divide, where ceremonial resources are collected, vision quests take place, elk are killed, and hunting offerings are placed to honor it (figure 8.5).

Figure 8.5. A Blackfeet hunter holds an elk offering.

Significantly, the mountains immediately to the south of the reservation have become the repository of origin stories and the home of sacred beings that in pre-reservation times were associated with landmarks in Glacier National Park and other places to the north, but which are no longer connected to people as closely as the landmarks on the modern hunting ground. Although this transposition of sacred space cannot be generalized to the entire tribe, it is nonetheless characteristic of hunters who grew up in rural communities closest to the Badger–Two Medicine and Birch regions of the forest. Among these community members, there is a strong belief that the power that once resided on the peaks of Glacier National Park migrated south once the shrines and other sacred sites could no longer cared for by the Blackfeet but used by non-Blackfeet folk (Zedeño et al. 2006:18). This shift in ritual space has allowed hunters to maintain the connection between the ancient and the contemporary by flexing core values within acceptable cultural parameters.

Conclusion

The Blackfeet mountain hunter was born amid multiscalar, internal and external, and variously paced changes that challenged the hunting ethos and the Blackfeet as a people in untold ways (figure 8.6). Interrelated historical events that brought about dramatic changes in the hunters' relationships with prey and place were resolved by behaviors that first aimed at sheer day-to-day survival but that soon encompassed deliberate acts of assertion and future planning. These actions both departed from tradition, as hunters needed to accommodate new conditions, and followed ritual and ecological knowledge and dispositions toward elk and the Rocky Mountains that were established centuries, if not millennia, ago. To a large extent, the Blackfeet transitioned from community-wide bison hunters to community-of-practice elk hunters successfully because of the prairie-mountain continuum that characterized their hunting ethos. But this transition also required flexibility and manipulation. As their new hunting identity emerged in the first half of the twentieth century, the Blackfeet had to negotiate a middle ground, where they surrendered the bison-less prairie to modern development and sociopolitical relations in exchange for the continuation of their god-given right to hunt in the mountains, which became non-negotiable.

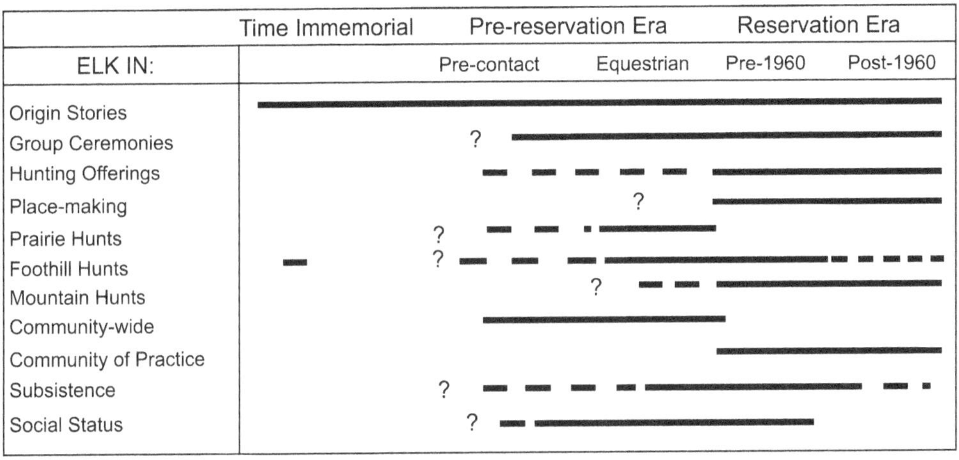

	Time Immemorial	Pre-reservation Era		Reservation Era	
ELK IN:		Pre-contact	Equestrian	Pre-1960	Post-1960
Origin Stories					
Group Ceremonies					
Hunting Offerings					
Place-making					
Prairie Hunts					
Foothill Hunts					
Mountain Hunts					
Community-wide					
Community of Practice					
Subsistence					
Social Status					

Figure 8.6. Continuity and change in the Blackfeet hunting ethos.

The impact of localized human activity on the mountain hunting ground is only beginning to outline itself—for example, in the overexploitation of elk herds along easily accessible slopes on reservation and forest land, in the colonization of improved springs by beaver and concomitant flooding of dry meadows, in the manipulation of mineral licks to attract elk to new areas, and in the effect of ever-changing hunting regulations and range management strategies on prey and hunting ground. We need at least another 50 years to fully understand the effect of mountain hunting on slow and stable components of this environment; yet, it is still possible to track key elements of this modern expression of an ancient adaptation through the archaeology of twentieth-century mountain hunting as well as the testimony and practice of Blackfeet hunters.

II

Comments and Considerations

9

Forging Collaborations between Ecology and Historical Ecology

When I was a graduate student, my fellow ecologists and I looked down on "applied ecology" (studies addressing practical problems, such as environmental impacts) and sought to do research on "pristine" ecosystems. Today, these views seem naïve (Kidder, this volume). Modern society faces many problems that are ecological in nature, and ecologists are turning out in droves to develop solutions. At the same time, we have realized that humans have been affecting ecosystems for tens of thousands of years (Thomas 1956; Redman 1999). "Pristine" ecosystems, as they're usually understood (free from human influence), may not exist (Denevan 1992). Instead, to understand how natural systems work, we must consider how humans affect them.

Ecologists have gotten fairly good at elucidating current human impacts on the biosphere. When we see large buildings, cleared fields or fishing boats, we realize that these human artifacts are likely clues to human impacts on natural systems (Jackson et al. 2001; Worm et al. 2006). But we struggle to understand the nature and extent of human activities in the past, many of which (fire, hunting, species introductions) did not leave clues that are readily seen by the untrained observer today (Briggs et al. 2006; Dambrine et al. 2007; Bover and Alcover 2008; Rick and Erlandson 2008). Ecologists need to collaborate with historical ecologists to gain a more complete understanding of these past human effects on natural systems. By historical ecologists, I mean those scholars who seek to understand the long-term dynamics between human decisions and actions and ecosystems (Balée 2006). In many cases, archaeological studies, such as the ones found in this book, have led the way in such endeavors. In turn, ecologists can bring a variety of perspectives and tools to these collaborations that would enhance the rigor of our understanding of the past.

Today, ecologists and historical ecologists study many of the same questions (Thompson, this volume). Humans and the environment affect each other, and affect other species, in complex ways (Rick, this volume)(figure 9.1). Modern ecologists seek to understand these complex interactions (Liu et al. 2007). Historical ecologists seek to understand the same issues in the past (Balée, this volume). Both could benefit from interacting with each other, so that ecologists could better understand how the past affects the present, and historical ecologists could access a range of approaches and ideas that would offer new insights into historical data. Both share the challenge of working with complex systems, in which multiple species and drivers can affect each other through multiple direct and indirect pathways (Milner, this volume). As a result, inferring the primary causal pathways driving variation is difficult, because many potential links exist. For example, if a particular plant used in herbal remedies has recently become rare, is this due to climate change, to humans overharvesting the plant, to humans suppressing fire, to humans suppressing a mutualist of the plant, to humans introducing an exotic consumer or competitor of the plant, or to humans suppressing an herbivore that eats a competitor of the plant's? Ecologists and historical ecologists might consider the same list of alternative hypotheses in trying to explain an ecological pattern. Ecologists have some advantages in that they can monitor ongoing changes and conduct experiments to examine possible drivers of current changes. Historical ecologists cannot do experiments in the past; however, they have the advantage of being able to examine interactions over longer time periods, and thus, potentially, over a wider range of conditions than those existing in the present (Gilman et al., this volume). Moreover, since the questions that they ask overlap heavily, and many of the species that they study overlap across time, there is the potential for collaborations between ecologists and historical ecologists to be mutually informative.

This book and the broader field of historical ecology bear witness to the insights that can emerge when the fields of ecology and anthropology inform each other in cross-disciplinary studies of historical ecology (Balée and Erickson 2006; Briggs et al. 2006). But there is room for a more effective infusion of ecology into historical ecology and vice versa. In the following sections, I offer some thoughts about how each field can benefit from the other, and some practical steps toward better collaborations.

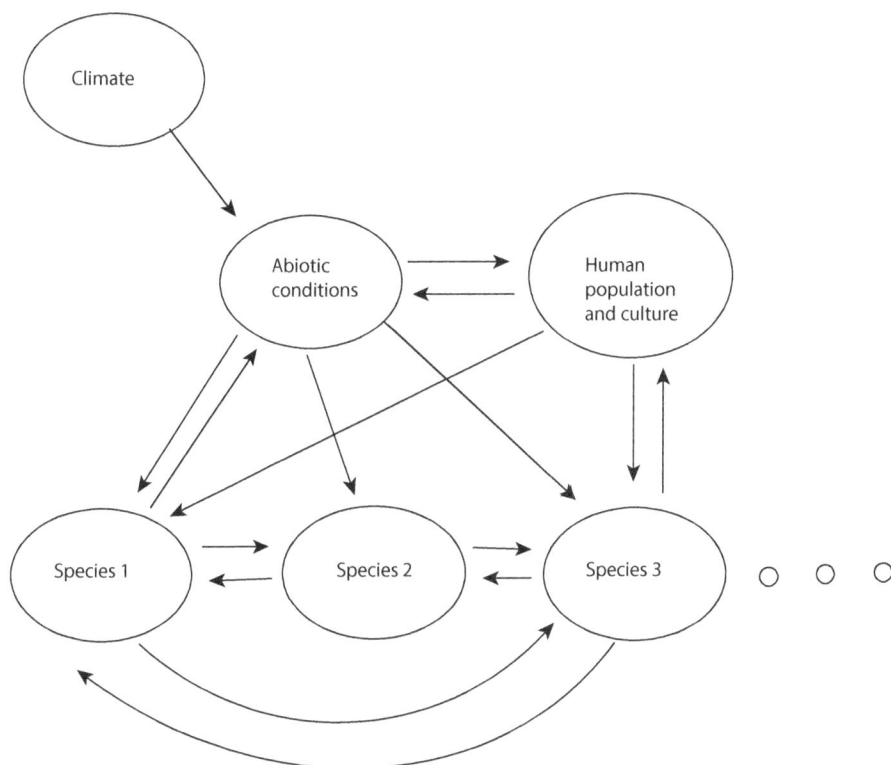

Figure 9.1. Model of socio-ecological system. Humans are embedded in ecological systems in complex ways. Climate affects local abiotic conditions (e.g., temperature, precipitation, length of growing season). Abiotic conditions affect the population dynamics of humans and other species (for clarity, only three nonhuman species are shown, but ecological communities contain many more). Humans and other species may also affect abiotic conditions (e.g., forests affect light, temperature and humidity; beavers affect wetland development and stream flow; oyster reefs change water flow patterns and water clarity; human agriculture affects river sediment loads). The various species in the community affect each other through complex networks of predation, competition, and mutualism, and the densities of selected species used as human resources may in turn affect human populations. Finally, human impacts and responses are mediated not just by human population density, but also by cultural practices.

How Ecology Can Benefit from Historical Ecology

Ecologists tend to be focused on the present—on how the natural systems that they study currently work. It is very easy for us to be deceived into thinking that how they work now is how they have always worked. When I first began conducting research on Sapelo Island in Georgia, I assumed, without really thinking about it, that the pine and hardwood forests that covered most of the island had always been there. I was surprised to see photographs that showed the island mostly lacking trees a hundred years earlier, when it was instead agricultural and range land. Later, Victor Thompson explained to me that the mounds of oyster shell that I had been stumbling over (Thompson et al., this volume) were evidence that Native Americans had shaped the ecological communities and physical landscapes of the coast for thousands of years (Thompson et al. 2004; Quitmyer and Reitz 2006; Thomas 2008; Thompson and Turck 2009, 2010). I may be more oblivious than most ecologists, but I think that, as a rule, ecologists do not fully grasp how extensively the world that we live in has been altered by human activity. We are aware of current impacts—overfishing of the oceans, the transformation of landscapes by agriculture and urbanization, pollution, and so on—but we are largely unaware of the impacts that occurred hundreds or thousands of years ago, and yet may still be affecting ecological patterns and processes. There are at least three ways that ecologists can benefit from interacting with historical ecologists.

First, historical ecology can teach ecologists about how the past may be affecting the present. I was mistaken in thinking that the Georgia coast was pristine. Native Americans collected vast amounts of shellfish from the coast and built extensive piles of shells that altered the terrestrial landscape (Thompson et al. 2004; Reitz et al. 2009; Thompson et al., this volume). Early European colonists extracted lumber from the forests, farmed in ways that filled the rivers with upland sediments, and created marsh islands out of piles of ballast stones offloaded from shipping (Sullivan 2001). Later impacts include logging, agriculture, urbanization, and recreational and commercial fisheries. An appreciation for historical ecology can help me understand how these past activities still affect the present. In short, in order for me to understand how the Georgia coast works now, I need to understand its past.

Second, historical ecology can also inform discussions that ecologists have about conservation by giving us a more sophisticated understanding about what is "natural" (Costa et al. 2009). Suppose we want to conserve an area of coastal Georgia. A naïve approach would be to simply protect it from current threats, such as fishing, invasive species, and pollution. But by doing so, we are accepting the various anthropogenic impacts of Native Americans and early Europeans as "natural." On the other hand, returning the coast to the conditions it experienced before humans arrived might be very difficult, assuming that we even know what those conditions were. The decision about what the "target" of conservation and restoration should be is a political one, not a scientific one, but only historical ecology can clarify what the options are.

Third, ecologists are increasingly interested in studying humans as part of natural systems (Liu et al. 2007). Ecologists are aware that human beings affect natural systems through a wide variety of mechanisms, including consumption, altering nutrient cycling, and land-use change, and that natural systems affect human populations and culture, down to the minutiae of decisions about zoning regulations. Research on these "coupled human-natural systems" could be greatly informed by an understanding of how humans and natural systems have affected each other in the past (Balée, this volume). In particular, because the past, in sum, contains a wider range of environmental conditions and human cultures than exist at present, studying the past allows us to consider a wider range of possible interactions and outcomes than we can study in the present.

How Historical Ecology Can Benefit from Ecology

Any practitioner of an interdisciplinary field will inevitably be lacking in expertise in one or the other of the "parent" disciplines. It simply is not possible to master the content of two fields as thoroughly as one can master a single one. For this reason, historical ecologists can benefit from collaborating with ecologists in at least two ways.

First, ecologists have developed sophisticated theories and models about populations, communities and ecosystems. An appreciation of these ideas could allow historical ecologists to learn more from their data by testing hypotheses about the past that otherwise might not occur to them.

Second, ecologists have developed sophisticated approaches to framing and testing hypotheses that could add rigor to theories proposed by historical ecologists. Studies of historical ecology are often presented as narratives. Ecologists would argue that these narratives could be made more explicit and rigorous if the ideas within them were framed as testable hypotheses, with clear criteria for accepting or rejecting the hypotheses. These hypotheses do not have to be simplistic—ecologists are used to framing hypotheses about systems that have multiple interacting sources of causation—but they can sharpen our thinking by making the process by which the sources of causation are evaluated as explicit as possible.

For example, ecologists typically summarize their data and test hypotheses about their data by using statistical procedures. Statistical summaries can provide measures of how much data vary that are explicit (because they are numerical) rather than vague (because they are verbal). Statistical tests can provide measures of trends over time or differences among groups that are explicit (because they assign a probability estimate) rather than vague (because the patterns are open to interpretation by the author and reader using an informal decision-making process that is not explicit). Statistical tests include methods for dealing with un-replicated time series—a common situation for historical ecologists studying a particular location over time. (Ecologists also may do un-replicated studies when dealing with environmental impacts or problems at large spatial scales.) More extensive application of these statistical approaches would help make historical ecology more rigorous and its logic more explicit.

Steps Toward Beneficial Collaborations between Historical Ecology and Ecology

Readers will note that the rosy picture that I paint of collaboration between historical ecology and ecology has not been fully realized in the case studies presented in this book. Given the potential benefits of collaboration, why don't ecologists and historical ecologists collaborate more often? The most obvious answer is that it is always uncomfortable to work outside the familiar territory of your own discipline, and forging collaborations with other disciplines requires extra effort. Because every discipline has its own set of questions, methods, and ways of communicating results, cross-disciplinary research requires work and flexibility to bridge these cultural gaps. From the perspective of an ecologist, I suggest three approaches on the part of historical ecologists that could lead to better collaboration between historical ecologists and ecologists, and move our fields forward toward deeper and more rigorous insights in future work.

1. Work at multiple sites and get "control" data. Ecologists, for the most part, will not find detailed descriptions of change over time at a single site compelling. Ecologists are used to thinking about average trends across multiple sites. They will wonder whether there was something unusual about the particular site that would make the data not representative for the region as a whole. The solution is to work at multiple sites—at least three, but ideally 10 or

more—so that trends can be presented as averages, with measures of variation. This does not mean that all the sites need be assumed to be identical. If there are features of individual sites that might lead to different patterns (perhaps differences in human population density, soil fertility, or distance to a particular resource), these differences can be included in analyses as covariates and their importance explicitly addressed. Because working at 10 sites is 10 times harder than working at one site, working at multiple sites requires that less work be done at each site. For example, when I have talked with Victor Thompson about possible collaborations to study small marsh islands in Georgia, his training led him to think about sampling individual islands intensely with hundreds of closely spaced shovel test pits. This approach is so labor-intensive that it is hard for him to sample more than one or two islands a year. In contrast, my ecological training led me to think about sampling 50 or 100 islands with perhaps a dozen random plots on each. Finding a sampling scheme that made sense to both of us was a major obstacle to working together.

An even more challenging problem for historical ecologists is to get control data. If all the information that historical ecologists have about, say, bat populations, comes from human trash piles, it is a major problem to disentangle (1) human effects on bats from (2) changes in human culture that affect food-collection decisions from (3) climate-driven changes in bat availability in nature. Historical ecologists have given a great deal of thought to how to disentangle these different potential sources of variation; however, an alternate approach would be to find some way to get data on bats in areas where humans are absent. Alternatively, if it were possible to study a number of sites that varied in human population density, it might be possible to analyze bat data as a function of human population size using a regression approach. If comparisons across space showed the same result as comparisons across time, it would strengthen the argument that the same driver (human population density) was responsible in both cases.

The best way to address these issues is to involve ecologists in the study from the start, when the sampling design is being decided. If historical ecologists instead wait until the data are collected, and then try to find an ecologist to collaborate on interpreting the data, they are likely to find that the ecologist will not be receptive, because he or she will consider the study design to be inappropriate for addressing ecological questions.

Having said this, the reality of research in historical ecology is that many studies will involve detailed analyses of single sites—no replication and no "controls." Given such a situation, historical ecologists are used to constructing verbal arguments for the relative importance of different processes in explaining change over time. For example, suppose the archaeological record shows an increase in the frequency of a particular plant in the human diet over time. A historical ecologist might argue for or against the importance of climate change, human alteration of soil conditions, and human cultural changes in mediating this dietary shift. Ecologists can add rigor to these arguments in the following two ways.

2. Collaborate with ecologists on experiments to inform hypotheses about the past.

The past is gone, and we cannot "rerun" it to determine what happened. But, in many cases, the species and habitats of interest to historical ecologists are still extant. Ecologists cannot re-create all aspects of ecological systems from 5,000 years ago. But they can construct experiments that assess some aspects of different historical scenarios. For example, if historical ecologists hypothesize that human farming enriched the soil and led to the invasion of a particular plant species, ecologists could test this hypothesis by growing the "invader," the "natives," and mixtures of these species across a range of soil conditions in pots or field plots. If there is an alternative hypothesis that climate change led to the invasion of the plant, ecologists could conduct an experiment that varied both soil conditions and local climate (by manipulating precipitation or temperature) in order to determine which more strongly affected the success of the plant. The results of the experiment would not conclusively prove what did or did not happen in the past, but they could inform our evaluation of how likely different scenarios are.

3. Collaborate with ecologists on models to inform hypotheses about the past.

In some cases, experiments may not be feasible. The species of interest may be extinct, or the spatial scales relevant to the hypothesis may be too large to be tractable. In these cases, it may still be possible to rigorously evaluate different scenarios about the past by constructing a mathematical model. For example, given reasonable parameter values in the model, how likely is it that a human population of a certain size, killing a certain number of seals per year, would reduce the seal population? By assessing the sensitivity of the model to a range of parameter values, models can test the sensitivity of given processes to variation in different drivers, helping to assess how likely it is that different drivers could produce given outcomes. Again, this would not conclusively prove what did or did not happen in the past, but it would inform our evaluation of how likely different scenarios are.

In summary, ecologists and historical ecologists are interested in many of the same questions. Historical ecologists can provide insights into natural systems that will benefit ecologists, and vice versa. By working together, we can advance our disciplines faster than by working apart. Humans depend on the functioning of natural systems for our own survival, and we mediate the fate of many species around us. By collaborating, ecologists and historical ecologists could gain a better understanding of how the workings of coupled human and natural systems have brought us to where we are today, and a clearer vision to guide our choices for how these systems might work in the future.

Acknowledgments

I thank Victor Thompson for inviting and commenting on this chapter, and the National Science Foundation for their support of the Georgia Coastal Ecosystems LTER program (OCE06–20959).

10

Observations about the Historical Ecology
of Small-Scale Societies

TRISTRAM R. KIDDER

We have met the enemy and he is us.
Walt Kelly, 1970

Walt Kelly's well-known line—uttered by his cartoon character Pogo—epit-
omizes the thesis of this book and the larger issues embedded in historical
ecology. If the question is, do humans at every level of social organization
and at all times transform the environment, and by how much, then the
answer is absolutely, and by a great deal. The chapters in this volume do a
superb job of providing empirical evidence that small-scale societies—in
this case, peoples practicing a subsistence-settlement strategy of hunting,
fishing, and foraging (and limited amounts of cultivation)—intervene in
their physical and biotic environment in ways that both transform human
cultures but also indelibly mark the landscape in ways that accumulate
through time and in part explain the configuration of the modern physical
and biological world. But Pogo's comment and the broader thesis of this
volume go deeper than just how and to what extent our actions and their
traces leave a mark on the globe. The chapters in this volume provide an
exclamation point on a generation of scholarship that has worked to demonstrate that humans are part of what we often define as nature, and not
apart from it. This work—in multiple fields, from anthropology to zoology—shows that the concept of a so-called natural world, separate from the
actions of humans, has not existed since the dawn of humanity some two
million years ago. In effect, this scholarship shows that there is no natural
world; but it also shows that the world we live in today is the product of cu-

mulative transformations—large and small—made by people, plants, animals, wind, weather, and time. Critically, this insight has major policy and political ramifications. This volume is not just about hunter-fisher-forager-farmers; it is about our modern world. If these low-level societies can transform environments and remake landscapes, then they teach us to more fully appreciate the capacities of modern and modernlike societies, which have a qualitatively larger impact on the environment (Redman 1999).

The papers in this volume make evident some crucial truths. First, all societies—no matter their size or scale of population, technology, political system or economy—can and do transform the world and have effects on local and global ecology. Scale does matter, but only in the degree of impact, not in the potential to have an impact. Time is perhaps the most crucial variable in this regard. Because smaller-scale societies have a diminished effect on the physical world as a result of their smaller populations and limited technological capacity, it takes longer for their impacts to be felt. As a result, the impacts of small-scale societies are usually more subtle and nuanced, and require an appreciation of how the histories of transformations have accumulated.

Second, it should now be a self-evident truth that small-scale societies can and do affect the environment and have been transforming the physical world in myriad ways from the onset of humans as social animals. This reality emphasizes modern conflicts about human influences on the environment: if small-scale societies can change their environment over time, what are the effects of modern societies and their capacity to transform the globe? One of the most interesting examples of how this debate may play out is found in the work of William Ruddiman, who has proposed an "Anthropocene hypothesis."

Readers should consult Ruddiman's work (Ruddiman 2003, 2007; Ruddiman 2005; Ruddiman et al. 2008), but in a nutshell he argues that human transformations of the environment in the Early to Middle Holocene— mostly the result of increasing human populations and extensive investment in land clearance and agriculture—altered the chemistry of the earth's atmosphere (by increasing carbon dioxide through burning and land clearance and methane through agricultural activities) to the extent that it changed global climates and has transformed human history by increasing temperatures and delaying glaciation (which, of course, have attendant spin-off effects). Ruddiman's hypothesis is far from settled, and there are considerable debates about its merits (Oldfield 2008:72–75 and references therein), but it raises a critical issue that is relevant to this volume and its thesis. Notably, Ruddiman makes a case that we humans have and continue to transform the so-called natural world in ways that have cumulative effects that have changed history and thus the shape of the present and future. Historical ecology makes a similar if less global claim. But in either case, the implication is clear. Present decisions about how we approach the many problems of the world require an understanding of how humans have acted as an agent to transform the environment (at many scales). The implications for contemporary policymaking are significant and suggest that even hunter-gatherers have something to teach us about the modern world.

Third, explaining social change requires detailed, high-resolution microhistories coupled with broad-scale understanding of larger historical trajectories. The strength of historical ecology lies in its ability to understand the place of history—the sequential step-by-step accumulation of events and activities—in the formation of and causal influence on change (Balée and Erickson 2006; Balée 1998). The chapters in this volume do a superb job of detailing these microhistories and in showing how these small-scale societies can cause and accumulate change in ways that have long-term and deep consequences.

Finally, we need to recognize that there is a risk of adopting an overly generalized approach to human-environment changes, because it might diminish our appreciation for the purposefulness of human action. This may be especially true with forager (small-scale) societies. In the past, these sorts of societies were understood to walk lightly on the landscape and to leave little or no trace of their activities and impacts on the environment; in more recent years, and as exemplified in these chapters, they are now seen as having a heavier footprint. The challenge, though, is how to understand this footprint. Is it the result of an accumulation of unplanned and unappreciated actions that over time lead to changes in the environment? Or is it, in fact, a far more conscious and planned process wherein people, and people as members of society, actively manipulate their environment, leading to both short-term, purposeful change and long-term accumulations of change? Or is it both? The latter is most surely correct. But the challenge of working with small-scale hunter-fisher-forager-farmers is that we may inadvertently fail to acknowledge that even simple social groups act with a purpose and their transformations of the landscape were often—certainly not always—done to suit a purpose at a specific point in time.

This is why microhistorical approaches are so critical. What we see as landscape history and the palimpsest of human activity may well be, and in many cases assuredly was, activity directed to a specific end. And here too we confront the issue of scale. Small-scale societies can act in ways that are increasingly understood to defy our conventional sense of their accomplishments. Hunters and gatherers in some instances embarked on projects that transformed environments in remarkably short periods of time to accomplish specific goals that are often different—at least directly so—from the nominally minimal environmental impact we expect for these kinds of societies. Thus, to the extent that I have a critique of this volume, it lies in the tendency to see hunter-gatherers as inadvertent agents of change. I want to be clear with this critique. I do not want to claim that all change is purposeful or that hunter-gatherers were in some way clairvoyant and could foresee the effects of their actions on future generations; far from it. Instead, what we should acknowledge is the capacity for hunters and gatherers to act in deliberate ways that they knew and understood to change their physical and biotic world, even if we at a temporal distance cannot ascribe to these changes consciousness or purpose. For example, it is evident to me that the builders of the Brazilian sambaquis knew and understood that they were transforming the physical environment, even if their actions were cumulative over generations and perhaps a thousand or more years. In fact, as Fish et al. note (this volume), the sambaquis were built specifically as a sign of change because that change symbolized the transformed social world that was marked by the altered physical place.

Another example is the Poverty Point site in northeast Louisiana. Here we can see not only evidence of the sorts of physical transformations that characterize any human interaction with the environment (e.g., changes in topography, vegetation, hydrology, etc.) but we also now have evidence that the changes in the physical world were purposeful, deliberate, and played out over considerable time and space.

Poverty Point is the largest hunter-gatherer community in North America and perhaps one of the largest such settlements in the world. Calculations of the land area covered by hunter-gatherers at the height of the occupation, ca. 3500–3200 cal. BP, range from 3 to 7 km^2. The settlement consists of at least four and probably five earthen mounds and six nested earthen ridges covering an area of roughly 1.5 km^2 and outlying habitation areas extending over a roughly 5 km-long area along the front of a Pleistocene terrace overlooking the Mississippi River floodplain. Estimates of earth moved to create the artificial mounds and to alter the topography to create the built environment range from 750,000 to 1,000,000 m³. Thus, as with the sambaquis, the construction of Poverty Point left an indelible mark on the landscape and altered local environments such that the imprint is still quite evident today. Moreover, the pattern of construction leaves no doubt that the builders had a plan for the site and that this plan evolved over the course of time as subsequent generations took the existing landscape and further modified it to suit contemporary needs and tastes (Gibson 2000; Gibson and Carr 2004; Kidder 2010, 2011; Kidder et al. 2008, 2009; Kidder and Sassaman 2009; Ortmann 2010).

But like any hunter-gatherer community, Poverty Point could simply be considered an outsized example of the cumulative and unintentional imprinting of human use on the landscape. Purposeful construction aside, what is the evidence that the occupants of the site deliberately set out to remake the environment in a way that suggests that the occupants wanted to alter the physical world to imprint on it their own plan? The evidence is derived from increasingly high-resolution microhistories and lies both in the site plan but also in new data emerging from the Jaketown site in west-central Mississippi.

Lee Arco's work at Jaketown (Arco 2009; Arco and Kidder 2010; Arco and Ortmann 2010) reveals that the site is temporally antecedent to Poverty Point but also appears to have been built according to a plan that was later borrowed and expanded at Poverty Point. It is hard to see these patterns as coincidental or accidental. Jaketown and Poverty Point are the largest Poverty Point sites, and their archaeological records are clearly similar, suggesting a shared cultural pattern (Ford et al. 1955; Webb 1982). Jaketown is the only settlement other than the type site with multiple (at least three) confirmed Poverty Point-age earthworks. Although the full extent of Jaketown's constructed landscape remains unclear, the construction chronologies of the dated earthworks at Jaketown and Poverty Point indicates synchronous mound-building activity at both sites. However, Jaketown's initial Poverty Point culture occupation (ca. 4150 cal. BP) predates the type of site by perhaps 600 years and the earliest dated earth-moving activity at Jaketown is roughly coeval with the construction of Poverty Point's first mound (Mound B) ca. 3570 cal. BP. The antecedent occupation at Jaketown and the similarity between the site's natural landscape and the subsequently built environment of Poverty Point provide information on the origin and development of landscape transformation at Poverty Point.

While Poverty Point may have been occupied by ca. 3500 cal. BP, the earliest occupants were content to live on the contemporary ground surface and to engage in limited earthwork building (the erection of Mound B and possibly Mound E). The site underwent a major structural reorganization between 3400 and 3300 cal. BP, marked by a construction project of unprecedented scale that completely transformed the landscape through, first, the erection of six nested earthen ridges, followed by (or contemporary with?) one small mound (Mound C) and finally the building of Mound A, the second-largest earthen mound in North America. These earthworks were constructed late in the site's history, long after the period of initial occupation. This differs from the pattern exhibited in many other societies, where grandiose monumental architecture typically occurs early in the history of social development.

Poverty Point has a complex history, and there is evidence to suggest that it was founded by a community or communities of immigrants who arrived at the site at a time when there were few if any local inhabitants (Kidder 2010; Kidder et al. 2009). Elsewhere I argue that if the peoples who founded Poverty Point had multiple origins and ethnicities, then perhaps the massive construction projects undertaken at Poverty Point after ca. 3400 cal. BP were about creating/re-creating a new, unified shared cosmology and cultural narrative to integrate a community whose members had varied geographic, ethnic, or social origins (Kidder 2010, 2011). Based on its temporal precedence to the occupation at Poverty Point and the material culture remains in Jaketown's earliest levels, Jaketown's occupants were likely part of this founding community. Late Archaic hunter-gatherers settled Jaketown more than 500 years before the main occupation at Poverty Point, and the new radiocarbon evidence from Jaketown indicates that it represents an early (if not the earliest) expression of Poverty Point culture.

The specific role that Jaketown and its Late Archaic inhabitants played in the formation and development of the Poverty Point site is not yet completely understood. However, the blueprint for much of Poverty Point's constructed landscape can be seen in the natural and human-modified landscape of Jaketown. Jaketown was built on a natural landscape formed by ridges and swales of an ancestral Mississippi River point bar. Today, this topography is obscured by later Holocene alluviation. An underfit Mississippi River channel marks the eastern edge of Jaketown, while a relict oxbow lake meander scar forms the western boundary. Between these two features were at least five point-bar ridges and their corresponding swales. These ridges were preferred places of habitation because of the advantages of elevation and drainage in the floodplain environment. At least one mound was situated inside the point-bar ridges at Jaketown, and at least one was found on the western edge of the ridge and swale complex. A third mound is located within the undulating point-bar topography.

The structure and layout of Poverty Point's earthen ridges bear a striking resemblance to the natural ridge and swale topography of Jaketown's Poverty Point-era landscape. A small, sluggish bayou or stream flowed immediately east of both Jaketown and Poverty Point during the Late Archaic occupations, and both sites contained a water-filled barrier demarcating the western edges of the sites (Ford et al. 1955:Figures 1–4; Kidder 2002:Figure 1). A natural oxbow lake formed this barrier at Jaketown; at Poverty Point, however, this feature was built through borrowing and transporting earth for construction of the mounds and ridges. The water barriers artificially created at Poverty Point mirror the natural water bodies present at Jaketown. Because much of Jaketown's Poverty Point-era landscape is deeply buried by later Holocene deposits, we cannot be certain of all the features at the site and the degree to which its final form was duplicated at Poverty Point. Given the consistently early dates from Jaketown and its clear material-cultural connection to Poverty Point, it is highly probable that the natural layout of Jaketown's Late Archaic landscape was an (if not *the*) inspiration for the built environment at Poverty Point.

Poverty Point is only one example of what is almost surely a purposeful transformation of a hunter-gatherer landscape and its environment. Unlike some of the other contexts documented in this volume where agency is unclear or uncertain (e.g., the chapters by Milner and Rick), we can be reasonably certain that these transformations were deliberate. These are not instances of people walking lightly on the land. Visitors to Poverty Point today can still see the physical imprint of the site on the landscape 3,500 years later.

We might also take note of Zedeño's argument (this volume) that human-environmental interaction is shaped by cultural practice. Even unintended consequences are the end product of intentional actions shaped by cultural choices built not solely around ecological and environmental needs, but also around historically formed and situated concepts, such as identity, values, and inter- and intra-group interactions. Small-scale societies may not always understand the ramifications of their footprint on the landscape, but it is evident that they knowingly attribute to the land cultural values (genealogy, history, and myth) that affect how they use resources, recognize landscapes, and justify their actions (Basso 1996; Kahn 1990, 1996).

Modern scholarship increasingly recognizes that the physical and biotic world we live in is the cumulative result of millennia of change brought about by wind, water, and organisms large and small. Ecologists understand that organisms of all types are capable of reshaping physical and biotic landscapes and that these changes accumulate through time to shape the modern world. The work of this volume demonstrates that humans are part of this tradition and have been for as long as we have been on this earth. Hunter-gatherers effect transformations on scales that are often far less obvious than societies that live in denser populations and that practice agriculture. But it is clear from the chapters in this volume as well as from earlier research that humans at all scales alter the environment. Pre-modern hunter-gatherers were more than termites or beavers, however, and we need to be careful not to fall into the trap of assuming that low-level societies were inherently qualitatively different from what are often assumed to be more complex social forms.

The most profound implication of these chapters is the demonstration that even small-scale societies affect the environment. The long-term policy implications of this conclusion seem to me to be important and far-reaching. Our hunter-gatherer ancestors may not have had the tools that allowed them to see the effects of their actions on the physical world, but modern societies cannot claim such ignorance. We have the tools to predict the outcomes of our interventions on the landscape, but can only use them if we recognize that those interventions are real and consequent, no matter their scale. We have much still to learn from our past, but the real question is, Will we heed these lessons? Santayana's dictum about those who don't heed the past being doomed to repeat it is too often trumped by Pogo's observation that we are our own worst enemy.

11

Epilogue

Contingency in the Environments of Foraging Societies

WILLIAM BALÉE

The substantive chapters herein concern relationships through time between foragers and landscapes, and in a few instances, between foragers and seascapes. Sometimes the time frame is historical, as when the evidence at hand is documentation in the form of ethnohistory or observational data in the form of ethnography in addition to archaeological inferences from the not too distant past (e.g., Zedeño, this volume). At other times, the evidence is associated with the *longue durée*, or what is increasingly being referred to as "deep time" by some of the authors (e.g., Rick, this volume; Fish et al., this volume). A concept of deep time in understanding the origins of landscapes modified by human-mediated disturbance frequently is only accessible through a variety of archaeological methods and procedures (e.g., Dean 2010). Substantive chapters in this volume represent these, the data produced, and the analysis deriving from them to show contingency and variability in prehistory among foragers and their impacts on landscapes and seascapes.

Different timescales and relative abundances of material evidence have implications for the interpretation of the findings reported, and for the reliability and validity in particular, of those findings. Overall, the material evidence herein is rich, perhaps because it is mostly still within the confines of the Holocene. The previous chapters for the most part discuss in scintillating detail Holocene foragers' relationship to their environments, the effects they have had on these, and the results the culturally modified landscapes and seascapes have exerted on attributes of their history and prehistory. As such, a common thread of historical ecology runs through these chapters.

An important common feature, moreover, concerning the groups discussed, is foraging. The rubric "forager" embraces a broad range of socio-cultural phenomena, and it is often heuristically broken down into two types: "simple" forager vs. "complex" forager (e.g., Kelly 1995). It is not the case that this typological dichotomy itself is problematic for what it avers—namely, palpable differences of political complexity between the two types. One can think of the stark difference between the ethnographic !Kung, with their ostracism of persons who might be tempted to show the slight-est hint of hubris, and the ethnohistorical Kwakiutl (now the Ka-ka-wa-ka) who found to be proper and fitting the ostentatious, self-aggrandizement of great, wealthy chiefs, as illustrative of the political contrasts I have in mind. Rather, the dichotomy simple vs. complex may be inapplicable to an underlying dimension of this volume—namely, whether foragers impact the environment on scales that can be detected reliably in the archaeologi-cal record, and if so, whether such impacts can be construed in terms of a dichotomy instead of a continuum. It seems that the social organization attendant upon the changes discussed herein is not always readily discern-ible from environmental legacies.

The most obvious human impacts on earth's landscapes and seascapes, historically and ethnographically, include documented changes of courses or directions and drainage patterns of natural rivers (as with the Chicago River, the flow of which was reversed by 180 degrees) (Cronon 1992); con-version of forest to pastures and savannas; eutrophication of waters due to runoff of fertilization nitrates; subsidence of heavy metals; creation of hazardous waste sites, superfund sites, and radioactive zones (e.g., Ukraine and Belarus in the Chernobyl disaster); acidification of the oceans; deple-tion of oxygen and pollution of the oceans (such as that due to massive oil spills, such as Exxon Valdez and more recently, Deepwater Horizon) (Broder 2010); extinctions of species; and anthropogenic global warming. The hunter-gatherers discussed herein were not responsible for those most obviously human-mediated disturbances of world environments.

It may not be, however, because they were hunter-gatherers per se. Of course, one of the original motivations for *fundamentally* altering earth's landscapes is to be found in agrarian technologies. In contrast, the people discussed in this book did not engage in such activities, though they had palpable effects on their environments, if only nuanced and not necessarily seen in major changes of disturbance-indicator biota (e.g., Gilman et al., this volume). These minor modifications require careful study, because it means that humans are not necessarily incompatible with existing species diversity and landscape heterogeneity, which, generally speaking, are desirable attributes of environments in Western philosophy and discourse on nature since the time of Plato (Balée 2010). The concept of nature perhaps requires revisiting, to be understood with the complexities that historical ecology brings to bear in the analysis of seemingly pristine landscapes and original biota. This book intimates a reacquainting with nature by providing new understandings in specific case studies along the lines of historical ecology.

This historical ecology is focused on people who did not impact the landscape with cultivation and agriculture, but what is perhaps most interesting is their vestiges on the landscape are parallel or analogous to agricultural impacts of the remote past. In most but not all cases, these foragers have had major impacts on the landscapes in which they lived, less like the more nuanced impacts one observes among contemporary foragers, for the most part. These impacts involved the potential introduction of invasive species (Rick, this volume), intensive utilization patterns that affected the genotype of otherwise nondomesticated nut trees (Habu and Hall, this volume), alterations of substrates and coastlines, which created conditions for redistribution and enrichment in certain locales of plants and animals (Thompson et al., this volume), together with changes in the age of harvested organisms, which in turn affected the size of the resource patch being exploited (Milner, this volume).

Interestingly, the arrival of agriculture does not uniformly precipitate marked changes in the landscape, including altered densities of disturbance indicators, such as disturbance rodents and perching birds (Gilman et al., this volume). The early cultivators of the U.S. Southwest and northwest Mexico had maize (Gilman et al., this volume). By way of comparison, in the Amazon basin, dependence on maize tends to leave a light signature on the landscape, as the people who grow it as the principal food crop have often exhibited also high residential mobility through time (Balée 1992). The minimal disturbance of these earliest cultivators in North America may be similar to trekking societies elsewhere.

What the archaeological record in this volume shows is differentiation of societies in terms of complexity, space, and time, and the dissimilar effects of these ensembles on the environment, both at any given point in time and over the *longue durée*. Whether they are agricultural or not, human impacts on resources, however often these are compared to traces and residues, frequently extend across centuries, with effects most likely unintended by their originators. This volume illuminates, through the application of new data, knowledge about ancient hunter-gatherers on a variety of landscapes and seascapes across several continents, and enhances understanding of their interactions with local resources and biota over time. The questions that arise in the wake of these studies concern what we can learn from their interactions, and how this knowledge can be deployed, in a context of applied historical ecology. What and how can environmental mistakes be avoided, such as those documented herein, including introductions of invasive species (Rick, this volume) and overharvesting of bivalves in prime age and size classes (Milner, this volume)? In what ways can human populations and resource utilization strategies be adjusted to existing indices of diversity, even if the actual species undergo substitutions through time? It is possible they would do that anyway, but the documentation herein provides enlightened keys to answering these questions in light of human-mediated disturbance, landscape and seascape transformation, and the viewpoint of historical ecology.

Works Cited

Aarhus, Angela J. 2005. Abundance and Distribution of the Santa Catalina Island Shrew (*Sorex ornatus willetti*) on Santa Catalina Island, California. In *Proceedings of the Sixth California Islands Symposium,* edited by D. K. Garcelon and C. A. Schwemm, pp. 249–55. National Park Service Technical Publication CHIS-05-01, Institute for Wildlife Studies, Arcata.

Agenbroad, L. D. 1998. New Pygmy Mammoth (*Mammuthus exilis*) Localities and Radiocarbon Dates from San Miguel, Santa Rosa, and Santa Cruz Islands. In *Contributions to the Geology of the Northern Channel Islands, Southern California,* edited by P. Weigend, pp. 169–75. Pacific Section American Association of Petroleum Geologists, Bakersfield.

———. 2002a. California's Channel Islands: A One Way Trip in the Tunnel of Doom. In *Proceedings of the Fifth California Islands Symposium,* edited by D. Browne, K. Mitchell and H. Chaney, pp. 1–6. Santa Barbara Museum of Natural History, Santa Barbara.

———. 2002b. New Localities, Chronology, and Comparisons for the Pygmy Mammoth (*Mammuthus exilis*): 1994–98. In *Proceedings of the Fifth California Islands Symposium,* edited by D. Browne, K. Mitchell and H. Chaney, pp. 518–24. Santa Barbara Museum of Natural History, Santa Barbara.

———. 2009. *Mammuthus exilis* from the Channel Islands: Height, Mass, and Geologic Age. In *Proceedings of the Seventh California Islands Symposium,* edited by C. C. Damiani and D. K. Garcelon, pp. 15–19. Institute for Wildlife Studies, Arcata.

Agenbroad, L. D., J. R. Johnson, D. Morris, and T. W. Stafford Jr. 2005. Mammoths and Humans as Late Pleistocene Contemporaries on Santa Rosa Island. In *Proceedings of the Sixth California Islands Symposium,* edited by D. Garcelon and C. Schwemm, pp. 3–7. National Park Service Technical Publication CHIS-05-01. Institute for Wildlife Studies, Arcata.

Aguilar, A., G. Roemer, S. Debenham, M. Binns, D. Garcelon, and R. K. Wayne. 2004. High MHC Diversity Maintained by Balancing Selection in an Otherwise Genetically Monomorphic Mammal. *Proceedings of the National Academy of Sciences* 101:3490–94.

Aguilar, S. 2002. *Peromyscus leucopus.* Animal Diversity Web.http://animaldiversity.ummz. umich.edu/site/accounts/information/Peromyscus_leucopus.html (accessed February 15, 2009).

Akazawa, Takeru. 1980. Fishing adaptation of prehistoric hunter-gatherers at the Nittano site, Japan. *Journal of Archaeological Science* 7:325–44.

———. 1987. Variability in the types of fishing adaptation of the Later Jomon people, ca. 2500–300 B.C. In *The Archaeology of Prehistoric Coastlines,* edited by G. Bailey and J. Parkington, pp. 78–92. Cambridge University Press, Cambridge.

Ainis, A. A., and Vellanoweth, R. L. 2012. Expanding the chronology for the extinct giant island deer mouse (*Peromyscus nesodytes*) on San Miguel Island, California, U.S.A. *Journal of Island and Coastal Archaeology* 7:146–152.

Ali, J. R., and M. Huber. 2010. Mammalian Biodiversity on Madagascar Controlled by Ocean Currents. *Nature* 463:653–56.

Ames, Kenneth. 1991. The Archaeology of the *Longue Durée*: Temporal and Spatial Scale in the Evolution of Social Complexity on the Southern Northwest Coast. *Antiquity* 65(249):935–45.

Andersen, S. H. 1989. Norsminde. A "kokkenmødding" with Late Mesolithic and Early Neolithic occupation. *Journal of Danish Archaeology* 8(3):3–40.

———. 2000. "Køkkenmøddinger" (Shell Middens) in Denmark: a survey. *Proceedings of the Prehistoric Society* 66:361–84.

———. 2005. *Køkkenmøddingerne ved Krabbesholm. Ny forskning I stenalderens kystloopladser.* Denmark: National Museets Arbejdsmark.

———. 2008. A report on recent excavations at the shell midden of Havnø in Denmark. *Mesolithic Miscellany* 19(1):2–6.

Anderson, A. 2009. The Rat and the Octopus: Initial Human Colonization and the Prehistoric Introduction of Domestic Animals to Remote Oceania. *Biological Invasions* 11:1503–19.

Anderson, D. G., K. A. Maasch, D. H. Sandweiss, and P. A. Mayewski. 2007. Climate and Culture Change: Exploring Holocene Transitions. In *Climate Change and Cultural Dynamics: A Global Perspective on Mid-Holocene Transitions,* edited by D. G. Anderson, K. Maasch, and D. H. Sandweiss, pp. 1–24. Academic Press, New York.

Anderson, David G., Kirk A. Maasch, and Daniel H. Sandweiss, ed. 2007. *Climate Change and Cultural Dynamics: A Global Perspective on Mid-Holocene Transitions.* Academic Press, London.

Anderson, Derek, and María Nieves Zedeño. 2009. *Returning to the Country: Hunter-Gatherer Territory Formation.* Paper presented at the 74th Annual Meeting of the Society for American Archaeology, Atlanta.

Andrus, C. Fred T., and Victor D. Thompson. 2012. Determining the Habitats of Mollusk Collection at the Sapelo Island Shell Ring Complex, USA using Oxygen Isotope Sclerochronology. *Journal of Archaeological Science* 39:215–228.

Angulo, R. J., P.C.F. Giannini, K. Suguio, and L.C.R. Pessenda. 1999. Relative sea level changes during the last 550 years in the Laguna-Imbituba region (Santa Catarina, Brazil) based on vermited radiocarbon ages. *Marine Geology* 159:323–39.

Angulo, Rodolfo, Guilherme C. Lessa, and Maria Cristina de Souza. 2006. A critical review of mid- to late-Holocene sea level fluctuations on the eastern Brazilian coastline. *Quaternary Science Reviews* 25:486–506.

Aomori-ken Maizo Bunkazai Chosa Center [Archaeological Center of Aomori Prefecture]. 2007. *Sannai Iseki II, Sannai Maruyama (9) Iseki* [The Sannai Site, Vol. II; the Sannai Maruyama No. 9 Site]. Aomori-ken Kyoiku Iinkai [Board of Education of Aomori Prefecture], Aomori.

———. 2008. *Sannai Maruyama (9) Iseki II* [The Sannai Maruyama No. 9 Site, Vol. II]. Aomori-ken Kyoiku Iinkai [Board of Education of Aomori Prefecture], Aomori.

Arco, Lee J. 2009. *Geoarchaeology of the Buried Poverty Point Landscape at Jaketown.* Paper presented at the 65th annual meeting of the Southeastern Archaeological Conference, Mobile.

Arco, Lee J., and Tristram R. Kidder. 2010. *NSF Doctoral Dissertation Improvement Grant: Geoarchaeological Investigation of the Jaketown Site: A Late Archaic Poverty Point Settlement in the Lower Mississippi Valley.* Final Report: 0827097 to the National Science Foundation. Department of Anthropology, Washington University, St. Louis.

Arco, Lee J., and Anthony L. Ortmann. 2010. *Jaketown's Buried Landscape: Recent Research at a Poverty Point Settlement in the Yazoo Basin, Mississippi.* Invited paper presented at the symposium "Current Research on the Poverty Point Culture," 75th annual meeting of the Society for American Archaeology, St. Louis.

Arnold, J. E. 1987. *Craft Specialization in the Prehistoric Channel Islands, California.* University of California Publications in Anthropology 18. University of California Press, Berkeley.

———. 1992. Complex Hunter-Gatherer-Fishers of Prehistoric California: Chiefs, Specialists, and Maritime Adaptations of the Channel Islands. *American Antiquity* 57:60–84.

Ashley, M. V. 1989. Absence of Differentiation in Mitochondrial DNA of Island and Mainland Harvest Mice, *Reithrodontomys megalotis. Journal of Mammalogy* 70:383–86.

Ashley, M., and C. Wills. 1979. Analysis of Mitochondrial DNA Polymorphisms Among Channel Island Deer Mice. *Evolution* 41:854–63.

———. 1987. Analysis of Mitochondrial DNA Polymorphisms Among Channel Island Deer Mice. *Evolution* 41:854–63.

———. 1989. Mitochondrial DNA and Allozyme Divergence Patterns are Correlated Among Island Deer Mice. *Evolution* 43:646–50.

Ashmore, Wendy. 2002. "Decisions and dispositions": socializing spatial archaeology. *American Anthropologist* 104:1172–83.

Badenhorst, S., and J. C. Driver. 2009. Faunal Changes in Farming Communities from Basketmaker II to Pueblo III (A.D. 1–1300) in the San Juan Basin of the American Southwest. *Journal of Archaeological Science* 36:1832–41.

Bailey, G. N., and A. S. Craighead. 2003. Late Pleistocene and Holocene Coastal Palaeoeconomies: A reconsideration of the molluscan evidence from northern Spain. *Geoarchaeology: An International Journal* 18(2):175–204.

Bailey, G. N., and N. J. Milner. 2002. Coastal hunters and gatherers and social evolution: marginal or central? *Before Farming: the Archaeology of Old World Hunter-Gatherers* 3–4 (1):1–15.

———. 2008. Molluscan archives from European Prehistory. In *Early Human Impact on Megamolluscs, edited by A. Antczak & R. Cipriani,* pp. 111–34. BAR International Series, No. 1865. British Archaeological Reports, Oxford.

Bailey, G., J. Barrett, O. Craig, and N. Milner. 2008. Historical Ecology of the North Sea Basin: an archaeological perspective and some problems of methodology. In *Human Impacts on Ancient Marine Ecosystems,* edited by J. Erlandson & R. Torrey, pp. 215–42. University of California Press, Berkeley.

Balée, William. 1992. People of the fallow: A historical ecology of foraging in lowland South America. In *Conservation of Neotropical Forests: Building on Traditional Resource Use,* edited by K. H. Redford and C. Padoch, pp. 35–57. New York: Columbia University Press.

———. 1994. *Footprints of the Forest: Ka'apor Ethnobotany: The Historical Ecology of Plant Utilization by an Amazonian People.* Columbia University Press, New York.

———. 1998. Historical Ecology: Premises and Postulates. In *Advances in Historical Ecology,* edited by W. L. Balée, pp. 13–29. Columbia University Press, New York.

———. (editor). 1998. *Advances in Historical Ecology.* Columbia University Press, New York.

———. 2006. The Research Program of Historical Ecology. *Annual Review in Anthropology* 35:75–98.

———. 2010. Contingent diversity on anthropic landscapes. *Diversity* 2(2):163–81.

Balée, William, and W. Erickson. 2006. Time, complexity, and historical ecology. In *Time and Complexity in Historical Ecology: Studies in the Neotropical Lowlands,* edited by W. Balée and W. Erickson, pp. 1–17. Columbia University Press, New York.

———. (editors). 2006. *Time and Complexity in Historical Ecology: Studies in the Neotropical Lowlands.* Columbia University Press, New York.

Ballenger, Jesse A., and María Nieves Zedeño. 2009. *If We Build It, Will They Come? Planning and Execution of Late Prehistoric Communal Bison Hunts.* Paper presented at the 69th Plains Anthropological Conference, Norman.

Bamforth, D. B. 1986. Technological Efficiency and Tool Curation. *American Antiquity* 51:38–50.

Baptista, C.M.M. 2001. *Os marisqueiros de Vila do Bispo. Ensaio Etnográfico.* Junta de Freguesia de Vila do Bispo, Vila do Bispo.

Barbosa, Márcia, M. D. Gaspar, and D. Barbosa. 1994. A organização especial das estruturas habitacionais e distribução dos artefatos no sitio Ilha da Boa Vista I, Cabo Frio, RJ. *Revista do Museu de Arqueologia e Etnologia* 4:31–38. Museu de Arqueologia e Etnologia de Universidade de São Paulo, São Paulo.

Barrow, C. J. 1999. Environmental Management: *Principles and Practice,* Routledge Press, London.

Basso, K. H. 1996. Wisdom Sits in Places: Notes on a Western Apache Landscape. In *Senses of Place,* edited by S. Feld and K. H. Basso, pp. 53–90. School of American Research Press, Santa Fe, New Mexico.

Bastien, Betty. 2004. *Blackfoot Ways of Knowing.* University of Calgary Press, Calgary, Alberta.

Baumhoff, M. A. 1981. The carrying capacity of hunter-gatherers. In *Affluent Foragers,* edited by S. Koyama and D. H. Thomas, pp. 77–90. Senri Ethnological Studies 9. Osaka, Japan: National Museum of Ethnology.

Bayham, F. E. 1979. Factors Influencing the Archaic Pattern of Animal Exploitation. *Kiva* 44:219–35.

Bayham, F. E., and P. Hatch. 1985. Archaeofaunal Remains from the New River Area. In *Hohokam Settlement and Economic System in the Central New River Drainage, Arizona,* edited by D. E. Doyel and M. D. Elson, pp. 405–33. Soil Systems Publication in Archaeology No. 4., Phoenix.

Beale, N. H. 2007. *Archaic Projectile Points and Cultural Differences in the Southern Southwest.* Unpublished Master's Thesis, Department of Anthropology, University of Oklahoma, Norman.

Beck, A. 1972. A variação do conteúdo cultural dos sambaquis, litoral de Santa Catarina. Ph.D. dissertation, Universidad de São Paulo, São Paulo.

Beidl, Jacqueline. 1992. *The Blackfeet and the Badger-Two Medicine: An Evaluation of Potential Traditional Cultural Significance Drawn from Archival Sources.* USDA Forest Service, Lewis and Clark National Forest and Lincoln National Forest. Submitted to USDA Forest Service, Lincoln National Forest.

Bettinger, Robert. 1991. *Hunter-Gatherers: Archaeological and Evolutionary Theory.* Plenum Press, New York.

Bickford, V., and P. Martz. 1980. Test Excavations at Cottonwood Creek, Catalina Island, California. *Pacific Coast Archaeological Society Quarterly* 16:106–24.

Binford, L. R. 1973. Interassemblage Variability: The Mousterian and the "Functional" Argument. In *The Explanation of Culture Change,* edited by C. Renfrew, pp. 227–54. Duckworth Press, London.

———. 1979. Organization and Formation Processes: Looking at Curated Technologies. *Journal of Anthropological Research* 35:255–73.

———. 1980. Willow smoke and dogs' tails: hunter-gatherer settlement systems and archaeological site formation. *American Antiquity* 45:4–20.

———. 2001. *Constructing Frames of Reference.* University of California Press, Berkeley.

Binford, S. R., and L. R. Binford. 1968. *New Perspectives in Archaeology,* Aldine Publishing, Chicago.

Blanton, R. E., S. A. Kowalewski, G. Feinman, and J. Appel. 1981. *Ancient Mesoamerica.* Cambridge: Cambridge University Press.

Bleed, P. 1986. The Optimal Design of Hunting Weapons: Maintainability or Reliability. *American Antiquity* 51:737–47.

Blench, R. 2007. New Paleozoogeographical Evidence for the Settlement of Madagascar. *Azania* 42:69–82.

Bliege Bird, R., D. W. Bird, B. F. Codding, C. Parker, J. Holland Jones. 2008. The "fire stick farming" hypothesis: Australian Aboriginal foraging strategies, biodiversity and anthropogenic fire mosaics. *Proceedings of the national Academy of Sciences,* USA 105:14796–14801.

Bover, P., and J. A. Alcover. 2008. Extinction of the autochthonous small mammals of Mallorca (Gymnesic Islands, Western Mediterranean) and its ecological consequences. *Journal of Biogeography* 35:1112–22.

Bowser, B. J., and M. N. Zedeño. 2009. *The Archaeology of Meaningful Places.* University of Utah Press, Salt Lake City.

Boyadjian, C. H., S. Eggers, and K. Reinhard. 2007. Dental wash: a new method of estimating microfossil content in prehistoric teeth. *Journal of Archaeological Science* 34:1622–28.

Braje, T. J. 2010. *Modern Oceans, Ancient Sites: Archaeology and Marine Conservation on San Miguel Island, California.* University of Utah Press, Salt Lake City.

Braje, T. J., J. M. Erlandson, T. C. Rick, P. K. Dayton, and M. Hatch. 2009. Fishing from Past to Present: Long-term Continuity and Resilience of Red Abalone Fisheries on California's Northern Channel Islands. *Ecological Applications* 19:906–19.

Braje, T. J., T. C. Rick, J. M. Erlandson, and R. L. DeLong. 2010. The Archaeology and Historical Ecology of California Channel Island Marine Mammals. In *Human Impacts on Ancient Seals, Sea Lions, and Sea Otters: Integrating Archaeology and Ecology in the Northeast Pacific,* ed. T. J. Braje, and T. C. Rick. University of California Press, Berkeley, in press.

Braudel, Ferdnand. 1980. *On History.* University of Chicago Press, Chicago.

Briggs, J. M., H. Schaafsma, and D. Trenkov. 2007. Woody Vegetation Expansion in a Desert Grassland: Prehistoric Human Impact? *Journal of Arid Environments* 69(3):458–72.

Briggs, J. M., K. A. Spielmann, H. Schaafsma, K. W. Kintigh, M. Kruse, K. Morehouse, and K. Schollmeyer. 2006. Why Ecology Needs Archaeologists and Archaeology Needs Ecologists. *Frontiers in Ecology and the Environment* 4(4):180–88.

Brink, Jack W. 2008. *Imagining Head-Smashed-In.* Athabasca University Press, Edmonton, Canada.

Broder, John M. 2010. Scientists warn oil spill could threaten Florida. *New York Times.* 17 May.

Brooks, M., D. J. Colquhoun, and a. P.A.S. Janice G. Brown. 1989. Sea Level Change, Estuarine Development, and Temporal Variability in Woodland Period Subsistence-settlement Patterning on the Lower Coastal Plain of South Carolina. In *Studies in South Carolina Archaeology in Honor of Robert L. Stephenson,* edited by A. C. Goodyear and G. T. Hanson, pp. 91–100. Anthropological Studies 9. South Carolina Institute of Archaeology and Anthropology, University of South Carolina, Columbia.

Bryan, A. L. 1993. Sambaqui at Forte Marechal Luz, State of Santa Catarina, Brazil. In *Brazilian Studies,* edited by A. L. Bryan and R. Gruhn, pp. 1–113. Corvallis: Center for the Study of First Americans, Oregon State University.

Bullchild, Percy. 1985. *The Sun Came Down: The History of the World as my Blackfeet Elders Told It.* Harper and Row, New York.

Bye, R., and E. Linares. 2000. Relationships between Mexican Ethnobotanical Diversity and Indigenous Peoples. In *Biodiversity and Native America*, edited by P. E. Minnis and W. J. Elisens, pp. 44–73. University of Oklahoma Press, Norman.

Calderón, V. 1964. *O Sambaqui de Pedra Oca*. Instituto de Ciencias Sociais 2. Salvador: Universidade da Bahia.

Caldwell, J. R. 1958. *Trend and Tradition in the Prehistory of the Eastern United States*. American Anthropologist Memoir 88, Washington, D.C.

Campbell, Gregory R. 2008. Beyond means to meaning: using distributions of shell shapes to reconstruct past collecting strategies. *Environmental Archaeology* 13 (2):111–21.

Campbell, Gregory R., and Thomas A. Foor. 2002. *An Ethnohistorical and Ethnographic Evaluation of Blackfeet Religious and Traditional Cultural Practices in East Glacier National Park and the Surrounding Mountains*. Submitted to Glacier National Park, The University of Montana, Missoula.

Capella, A. 2008. Spain's great barnacle battle. http://www.timesonline.co.uk/tol/travel/holiday_type/food_and_travel/article5370129.ece (accessed November 26, 2009).

Carr, R. F., and J. E. Hazard. 1961. Map of the Ruins of Tikal, El Petén, Guatemala. *Tikal Reports*, No. 11, *Museum Monographs*. The University Museum, Philadelphia.

Castro Faria, L. de. 1959. O problema da proveção dos sambaquis. *Arquivos do Museu Nacional* 49:95–138.

Claassen, C. 1998. *Shells*. Cambridge University Press, Cambridge.

Clark, G. 1970. *Aspects of Prehistory*. University of California Press, Berkeley.

Collins, P. W. 1980. Food Habits of the Island Fox (*Urocyon littoralis littoralis*) on San Miguel Island, California. In *Proceedings of the Second Conference on Scientific Research in the National Parks* 12:152–64. Terrestrial Biology; Zoology. NTIS.PB81–100133. National Park Service, Washington, D. C.

———. 1991a. Interaction Between Island Foxes (*Urocyon littoralis*) and Indians on Islands off the Coast of Southern California: I. Morphological and Archaeological Evidence of Human Assisted Dispersal. *Journal of Ethnobiology* 11:51–81.

———. 1991b. Interaction Between Island Foxes (*Urocyon littoralis*) and Native Americans on Islands off the Coast of Southern California: II. Ethnographic, Archaeological, and Historical Evidence. *Journal of Ethnobiology* 11:205–29.

———. 1993. Taxonomic and Biogeographic Relationships of the Island Fox (*Urocyon littoralis*) and Gray Fox (*U. cinereoargenteus*) from Western North America. In *Third California Islands Symposium: Recent Advances in Research on the California Islands*, edited by F. G. Hochberg, pp. 351–90. Santa Barbara Museum of Natural History, Santa Barbara.

———. 1998. Santa Catalina Island Shrew, *Sorex ornatus willetti*. In *Terrestrial Mammal Species of Special Concern in California*, edited by B. C. Bolster, pp. 19–21. California Department of Fish and Game, Sacramento.

Collins, P. W., and S. B. George. 1990. Systematics and Taxonomy of Island and Mainland Populations of Western Harvest Mice (*Reithrodontomys megalotis*) in Southern California. *Natural History Museum of Los Angeles County Contributions in Science* 420:1Collins, P. W., J. Storrer, and K. Rindlaub. 1979. Vertebrate Zoology: Biology of the Deer Mouse. In *A Natural Resources Study of the Channel Islands National Park, California*, edited by D. M. Power, Chapter XI. Final Technical Report to the Denver Service Center, National Park Service, Washington, DC.

Collins, P. W., D. A. Guthrie, T. C. Rick, and J. M. Erlandson. 2005. Analysis of Prey Remains Excavated from an Historic Bald Eagle Nest Site on San Miguel Island, California. In *Proceedings of the Sixth California Islands Symposium, edited by D. Garcelon and C. Schwemm, pp. 103–120. National Park Service Technical Publication CHIS-05-01, Institute for Wildlife Studies, Arcata.

Colquhoun, Donald J. and Mark J. Brooks. 1986. New Evidence from the Southeastern U.S. for Eustatic Components in the Late Holocene Sea Levels. Geoarchaeology 1:275–91.

Colten, R. H. 2001. Ecological and Economic Analysis of Faunal Remains from Santa Cruz Island. In The Origins of a Pacific Coast Chiefdom: The Chumash of the Channel Islands, edited by J. E. Arnold, pp. 199–219. University of Utah Press, Salt Lake City.

Cook, J. A., A. A. Eddingsass, J. L. Loxterman, S. Ebbert, and S. O. MacDonald. 2010. Insular Arctic Ground Squirrels (Spermophilus parryii) of the North Pacific: Indigenous or Exotic? Journal of Mammalogy 91:1401–12.

Coonan, T. J., C. A. Schwemm, G. W. Roemer, and G. Austin. 2002. Population Decline of Island Foxes (Urocyon littoralis littoralis) on San Miguel Island. In Proceedings of the Fifth California Islands Symposium, edited by D. Browne, K. Mitchell, and H. Chaney, pp. 289–97. Santa Barbara Museum of Natural History, Santa Barbara.

Coonan, T. J., K. Rutz, D. K. Garcelon, B. C. Latta, M. M. Gray, and E. T. Ashehoug. 2005. Progress in Island Fox Recovery Efforts on the Northern Channel Islands. In Proceedings of the Sixth California Islands Symposium, edited by D. Garcelon and C. Schwemm, pp. 263–73. National Park Service Technical Publication CHIS-05-01, Institute for Wildlife Studies, Arcata.

Coonan, T. J., C. A. Shwemm, and D. K. Garcelon. 2010. Decline and Recovery of the Island Fox: A Case Study for Population Recovery. Cambridge University Press, Cambridge.

Cormier, L. A. 2006. Between the Ship and Bulldozer: historical Ecology of the Guajà Subsistence, Sociality, and Symbolism After 1500. In Time and Complexity in Historical Ecology: Studies in the Neotropical Lowlands, edited by W. Balêe and C. L. Erickson, pp. 341–64. Columbia University Press, New York.

Costa, K.S.M., M. M. Costa, and M. C. Lukas. 2009. Volcanic eruptions and the forgotten pearls. Ocean and Coastal Management 52:229–32.

Crawford, Garry W. 2006. East Asian plant domestication. In Archaeology of East Asia, ed. M. T. Stark, 77–95. Blackwell, Malden.

———. 2008. The Jomon in early agriculture discourse: issues arising from Matsui, Kanehara and Pearson. World Archaeology 40(4):445–65.

Cronon, William. 1992. Nature's Metropolis: Chicago and the Great West. New York: W. W. Norton.

Crook, Morgan R. 1984. Evolving Community Organization on the Georgia Coast. Journal of Field Archaeology 11:247–63.

———. 1995. Mississippi Period Archaeology of the Georgia Coastal Zone. Laboratory of Archaeology Series, Report No. 23. University of Georgia, Athens.

Crooks, K. R. 1994a. Demography and Status of the Island Fox and the Island Spotted Skunk on Santa Cruz Island, California. The Southwestern Naturalist 39:257–62.

———. 1994b. Den-Site Selection in the Island Spotted Skunk of Santa Cruz Island, California. The Southwestern Naturalist 39:354–57.

———. 1999. Western Spotted Skunk. In Smithsonian Book of North American Mammals, edited by D. E. Wilson and S. Ruff, pp. 183–85. National Museum of Natural History, Smithsonian Institution, Washington, D.C.

Crooks, K. R., and D. Van Vuren. 1994. Conservation of the Island Spotted Skunk and Island Fox in a Recovering Island Ecosystem. In The Fourth California Islands Symposium: Update on the Status of Resources, edited by W. L. Halvorson and G. J. Maender, pp. 379–86. Santa Barbara Museum of Natural History, Santa Barbara.

———. 2002. Update on the Status of the Island Spotted Skunk. In *Proceedings of the Fifth California Islands Symposium*, edited by D. Browne, K. Mitchell, and H. Chaney, pp. 298–99. Santa Barbara Museum of Natural History, Santa Barbara.

Crumley, Carole L. 1994a. *Historical Ecology: Cultural Knowledge and Changing Landscapes*, School of American Research Advanced Seminar. School of American Research, Santa Fe.

———. 1994b. Historical Ecology: A Multidimensional Ecological Orientation. In *Historical Ecology: Cultural Knowledge and Changing Landscapes*, edited by Carole L. Crumley, pp. 1–16. SAR Press, Santa Fe.

———. 1994c. Epilogue. In *Historical Ecology: Cultural Knowledge and Changing Landscapes*, edited by Carole L. Crumley, pp. 229–42. School of American Research, Santa Fe.

———. 2007. Historical Ecology: Integrated Thinking at Multiple Temporal and Spatial Scales. In *The World System and The Earth System: Global Socio-Environmental Change and Sustainability Since the Neolithic*, edited by A. Hornborg and C. Crumley, pp. 15–28. Left Coast Press, Walnut Creek.

Cushing, J., M. Daily, E. Noble, L. Roth, and A. Wenner. 1984. Fossil Mammoths from Santa Cruz Island, California. *Quaternary Research* 21:376–84.

Dambrine, E., J. L. Dupouey, L. Laut, L. Humbert, M. Thinon, T. Beaufils, and H. Richard. 2007. Present forest biodiversity patterns in France related to former Roman agriculture. *Ecology* 88:1430–39.

Davis, J. H. 1956. Influences of Man Upon Coast Lines. In *Man's Role in Changing the Face of the Earth*, edited by W. Thomas, Jr., pp. 504–21, University of Chicago Press, Chicago.

Davis, M. A. 2009. *Invasion Biology*. Oxford University Press, New York.

Dean, R. M. 2003. *People, Pests, and Prey: The Emergence of Agricultural Economies in the Desert Southwest*. University of Arizona, Tucson. University Microfilms, Ann Arbor, Michigan.

———. 2005. Site-Use Intensity, Cultural Modification of the Environment, and the Development of Agricultural Communities in Southern Arizona. *American Antiquity* 70:403–31.

———. (editor). 2010. *The Archaeology of Anthropogenic Environments*. Center for Archaeological Investigations, Occasional Paper no. 37. Carbondale, IL: Southern Illinois University Carbondale.

Deaver, Sherri. 1988. *Blackfeet Use of the Badger-Two Medicine*. Ethnoscience. Submitted to USDA Forest Service, Lewis and Clark National Forest.

DeBlasis, P. 2005. *Os sambaquis vistos através de um sambaqui*. Tese de Livre-Docência, Faculdade de Filosofia, Letras e Ciências Humanas de Universidade de São Paulo, São Paulo.

DeBlasis, P., S. Fish, M. D. Gaspar, and P. Fish. 1998. Some references for the discussion of complexity among the sambaqui mound-builders from the southern shores of Brasil. *Revista de Arqueologia Americana* 15:75–105.

DeBlasis, P., A. Kneip, R. Scheel-Ybert, P. Giannini, and M. D. Gaspar. 2007. Sambaquis e paisagem: dinâmica natural e arqueologia regional no litoral do sul do Brasil. *Arqueologia Suramericana* 3:29–61.

De Masi, M.A.N. 2001. Pescadores coletores da costa sul do Brasil. *Pesquisas* (serie Antropologia) 57:1–136.

Dempsey, Hugh A. 2001. Blackfoot. In *Handbook of North American Indians, Vol. 13, Plains*, edited by R. DeMallie, pp. 604–28. Smithsonian Institution Press, Washington, D.C.

Denevan, W. 1992. The pristine myth: the landscape of the Americas in 1492. Current Geographic Research. *Annals of the Association of American Geographers* 82:369–85.

DePratter, Chester B. 1976. The Refuge Phase on the Coastal Plain of Georgia. *Early Georgia* 4:1–13.

———. 1977. Environmental Changes on the Georgia Coast During the Prehistoric Period. *Early Georgia* 5:1–14.

———. 1978. Prehistoric Settlement and Subsistence Systems, Skidaway Island, Georgia. *Early Georgia* 6:65–80.

———. 1979. Shellmound Archaic on the Georgia Coast. *South Carolina Antiquities* 11:1–69.

———. 1991. *W.P.A. Archaeological Excavations in Chatham County, Georgia: 1937–1942.* University of Georgia Laboratory of Archaeology Series Report Number 29, Athens.

DePratter, Chester B., and James D. Howard. 1977. History of Shoreline Changes Determined by Archaeological Dating: Georgia Coast, United States of America. *Transactions of the Gulf Coast Association of Geological Societies* 27:251–58.

———. 1980. Indian Occupation and Geologic History of the Georgia Coast: A 5000 year Summary. In *Excursions in Southeastern Geology: The Archaeology of the Georgia Coast, vol. 20,* edited by J. Howard, C. B. DePratter, and R. W. Frey, pp. 1–65. Geological Society of America, Guidebook, Atlanta.

———. 1981. Evidence for a Sea Level Lowstand Between 4500 and 2400 years B.P. on the Southeast Coast of the United States. *Journal of Sedimentary Petrology* 51:1287–95.

DePratter, Chester B., and Victor D. Thompson. *In Preparation.* Past Shorelines of the Georgia Coast. In *Native American Archaeology of the Georgia Coast,* edited by Victor D. Thompson, and David Hurst Thomas, Anthropological Papers of the American Museum of Natural History, New York.

Dew, M. A. 2007. *Unsettling Times: The Growth and Subsequent Depopulation of the Ancient San Simon Basin in Southeastern Arizona.* Unpublished Master's Thesis, Department of Anthropology, University of Oklahoma, Norman.

Diamond, Jared. 2005. *Collapse: How Societies Choose to Fail or Succeed.* Viking, New York.

Dickey, D. R. 1929. The Spotted Skunk of the Channel Islands of Southern California. *Proceedings of the Biological Society of Washington* 42:157–60.

Diehl, M. W. 2001. Macrobotanical Remains and Land Use: Subsistence and Strategies for Food Acquisition. In *Excavations in the Santa Cruz River Floodplain: The Early Agricultural Period Component at Los Pozos,* edited by D. A. Gregory, pp. 195–208. Center for Desert Archaeology Anthropological Papers No. 21, Tucson.

Diehl, M. W., and J. A. Waters. 2006. Aspects of Optimization and Risk During the Early Agricultural Period. In *Behavioral Ecology and the Transition to Agriculture,* edited by D. J. Kennett and B. Winterhalder, pp. 63–86. University of California Press, Berkeley.

Dincauze, D. F. 2000. *Environmental Archaeology: principles and practice.* Cambridge University Press, Cambridge.

Di Peso, C. C., J. B. Rinaldo, and G. Fenner. 1974. *Casas Grandes: A Fallen Trading Center of the Gran Chichimeca.* Amerind Foundation and Northland Press, Dragoon and Flagstaff, AZ.

Donnan, D. 2003. What has happened to the natives? *Shellfish news* 16:10–11.

Doolittle, W. 2000. *Cultivated Landscapes of Native North America.* Oxford University Press, Oxford.

Driver, J. C. 2002. Faunal Variation and Change in the Northern San Juan Region. In *Seeking the Center Place: Archaeology and Ancient Communities in the Mesa Verde Region,* edited by M. D. Varien and R. H. Wilshusen, pp. 143–60. University of Utah Press, Salt Lake City.

Driver, J. C., and J. R. Woiderski. 2008. Interpretation of the "Lagomorph Index" in the American Southwest. *Quaternary International* 185:3–11.

Drost, C. A., L. Gekzis, and P. Power. 2009. Distribution and Abundance of Harvest Mice and Deer Mice on Santa Cruz Island in relation to feral animal removal. In *Proceedings of the Seventh California Islands Symposium*, edited by C. C. Damiani and D. K. Garcelon, pp. 349–61. Institute for Wildlife Studies, Arcata.

Duvall, David C. 1904–11. *Papers (Vol. 1)*. Typed manuscripts. American Museum of Natural History, New York.

Eastoe, C. J., S. Fish, P. Fish, M. D. Gaspar, and A. Long. 2002. Reservoir corrections for marine samples from the south Atlantic Coast, Santa Catarina state, Brazil. *Radiocarbon* 44:145–48.

Eder, J. 1978. The Caloric Returns to Food Collecting: Disruption and Change Among the Batak of the Philippine Tropical Forest. *Human Ecology* 6:55–69.

Egan, D., and E. A. Howell. (editors). 2001. *The Historical Ecology Handbook: A Restorationist's Guide to Reference Ecosystems*. Island Press, Washington D.C.

Elliot, D. G. 1904. Descriptions of Apparently New Species and Subspecies of Mammals and a New Generic Name Proposed. Field Columbian Museum, 90. Zool. Ser., 3:263–70.

Elliott, Daniel T., and Kenneth E. Sassaman. 1995. *Archaic period archaeology of the Georgia coastal plain and coastal zone*. Georgia Archaeological Research Design Paper 11. University of Georgia, Athens.

Ellis, C. J. 1997. Factors Influencing the Use of Stone Projectile Tips An Ethnographic Perspective. In *Projectile Technology*, edited by H. Knecht, pp. 37–74. Plenum Press, New York.

Erickson, Clark L. 2008. Amazonia: The Historical Ecology of a Domesticated Landscape. In Handbook of South American Archaeology, edited by. H. Silverman and W. Isbell, pp. 157–83, Springer, New York.

Erlandson, Jon M. 2001. The Archaeology of Aquatic Adaptations: Paradigms for a New Millennium. *Journal of Archaeological Research* 9:287–350.

Erlandson, J. M., and T. C. Rick. 2008. Archaeology, marine ecology and human impacts on marine environments. In *Human Impacts on Ancient Marine Ecosystems: A Global Perspective*, edited by T. C. Rick and J. M. Erlandson, pp. 1–19. University of California Press, Berkeley.

———. 2010. Archaeology Meets Marine Ecology: The Antiquity of Maritime Cultures and Human Impacts on Marine Fisheries and Ecosystems. *Annual Review of Marine Science* 2:231–51.

Erlandson, J. M., T. C. Rick, and C. Peterson. 2005. A Geoarchaeological Chronology of Holocene Dune Building on San Miguel Island, California. *The Holocene* 15:1227–35.

Erlandson, J. M., T. C. Rick, T. L. Jones, and J. Porcasi. 2007. One If By Land, Two If By Sea: Who Were the First Californians? In *California Prehistory: Colonization, Culture, and Complexity*, edited by T. L. Jones and K. A. Klar, pp. 53–62. Altamira Press, Walnut Creek.

Erlandson, J. M., T. C. Rick, T. J. Braje, A. Steinberg, and R. L. Vellanoweth. 2008. Human Impacts on Ancient Shellfish: A 10,000 Year Record from San Miguel Island, California. *Journal of Archaeological Science* 35:2144–52.

Erlandson, J. M., T. C. Rick, T. J. Braje, M. Casperson, B. Culleton, Brian Fulfrost, T. Garcia, D. A. Guthrie, N. Jew, D. J. Kennett, M. Moss, L. Reeder, Craig Skinner, J. Watts and L. Willis. 2011. Paleoindian Seafaring, Maritime Technologies, and Coastal Foraging on California's Channel Islands. *Science* 331:1181–85.

Ewers, John C. 1958. *The Blackfeet: Raiders on the Northwestern Plains*. University of Oklahoma Press, Norman.

——. 2001. *The Horse in Blackfoot Indian Culture: With Comparative Material From other Western Tribes.* Reprinted by University Press of the Pacific, Honolulu, Hawaii.

Fagan, Brian. 2000. *The Little Ice Age: How Climate Made History 1300–1850.* Basic Books, New York.

——. 2004. *The Long Summer: How Climate Changed Civilization.* Basic Books, New York.

——. 2008. *The Great Warming: Climate Change and the Rise and Fall of Civilizations.* Bloomsbury Press, New York.

Farr, William. 1984. *The Reservation Blackfeet (1882–1945): A Pictorial History of Survival.* University of Washington Press, Seattle.

Faulkner, P. 2009. Focused, intense and long-term: evidence for granular ark (*Anadara granosa*) exploitation from late Holocene shell mounds of Blue Mud Bay, northern Australia. *Journal of Archaeological Science* 36:821–34.

Feit, Harvey. 1994. The Enduring Pursuit: Land, Time, and Social Relationships in Anthropological Models of Hunter Gatherers and Subartic Hunters' Images. In *Key Issues in Hunter-Gatherer Research,* edited by E. Burch Jr., and L. Ellanna, pp. 421–39. Berg, London.

Figuti, L., and D. Klökler. 1996. Resultados preliminares dos vestígios zooarqueologicos do sambaqui Espinheiros II (Joinville, SC). *Revista do Museu de Arqueologia e Etnologia* 10:69–87. Universidade de São Paulo, São Paulo.

Fish, S. K. 2000. Hohokam Impacts on Sonoran Desert Environment. In *Imperfect Balance: Landscape Transformations in the Precolumbian America,* edited by D. L. Lentz, pp. 251–80. Columbia University Press, New York.

Fish, S. K., P. DeBlasis, M. D. Gaspar, and P. Fish. 2000. Eventos incrementais na construção de sambaquis litoral do estado de Santa Catarina. *Revista do Museu Arqueologia e Etnologia, Universidade de São Paulo* 10:69–87.

Fish, S. K., and P. R. Fish. 2010. Monumentality and complex hunter-gatherers in southeast coastal Brazil. In *Monumental Questions: Prehistoric Megaliths, Mounds, and Enclosures,* edited by David Calado, Maximilian Baldia, and Matthew Boulanger, pp. 231–36. BAR International Series 2123, London.

Fish, S. K., P. R. Fish, and J. Madsen. 1990. Sedentism and Settlement Pattern Mobility Prior to A.D. 1000 in the Tucson Basin. In *Perspectives in Southwestern Prehistory,* edited by P. Minnis and C. L. Redman, pp. 26–91. Westview Press, Boulder.

——. 1992. Early Sedentism and Agriculture in the Northern Tucson Basin. In *The Marana Community in the Hohokam World,* edited by S. K. Fish, P. R. Fish, and J. Madsen, pp. 11–19. Anthropological Papers of the University of Arizona 56. University of Arizona Press, Tucson.

Floyd, C. H., D. H. Van Vuren, K. R. Crooks, K. L. Jones, D. K. Garcelon, N. M. Belfiore, J. W. Dragoo, and B. May. 2011. Genetic Differentiation of Island Spotted Skunks, Spilogale gracilis amphiala. *Journal of Mammalogy* 92:148–58.

Foley, Michael F. 1986. An Historical Analysis of the Administration of the Blackfeet Indian Reservation by the United States, 1855–1950s. Manuscript in the author's possession, Bureau of Applied Research in Anthropology, University of Arizona, Tucson.

Ford, James A., Philip Phillips and William G. Haag. 1955. The Jaketown Site in West-Central Mississippi. *Anthropological Papers Vol.45, Pt. 1.* American Museum of Natural History, New York.

Foster, J.B. 1965. The Evolution of the Mammals of the Queen Charlotte Islands, British Columbia. Occasional Papers of the British Columbia Provincial Museum 14.

Fredrickson, E. L., R. E. Estell, A. Laliberte, and D. M. Anderson. 2006. Mesquite Recruitment in the Chihuahuan Desert: Historic and Prehistoric Patterns with Long-term Impacts. *Journal of Arid Environments* 65(2):285–95.

Freeman, A.K.L. 1999. Status of the Middle Archaic in Southern Arizona. In *Excavations in the Santa Cruz River Floodplain: The Middle Archaic Component at Los Pozos*, edited by D. A. Gregory, pp. 75–84. Center for Desert Archaeology Anthropological Papers No. 20, Tucson.

Frison, George C. 2004. *Survival by Hunting: Prehistoric Animal Predators and Animal Prey*. University of California Press, Berkeley.

Fuji, Norio. 1984. *Koko Kafungaku* [Archaeo-palynology]. Yuzankaku, Tokyo.

Gamble, L. H. 2002. Archaeological evidence for the origin of the plank canoe in North America. *American Antiquity* 67:301–15.

Gaspar, M. D. 1991. *Aspectos da Organização de um Grupo de Pescadores, Coletores e Caçadores*. Ph.D. Dissertation, Universidade de São Paulo, São Paulo.

———. 1998. Considerations of the sambaquis of the Brazilian coast. *Antiquity* 72:592–615.

———. 2000. *Sambaquis: Arqueologia do Litoral*. Rio de Janeiro: Jorge Zahar Editora.

Gaspar, M. D., P. DeBlasis, S. Fish, and P. Fish. 2008. Sambaqui (shell mound) societies of coastal Brazil. In *Handbook of South American Archaeology*, edited by H. Silverman and W. Isbell pp. 319–38. Springer, New York.

Gayes, Paul T., David B. Scott, Eric S. Collins, and Douglas D. Nelson. 1992. A Late Holocene Sea-Level Fluctuation in South Carolina. In *Quaternary Coasts of the United States: Marine and Lacustrine Systems*, edited by C. H. Fletcher III and J. F. Wehmiller, pp. 155–60. SEPM Society for Sedimentary Geology, Special Publication No. 48, Tulsa.

Gibson, Jon L. 2000. *The Ancient Mounds of Poverty Point: Place of Rings*. University Press of Florida, Gainesville.

———. 2004. The power of beneficent obligation in first mound-building societies. In J. L. *Signs of Power: The Rise of Cultural Complexity in the Southeast*, edited by J. Gibson and P. Carr, pp. 254–69. The University of Alabama Press, Tuscaloosa, Alabama.Gibson, Jon L., and Philip J. Carr, ed. 2004. *Signs of Power: The Rise of Complexity in the Southeast*. University of Alabama Press, Tuscaloosa, Alabama.

Gill, A. E. 1976. Genetic divergence of insular populations of deer mice. *Biochemical Genetics* 14:835–48.

———. 1980. Evolutionary Genetics of California Islands *Peromyscus*. In *The California Islands: Proceedings of a Multidisciplinary Symposium*, edited by D. M. Power, pp. 719–44. Santa Barbara Museum of Natural History, San Barbara.

Gillespie, Jason. 2008. Enculturing an Unknown World: Caches and Clovis Landscape Ideology. *Canadian Journal of Archaeology* 31:179–89.

Gillespie, W. 1994. Vertebrate Faunal Remains from Five Schuk Toak Site. In *Archaeological Studies of the Avra Valley, Arizona: Excavations in the Schuk Toak District: Vol. 2. Scientific Studies and Interpretation*, edited by A. Dart, pp. 215–42. Anthropological Papers No. 16. Center for Desert Archaeology, Tucson.

Gilman, P. A. 1995. Multiple Dimensions of the Archaic-to-Pit Structure Period Transition in Southeastern Arizona. *Kiva* 60:619–32.

———. 1996. *Archaeological Survey Along the Northern San Simon River, 1994: A Joint Project Between the Safford District, Bureau of Land Management, and the University of Oklahoma*. Report on file at the Bureau of Land Management, Safford, AZ.

———. 1997. *Wandering Villagers: Pit Structures, Mobility and Agriculture in Southeastern Ari-*

zona. Arizona State University Anthropological Research Papers No. 49. Arizona State University, Tempe.

Gilman, P. A., V. S. Powell, and D. L. Dycus. 1996. The Role of Agriculture and Residential Movements in the Late Archaic and Early Pit Structure Periods of Southeastern Arizona. In *Early Formative Adaptations in the Southern Southwest,* edited by B. J. Roth, pp. 73–84. Prehistory Press, Madison, WI.

Goldstein, D. B., G. W. Roemer, D. A. Smith, D. E. Reich, A. Bergman, and R. K. Wayne. 1999. The Use of Microsatellite Variation to Infer Population Structure and Demographic History in a Natural Model System. *Genetics* 151:797–801.

Gragson, T. 2005. Time and Service to Historical Ecology. *Ecological and Environmental Anthropology* 1:1–9.

Grayson, D. K. 1991. The Archaeological Record of Human Impacts on Animal Populations. *Journal of World Prehistory* 15(1):1–68.

———. 2001. The Archaeological Record of Human Impacts on Animal Populations. *Journal of World Prehistory* 15:1–68.

Gregory, D. A. (editor). 1999. *Excavations in the Santa Cruz Floodplain: The Middle Archaic Component at Los Pozos.* Anthropological Papers 20. Center for Desert Archaeology, Tucson.

Gregory, D. A., and M. W. Diehl. 2002. Duration, Continuity, and Intensity of Occupation at a Late Cienega Phase Settlement in the Santa Cruz River Floodplain. In *Traditions, Transitions, and Technologies: Themes in Southwestern Archaeology,* edited by S. H. Schlanger, pp. 200–223. University Press of Colorado, Boulder.

Greiser, Sally T. 1994. Late Prehistoric Cultures of the Montana Plains. In *Plains Indians, A.D. 500–1500,* edited by K. H. Schleisier, pp. 34–55. University of Oklahoma Press, Norman.

Greiser, Sally T., and T. Weber Greiser. 1993. *Blackfoot Culture, Religion, and Traditional Practices in the Badger-Two Medicine Area and Surrounding Mountains.* Historical Research Associates. Submitted to USDA Forest Service, Lewis and Clark National Forest.

Grinnell, George B. 1962. *Blackfoot Lodge Tales: The Story of a Prairie People.* University of Nebraska Press, Lincoln.

Grinnell, J., and J. Dixon. 1918. Natural History of the Ground Squirrels of California. *Monthly Bulletin of the State Commission of Horticulture* 7:597–708.

Grootes, P. M., M. Struiver, J.W.C. White, C. Johnsen, and J. Jouzel. 1993. Comparison of oxygen isotope records from the GISP 2 and GRIP Greenland Ice Core. *Nature* 366:552–54.

Gunn, J., C. L. Crumley, E. Jones, and B. K. Young. 2004. A Landscape analysis of Western Europe during the Middle Ages. In *The Archaeology of Global Change: The Impacts of Humans on Their Environments,* edited by C. L. Redman, S. R. James, P. R. Fish, and J. D. Rogers, pp. 165–86. Smithsonian Institution, Washington, D.C.

Guthrie, D. A. 1980. Analysis of Avifauna and Bat Remains from Midden sites on San Miguel Island. In *The California Islands: Proceedings of a Multidisciplinary Symposium,* edited by D. M. Power, pp. 689–702. Santa Barbara Museum of Natural History, Santa Barbara.

———. 1993. New Information on the Prehistoric Fauna of San Miguel Island, California. In *Third California Islands Symposium, Recent Advances in Research on the California Islands,* edited by F. G. Hochberg, pp. 405–16. Santa Barbara Museum of Natural History, Santa Barbara.

———. 1998. Fossil Vertebrates from Pleistocene Terrestrial Deposits on the Northern Channel Islands, Southern California. In *Contributions to the Geology of the Northern Channel*

Islands, Southern California, edited by P. Weigend, pp. 187–92. Pacific Section American Association of Petroleum Geologists, Bakersfield.

———. 2005. Distribution and Provenance of Fossil Avifauna on San Miguel Island. In *Proceedings of the Sixth California Islands Symposium,* edited by D. Garcelon and C. Schwemm, pp. 35–42. National Park Service Technical Publication CHIS-05-01, Institute for Wildlife Studies, Arcata.

Guthrie, D. A., H. W. Thomas, and G. L. Kennedy. 2002. A new species of extinct late Pleistocene Puffin (Aves: Alcidae) from the southern California Channel Islands. In *Proceedings of the Fifth California Islands Symposium,* edited by D. R. Browne, K. L. Mitchell, and H. W. Chaney, pp. 525–30. Santa Barbara Museum of Natural History, Santa Barbara.

Habu, Junko. 2001. *Subsistence-Settlement Systems and Intersite Variability in the Moroiso Phase of the Early Jomon Period of Japan.* International Monographs in Prehistory, Ann Arbor.

———. 2002. Jomon collectors and foragers: regional interactions and long-term changes in settlement systems among prehistoric hunter-gatherers in Japan. In *Beyond Foraging and Collecting: Evolutionary Change in Hunter-Gatherer Settlement Systems,* edited by B. Fitzhugh and J. Habu, pp. 53–72. Kluwer/Plenum, New York.

———. 2004. *Ancient Jomon of Japan.* Cambridge University Press, Cambridge.

———. 2005. Jomon cultural landscapes, clay figurines and gender archaeology [Jenda kokogaku kara mita Jomon dogu to bunka-teki keikan]. *Annual Bulletin of the Sannai Maruyama Site* [Tokubetsu Shiseki Sannai Maruyama Iseki Nenpo] 8:92–96.

———. 2006. The archaeology of Sannai Maruyama in the context of world hunter-gatherer archeology: mechanisms of long-term change in cultural landscapes [Sekai no shuryo saishumin kenkyu kara mita Sannai Maruyama: bunka keikan no choki-teki henka to sono mekanizumu]. *Annual Bulletin of the Sannai Maruyama Site* [Tokubetsu Shiseki Sannai Maruyama Iseki Nenpo] 9:48–55.

———. 2008. Growth and decline in complex hunter-gatherer societies: a case study from the Jomon period Sannai Maruyama site, Japan. *Antiquity* 82:571–84.

———. 2009. Working with Japanese colleagues: excavation of a Jomon pit-dwelling and storage pits at Goshizawa Matsumori. *The SAA* (*Society for American Archaeology*) *Archaeological Record* 9(3):18–21.

Habu, Junko, and Clare Fawcett. 1999. Jomon archaeology and the representation of Japanese origins. *Antiquity* 73:587–93.

———. 2008. Science or narratives? Multiple interpretations of the Sannai Maruyama site, Japan. In *Evaluating Multiple Narratives: Beyond Nationalist, Colonialist, Imperialist Archaeologies,* edited by J. Habu, C. Fawcett, and J. M. Matsunaga, pp. 91–117. Springer, New York.

Habu, Junko, and Mark E. Hall, 2010. Climate change and the Jomon culture: a perspective from historical ecology. Paper presented at the Symposium on Climate Change and Subsistence in Prehistoric Japan. University of California, Berkeley and the Japan Society for the Promotion of Science, June 19–20, Berkeley.

Habu, Junko, Minkoo Kim, Mio Katayama, and Hajime Komiya. 2001. Jomon subsistence-settlement systems at the Sannai Maruyama site. *Bulletin of the Indo-Pacific Prehistory Association* 21:9–21.

Habu, Junko, and Yo-Ichiro Sato. 2008. Analyses of soil samples collected from the north wall of the 6th Excavation Area, the Sannai Maruyama site (a preliminary report) [Sannai Maruyama Iseki dai 6 ji chosa chiten hokuheki kara saishu shita dojo sample no bunseki kekka (chukan hokoku)]. *Annual Bulletin of the Sannai Maruyama Site* [Tokubetsu Shiseki Sannai Maruyama Iseki Nenpo] 11:24–39.

Hall, E. R. 1981. *The Mammals of North America* (2nd edition) vol. 2. John Wiley and sons, New York.

Hames, R. B., and W. T. Vickers. 1982. Optimal Diet Breadth Theory as a Model to Explain Variability in Amazonian Hunting. *American Ethnologist* 9:358–78.

Hard, R. J., and J. R. Roney. 2005. The Transition to Farming on the Rio Casas Grandes and in the Southern Jornada Mogollon Region. In *The Late Archaic Across the Borderlands: From Foraging to Farming,* edited by B. J. Vierra, pp. 141–86. University of Texas Press, Austin.

Hastorf, C. A. 2006. Domesticated Food and Society in Early Coastal Peru. In *Time and Complexity in Historical Ecology: Studies in the Neotropical Lowlands,* edited by W. Balée, pp. 87–126. Columbia University Press, New York.

Hatayama, Tsuyoshi. 1997. *Jomon-jin no Matsuei tachi: Hie to Konomi no Seikatsu-shi* [Descendants of the Jomon People: Lifeways with Barnyard Millets and Nuts]. Sairyu-sha, Tokyo.

Hayashida, Frances M. 2005. Archaeology, ecological history and conservation. *Annual Review of Anthropology* 34:43–65.

Hayden, B., N. Franco, and J. Spafford. 1996. Evaluating Lithic Strategies and Design Criteria. In *Stone Tools: Theoretical Insights into Human Prehistory,* edited by George H. Odell, pp. 9–45. Plenum Press, New York.

Hayden, B. P., and R. Dolan. 1979. Barrier Island, Lagoons, and Marshes. *Journal of Sediment Petrology* 49:1061–1072.

Hayes, M. O., V. J. Henry, T. F. Moslow, A. M. Wojtal, G. A. Zarillo, and L. F. Lens. 1980. Coastal environments of Georgia and South Carolina. In *Excursions in Southeastern Geology II,* edited by R. W. Frey and T. L. Neathery, pp. 281–310. American Geological Institute, Falls Church.

Heizer, R. 1968. New observations on La Venta. In *Dumbarton Oaks Conference on the Olmec,* edited by E. Benson and M. Coe, pp. 71–78. Washington, D.C., Dumbarton Oaks Research Library and Collection.

Henshaw, H. W. 1876. Notes on the mammals taken and observed in California in 1875 by H. W. Henshaw. In *Annual Report Upon the Geographical Surveys West of the One Hundredth Meridian, in California, Nevada, Utah, Colorado, Wyoming, New Mexico, Arizona, and Montana.* Appendix JJ., edited by G. M. Wheeler, pp. 305–12.

Hervert, J. J., and P. R. Krausman. 1986. Desert Mule Deer Use of Water Developments in Arizona. *Journal of Wildlife Management* 50:670–76.

Howald, G. R., K. R. Faulkner, B. Tershy, B. Keitt, H. Gellerman, E. M. Creel, M. Grinnell, S. T. Ortega, and D. A. Croll. 2005. Eradication of Black Rats from Anacapa Island: Biological and Social Considerations. In *Proceedings of the Sixth California Islands Symposium,* edited by D. K. Garcelon and C. A. Schwemm, pp. 299–312. National Park Service Technical Publication CHIS-05-01, Institute for Wildlife Studies, Arcata.

Howard, J. D., and R. W. Frey. 1985. Physical and biogenic aspects of backbarrier sedimentary sequences, Georgia Coast, USA. *Marine Geology* 63:77–127.

Howell, A. H. 1938. Revision of the North American Ground Squirrels with a Classification of the North American Sciuridae. *North American Fauna* 56.

Huckell, B. B. 1995. *Of Marshes and Maize: Preceramic Agricultural Settlements in the Cienega Valley, Southeastern Arizona.* Anthropological Papers of the University of Arizona No. 59. University of Arizona Press, Tucson.

———. 1996. The Archaic Prehistory of the North American Southwest. *Journal of World Prehistory* 10:305–73.

Huckell, B. B., L. W. Huckell, and M. S. Shackley. 1999. McEuen Cave. *Archaeology Southwest* 13(1):12.

Hudson, T., T. C. Blackburn, R. Curletti, and J. Timbrook. 1977. *The Eye of the Flute: Chumash Traditional History and Ritual as Told by Fernando Librado Kitsepawit to John P. Harrington.* Santa Barbara Museum of Natural History, Santa Barbara.

Hume, C. 1958. *Skunks as Pets.* All Pets Books, Inc., Fond du Lac, WI.

Hurt, W. R. 1974. Interrelationships between the Natural Environment and Four Sambaquis, Coast of Santa Catarina, Brazil. Bloomington: *Occasional Papers and Monographs* No. 1. Indiana University Museum, Bloomington.

Hutchinson, Dale L., Clark Spenser Larsen, Margaret J. Schoeninger, and Lynette Norr. 1998. Regional Variation in the Pattern of Maize Adoption and Use in Florida and Georgia. *American Antiquity* 63:397–416.

Ingold, Timothy. 2003. Three in one: how an ecological approach can obviate the distinctions between body, mind and culture. In *Imagining nature: practices of cosmology and identity,* edited by A. Roepstorff, N. Bubandt, and K. Kull, pp. 40–55. Aarhus University Press, Aarhus, Denmark.

Iversen, J. 2002. Stone age man's transformation and exploitation of the Primeval Forest. In *The Neolithisation of Denmark. 150 years of debate,* edited by A. Fischer and K. Kristiansen, pp. 195–210. J. R. Collis, Sheffield.

Jackson, J.B.C., M. X. Kirby, W. H. Berger, K. A. Bjorndal, L. W. Botsford, B. J. Bourque, R. H. Bradbury, R. Cooke, J. Erlandson, J. A. Estes, T. P. Hughes, S. Kidwell, C. B. Lange, H. S. Lenihan, J. M. Pandolfi, C. H. Peterson, R. S. Steneck, M. J. Tegner, and R. R. Warner. 2001. Historical Overfishing and the Recent Collapse of Coastal Ecosystems. *Science* 293:629–37.

Jackson, John C. 2000. *The Piikani Blackfeet.* Mountain Press Publishing Company, Missoula, Montana. Johnston, Susan. 2001. Food Choice is Shaped by Accessibility: How Sources of Food have Changed Overtime for the Blackfeet. *Nutritional Anthropology* 24(2):3–9.

James, S. R. 2004. Habitat Transformations and Animal Extinctions. In *The Archaeology of Global Change: The Impacts of Humans on Their Environments,* edited by C. L. Redman, S. R. James, P. R. Fish, and J. D. Rogers, pp. 28–62. Smithsonian Institution, Washington, D.C.

Jason, P. M., P. R. Krausman, and C. B. Vernon. 2005. Rainfall, Temperature, and Forage Dynamics Affect Nutritional Quality of Desert Mule Deer Forage. *Rangeland Ecology and Management* 58:360–65.

Jefferies, Richard W., and Christopher Moore. 2009. *In Search of Mission San Joseph de Sapala: Mission Period Archaeological Research on Sapelo Island, Georgia, 2003–2007.* Report submitted to the Georgia Department of Natural Resources, Historic Preservation Division, Atlanta.

Jerardino, A., G. M. Branch, and R. Navarro. 2008. Human impact on Precolonial marine environments of South Africa. In *Human impacts on ancient marine ecosystems. A global perspective,* edited by T. C. Rick and J. M. Erlandson, pp. 279–96. University of California Press, Berkeley.

Johnson, D. L. 1972. *Landscape Evolution on San Miguel Island, California.* Ph.D. Dissertation, Department of Geography University of Kansas, Lawrence, Kansas.

———. 1975. New Evidence on the Origins of the Island Fox, *Urocyon littoralis clementae,* and Feral Goats on San Clemente Island, California. *Journal of Mammalogy* 56:925–28.

———. 1980. Episodic Vegetation Stripping, Soil Erosion, and Landscape Modification in Prehistoric and Recent Historic Time, San Miguel Island, California. In *The California Islands:*

Proceedings of a Multidisciplinary Symposium, edited by D. Power, pp. 103–21. Santa Barbara Museum of Natural History, Santa Barbara.

———. 1983. The California Continental Borderland: Land bridges, Watergaps, and Biotic Dispersals. In *Quaternary Coastlines and Marine Archaeology: Towards the Prehistory of Land Bridges and Continental Shelves*, edited by P. M. Masters and N. Flemming, pp. 481–527. Academic Press, London.

Johnson, J. R., T. W. Stafford Jr., V. Ajie, and D. P. Morris. 2002. Arlington Springs Revisited. In *Proceedings of the Fifth California Islands Symposium*, edited by D. Browne, K. Mitchell, and H. Chaney, pp. 541–45. Santa Barbara Museum of Natural History, Santa Barbara.

Jones, Grant D. 1978. *The ethnohistory of the Guale coast through 1684*. Anthropological Papers of the American Museum of Natural History 55. American Museum of Natural History, New York.

Johnston, S. L. 2001. Food Choice Is Shaped by Accessibility: How Sources of Food Have Changed Over Time for the Blackfeet. *Nutritional Anthropology* 24:3–9.

Jones, K. L., D. H. Van Vuren, and K. R. Crooks. 2008. Sudden increase in a rare endemic carnivore: ecology of the island spotted skunk on Santa Cruz Island. *Journal of Mammalogy* 89:75–86.

Joyce, Rosemary A., and Jeanne Lopiparo. 2005. Postscript: Doing Agency in Archaeology. *Journal of Archaeological Method and Theory* 12:65–74.

Justice, N. D. 2002. *Stone Age Spear Points and Arrow Points of the Southwestern United States*. Indiana University Press, Indianapolis.

Kahn, M. 1990. Stone-Faced Ancestors: The Spatial Anchoring of Myth in Wamire, Papua New Guinea. *Ethnology* 29:51–66.

———. 1996. Your Place and Mine: Sharing Emotional Landscapes in Wamire, Papua New Guinea. In *Senses of Place*, edited by S. Feld and K. H. Basso, pp. 167–96. School of American Research Press, Santa Fe, New Mexico.

Kawahata, Hodaka, Hisashi Yamamoto, Ken'ichi Ohnkushi, Yusuke Yokoyama, Katsunori Kimoto, Hideaki Ohshima, and Hiroyuki Matsuzaki. 2009. Changes of environments and human activity at the Sannai-Maruyama ruins in Japan during the mid-Holocene Hypsithermal climatic interval. *Quaternary Science Reviews* 28:964–74.

Kay, Charles. 2002. Are Ecosystems Structured from the Top-Down or Bottom-Up? A New Look at an Old Debate. In *Wilderness and political Ecology: Aboriginal Influences and the Original State of Nature*, edited by C. Kay, and R. Simmons, pp. 484–98. Salt Lake City, Utah.

Keeley, L. 1988. Hunter-gatherer economic complexity and "population pressure": a cross-cultural analysis. *Journal of Anthropological Archaeology* 7: 373–411.

Keene, Deborah A. 2004. Reevaluating Late Prehistoric Coastal Subsistence and Settlement Strategies: New Data from Grove's Creek Site, Skidaway Island, Georgia. *American Antiquity* 69:671–89.

Kehoe, Alice. 1993. How the Ancient Peigans Lived. *Research in Economic Anthropology* 14:85–107.

Kehoe, Thomas F. 1978. Paleo-Indian Bison Drives: Feasibility Studies. *Plains Anthropologist* 23(82:2):79–83.

Kehoe, Thomas F. 2001. The Billy Big Spring Site, Montana. *Archaeology in Montana* 42(2):27–40.

Keleher, J. W. 1997. Chipped Stone Technological Strategies. In *Wandering Villagers: Pit Structures, Mobility and Agriculture in Southeastern Arizona*, edited by P. A. Gilman, 108–26. Arizona State University Anthropological Research Papers No. 49. Tempe.

Kelly, Robert L. 1995. *The Foraging Spectrum: Diversity in Hunter-Gatherer Lifeways*. Smithsonian Institution Press, Washington, D.C.

Kennett, D. J. 2005. *The Island Chumash: Behavioral Ecology of a Maritime Society.* University of California Press, Berkeley.

Kennett, D. J., J. P. Kennett, G. J. West, J. M. Erlandson, J. R. Johnson, I. L. Hendy, A. West, B. J. Culleton, T. L. Jones, and T. W. Stafford Jr. 2008. Wildfire and Abrupt Ecosystem Disruption on California's Northern Channel Islands at the Ållerød-Younger Dryas Boundary (13.0–12.9ka). *Quaternary Science Reviews* 27:2528–43.

Kennett, Douglas. J., Brendan J. Culleton, James P. Kennett, Jon M. Erlandson, and Kevin G. Cannariato. 2007. Middle Holocene climate change and population dispersal in Western North America. In Climate Change and Cultural Dynamics, edited by David G. Anderson, Kirk A. Maasch, and Daniel H. Sandweiss, 531–57. Elsevier Inc., New York.Kent, S. 1991. The Relationship between Mobility Strategies and Site Structure. In *The Interpretation of archaeological spatial patterning,* edited by Ellen M. Kroll, T. Douglas Price, pp. 33–60. Plenum Press, New York.

Kidder, T. R. 2002. Mapping Poverty Point. American Antiquity 67:89–101.

Kidder, Tristram R. 1998. The Rat that Ate Louisiana: Aspects of Historical Ecology in the Mississippi River Delta. In *Advances in Historical Ecology,* edited by W. Balée, pp. 141–68. Columbia University Press, New York.

———. 2010. Hunter-gatherer Ritual and Complexity: New Evidence from Poverty Point, Louisiana. In *Ancient Complexities: New Perspectives in Precolumbian North America,* edited by S. Alt, pp. 32–51. University of Utah Press, Salt Lake City.

———. 2011. Transforming Hunter-Gatherer History at Poverty Point. In *Hunter-Gatherer Archaeology as Historical Process,* ed. K. E. Sassaman and D. H. Holley, Jr., pp. 95–119. Amerind Foundation and University of Arizona Press, Tucson.

Kidder, Tristram R., Anthony L. Ortmann and Lee J. Arco. 2008. Poverty Point and the Archaeology of Singularity. *SAA Archaeological Record* 8(5):9–12.

Kidder, Tristram R., and Kenneth E. Sassaman. 2009. The View from the Southeast. In *Archaic Societies: Diversity and Complexity Across the Midcontinent,* edited by T. Emerson, D. McElrath and A. Fortier, pp. 667–94. State University of New York Press, Albany.

Kidder, Tristram R., Lee J. Arco, Anthony L. Ortmann, Timothy M. Schilling, Caroline Boeke, Rachel Bielitz and Katherine A. Adelsberger. 2009. Poverty Point Mound A: Final Report of the 2005 and 2006 Field Seasons. Louisiana Division of Archaeology and the Louisiana Archaeological Survey and Antiquities Commission, Baton Rouge.

Kirch, P. V. 1997. Microcosmic Histories: Island Perspectives on "Global" Change. *American Anthropologist* 99:30–42.

———. 2004. Oceanic Islands: Microcosms of "Global Change." In *The Archaeology of Global Change: The Impact of Humans on their Environment,* edited by C. Redman, S. James, P. Fish, and J. D. Rogers, pp. 13–27. Smithsonian Institution Press, Washington, D.C.

Kirch, Patrick V., and Terry L. Hunt. 1997. *Historical Ecology in the Pacific Islands: Prehistoric Environmental and Landscape Change.* Yale University Press, New Haven.

Kitagawa, Junko, and Yoshinori Yasuda. 2004. The influence of climatic change on chestnut and horse chestnut preservation around Jomon sites in Northeastern Japan with special reference to the Sannai Maruyama and Kamegaoka sites. *Quaternary International* 123–25:89–103.

Klökler, D. 2008. *For Body and Soul: Mortuary Ritual in Shell Mounds (Laguna-Brazil).* Ph.D. Dissertation, Department of Anthropology, University of Arizona, Tucson.

Kneip, Andreas. 2004. *O Povo da Lagoa: Uso do SIG para Modelamento e Simulacao na Area Arqueologia do Camacho*. Ph.D. Dissertation, Universidade de Sao Paulo, SP.

Kneip, L. M. 1977. Pescadores e coletores préhistóricos do litoral de Cabo Rop. RJ. *Coleção Museu Paulista, Série Erisalos* 2:145–69.

———. 1992. As habitacoes 1 e2 do sambaquie da Pontinha (Saquarema, RJ). *Anais da VI Reuniao da Sociedade de Arqueologia Brasileira* 2:730–37. Rio de Janeiro.

Kobayashi, Ken'ichi. 2004. Fuchaku tanka-butsu no AMS tanso nendai sokutei ni yoru Ento Doki no nendai kenkyu [Dates of Ento Pottery on the basis of AMS radiocarbon dating of attached charred remains]. *Annual Bulletin of the Sannai Maruyama Site* [Tokubetsu Shiseki Sannai Maruyama Iseki Nenpo] 8:81–91 (in Japanese).

Kodama, Daisei. 2003. Komakino stonecircle and its significance for the study of Jomon social structure. In *Hunter-Gatherers of the North Pacific Rim*, edited by J. Habu, J. M. Savelle, S. Koyama, and H. Hongo, pp. 235–61. Senri Ethnological Studies 72. National Museum of Ethnology, Senri, Osaka.

Kowalewski, S. 2008. Regional Settlement Pattern Studies. *Journal of Archaeological Research* 16:225–85.

Krausman, P. R., A. J. Kuenzi, R. C. Etchberger, K. R. Rautenstrauch, L. L. Ordway, and J. J. Hervert. 1997. Diets of Desert Mule Deer. *Journal of Range Management* 50:513–22.

Kuroyanagi, A., H. Kawahata, H. Narita, K. Ohkushi, and T. Aramaki. 2006. Reconstruction of paleoenvironmental changes based on the planktonic foraminiferal assemblages off Shimokita in the northwestern North Pacific. *Global and Planetary Change* 53:92–107.

Laing, I., P. Walker, and F. Areal. 2006. Return of the native—is European oyster (*Ostrea edulis*) stock restoration in the UK feasible? *Aquatic Living Resources* 19:283–87.

Lapinsky, Mike. 1998. *The Elk Mystique*. Stoneydale Press Publishing Company, Stevensville.

Larsen, Clark Spencer. 1982. *The Anthropology of St. Catherines Island: 3. Prehistoric Human Biological Adaptation*. Anthropological Papers of the American Museum of Natural History 57, New York.

———. 2002. *Bioarchaeology of the Late Prehistoric Guale: South End Mound I, St. Catherines Island, Georgia*. American Museum of Natural History, Anthropological Papers 84, New York.

Larsen, Clark Spencer, Mark C. Griffin, Dale L. Hutchinson, Vivian E. Noble, Lynette Norr, Robert F. Pastor, Christopher B. Ruff, Katherine F. Russell, Margaret J. Schoeninger, Michael Schultz, Scott W. Simpson, and Mark F. Teaford. 2001. Frontiers of contact: Bioarchaeology of Spanish Florida. *Journal of World Prehistory* 15:69–123.

Lasiak, T. 1992. Contemporary shellfish-gathering practices of indigenous coastal people in Transkei: some implications for interpretation of the archaeological record. *Suid-Afikaanse Tydskrif vir Wetenskap* 88:19–28.

Laurie, E. M. 2008. *An investigation of the Common Cockle (Cerastoderma edule L.). Collection practices at the kitchen midden sites of Norsminde and Krabbesholm, Denmark*. BAR International Series, No. 1834. British Archaeological Reports, Oxford.

Lima, T., and J. Mazz. 2000. La emergencia de complejidad entre los cazadores recolectores de la costa atlantica meridional sudamericana. *Revista de Arqueologia Americana* 17:129–75.

Linares, O. F. 1976. "Garden Hunting" in the American Tropics. *Human Ecology* 4: 331–49.

Littleton, Judith, and Harry Allen. 2007. Hunter-gatherer burials and the creation of persistent places in southeastern Australia. *Journal of Anthropological Archaeology* 26:283–98.

Liu, J., T. Dietz, S. R. Carpenter, M. Alberti, C. Folke, E. Moran, A. N. Pell, P. Deadman, T. Kratz, J. Lubchenco, E. Ostrom, Z. Ouyang, W. Provencher, C. L. Redman, S. H. Schneider, and W. W. Taylor. 2007. Complexity of coupled human and natural systems. *Science* 317:1513–16.

Lyman, R. L. 2006. Paleozoology in the Service of Conservation Biology. *Evolutionary Anthropology* 15:11–19.

Lyman, R. Lee, and Steve Wolverton. 2002. The Late Prehistoric-Early Historic Game Sink in the Northwestern United States. *Conservation Biology* 16:73–85.

Mabry, J. B. 2005. Changing Knowledge and Ideas about the First Farmers in Southeastern Arizona. In *The Late Archaic Across the Borderlands: From Foraging to Farming*, edited by B. J. Vierra, 41–83. University of Texas Press, Austin.

MacArthur, R. H., and E. O. Wilson. 1967. *The theory of island biogeography*. Princeton University Press, Princeton.

Madsen, A. P., S. Müller, C. Neergaard, C.G.J. Petersen, E. Rostrup, K.J.V. Steenstrup, and H. Winge. 1900. *Affaldsdynger fra Stenalderen i Danmark*. Undersøgte for Nationalmuseet København.

Maldonado, J. E., C. Vila, and R. K. Wayne. 2001. Tripartite Genetic Divisions in the Ornate Shrew (*Sorex ornatus*). *Molecular Ecology* 10:127–47.

Mannino, M. A. and K. D. Thomas. 2001. Intensive Mesolithic exploitation of coastal resources? Evidence from a shell deposit on the Isle of Portland (Southern England) for the impact of human foraging on populations of intertidal rocky shore molluscs. *Journal of Archaeological Science* 28:1101–14.

———. 2002. Depletion of a resource? The impact of prehistoric human foraging on intertidal mollusc communities and its significance for human settlement, mobility and dispersal. *World Archaeology* 33(3):452–74.

Marquardt, W. H. and C. L. Crumley. 1987. Theoretical Issues in the Analysis of Spatial Patterning. *Regional Dynamics: Burgundian Landscapes in Historical Perspective*, edited by Carole. L. Crumley and W. H. Marquardt, 1–18. Academic Press, San Diego.

Marrinan, Rochelle A. 1975. *Ceramics, Mollusks, and Sedentism: The Late Archaic Period on the Georgia Coast*. Unpublished Ph.D. dissertation, Department of Anthropology, University of Florida, Gainesville.

Martin, Louis, Kenitiro Suguio, and Jean-Marie Flexor. 1988. Hauts niveaux marins pleistocenes du litoral brésilien. *Palaeogeography, Palaeoclimatology, Palaeoecology* 68:231–239.

Marshal, J. P., P. R. Krausman, and V. C. Bleich. 2005. Dynamics of Mule Deer Forage in the Sonoran Desert. *Journal of Arid Environments* 60:593–609.

Martz, P. 2005. Prehistoric Subsistence and Settlement on San Nicolas Island. In *Proceedings of the Sixth California Islands Symposium*, edited by D. Garcelon and C. Schwemm, pp. 65–82. National Park Service Technical Publication CHIS-05-01, Institute for Wildlife Studies, Arcata.

———. 2008. *4000 Years on Ghalas-At: Part One of the San Nicolas Island Index Unit Analysis Program*. Naval Air Weapons Station, China Lake.

Masters, R., and M. Stewart. 1995. *White-tailed Deer*. Forest Stewardship Wildlife Management Notes No. 1. Publication No. L-267. Cooperative Extension Service, Oklahoma State University, Stillwater.

Matisoo-Smith, E. 2009. The Commensal Model for Human Colonization of the Pacific 10 Years on—What Can We Say and Where to Now? *Journal of Island and Coastal Archaeology* 4:151–63.

Maxwell, D. 2006. Vertebrates. In *Life on the Dunes: Fishing, Ritual, and Daily Life at Two Late*

Period Sites on Vizcaino Point: Archaeological Testing at CA-SNI-39 and CA-SNI-162, San Nicolas Island, CA, edited by B. Fagan, D. R. Grenda, D. Maxwell, A. H. Keller, and R. Ciolek-Torello, pp. 101–6. Statistical Research Press, Tucson.

McAnany, Patricia A., and Norman Yoffee, eds. 2010. *Questioning Collapse: Human Resilience, Ecological Vulnerability, and the Aftermath of Empire.* Cambridge University Press, New York.

McCabe, R. 2002. Elk and Indians: Then Again. In *North American Elk: Ecology and Management,* edited by D. E. Toweill, and J. W. Thomas, pp. 121–98. Smithsonian Institution Press, Washington, D.C.

McCay, B. J. and J. M. Acheson. 1987. Human Ecology of the Commons, In *The Question of the Commons: The Culture and Ecology of Communal Resources,* edited by B.J.B. McCay and J. M. Acheson, pp. 1–34. University of Arizona Press, Tucson.

McClintock, Walter. 1999. *The Old North Trail: Life, Legends and Religion of the Blackfeet Indians.* University of Nebraska Press, Lincoln.

McGovern, T. H., O. Vésteinsson, A. Fridriksson, M. Church, I. Lawson, I. A. Simpson, A. Einarsson, G. Cook, S. Perdikaris, K. J. Edwards, A. M. Thomson, W. P. Adderley, A. Newton, G. Lucas, R. Edvardsson, O. Aldred, and E. Dunbar. 2008. Landscapes of Settlement in Northern Iceland: Historical Ecology of Human Impact and Climate Fluctuation on the Millennial Scale. *American Anthropologist* 109:27–51.

Meese, D., R. A. Alley, T. Gow, P. M. Grootes, P. Mayewski, M. Ram, K. Taylor, E. Waddington, and G. Zielinski. 1994. *Preliminary Depth-Age Scale of the GISP Ice Core.* CRREL Special Report 94–1. Cold Regions Research and Engineering Laboratory, Hanover.

Mellink, E. 1985. Agricultural Disturbance and Rodents: Three Farming Systems in the Sonoran Desert. *Journal of Arid Environments* 8:207–22.

Metraux, Alfred. 1946a. The Caingang. *Handbook of South American Indians, Volume 1: The Marginal Tribes,* edited by Julian H. Steward, pp. 445–76. Smithsonian Institution, Bureau of American Ethnology, Bulletin 143. U.S. Government Printing Office, Washington, D.C.

———. 1946b. The Botocudo. *Handbook of South American Indians, Volume 1: The Marginal Tribes,* edited by Julian H. Steward, pp. 531–40. Smithsonian Institution, Bureau of American Ethnology, Bulletin 143. U.S. Government Printing Office, Washington, D.C.

Milner, N. 2002. *Incremental growth of the European Oyster, Ostrea edulis: seasonality information from Danish kitchenmiddens.* BAR International Series, No. 1057. British Archaeological Reports, Oxford.

Milner, N., and E. Laurie. 2009. Coastal perspectives on the Mesolithic Neolithic transition. In *Mesolithic Horizons. Papers presented at the Seventh International Conference on the Mesolithic in Europe, Belfast 2005,* edited by S. McCartan, R. Schulting, G. Warren and P. Woodman, pp. 134–39. Oxbow Books, Oxford.

Milner, N., J. Barrett, and J. Walsh. 2007. Marine resource intensification in Viking Age Europe: the molluscan evidence from Quoygrew, Orkney. *Journal of Archaeological Science* 34:1461–72.

Milner, N., O. E. Craig, G. N. Bailey, K. Pedersen, and S. H. Andersen. 2004. Something fishy in the Neolithic? A re-evaluation of stable isotope analysis of Mesolithic and Neolithic coastal populations. *Antiquity* 78:9–22.

Milton, K. 1984. Protein and Carbohydrate Resources of the Miku Indians of Northwestern Amazonia. *American Anthropologist* 86:7–27.

Minnis, P. E. 1985a. Domesticating People and Plants in the Greater Southwest. In *Prehistoric*

Food Production in North America, edited by R. I. Ford., pp. 114–28. Anthropological Papers No. 75. University of Michigan Museum of Anthropology, Ann Arbor.

———. 1985b. *Social Adaptation to Food Stress: A Prehistoric Southwest Examples.* University of Chicago Press, Chicago.

Molenaar, M. E. 2000. Encounters with the Inhabitants of [Alberta] in 1792–1793 as Recorded by Peter Fidler, Surveyor. *Yumtzilob* 12:7–56.

Moore, C. M., and P. W. Collins, 1995. *Urocyon littoralis. Mammalian Species* 489:1–7.

Moran, E. F. 1990. *The Ecosystem Approach in Anthropology: From Concept to Practice.* University of Michigan Press, Ann Arbor.

Moratto, Michael J. 1984. *California Archaeology.* New York: Academic Press.

Morrison, A. E., and E. E. Cochrane. 2008. Investigating shellfish deposition and landscape history at the Natia Beach site, Fiji. *Journal of Archaeological Science* 35:2387–99.

Morrison, A. E., and T. L. Hunt. 2007. Human impacts on the nearshore environment: an archaeological case study from Kaua'I, Hawaiian Islands. *Pacific Science* 61:325–45.

Murray, John R. 2006. Personal Communication.

Murray, K. G., K. Winnett-Murray, Z. A. Eppley, G. L. Hunt, Jr., and D. B. Schwartz. 1983. Breeding Biology of the Xantus' Murrelet. *Condor* 85:12–21.

Nabhan, G. P. 2000. Cultural Dispersal of Plants and Reptiles to the Midriff Islands of the Sea of Cortes: Integrating Indigenous Human Dispersal Agents into Island Biogeography. *Journal of the Southwest* 42:545.

Nakao, Sasuke. 1976. *Saibai Shokubutsu no Kigen* [Origins of Domesticated Plants]. Chuo Koron Sha, Tokyo.

Nelson, M. C. 1991. The Study of Technological Organization. In *Archaeological Method and Theory, Vol. 3*, edited by M. B. Schiffer, pp. 57–100. University of Arizona Press, Tucson.

Nelson, M. C., and K. G. Schollmeyer. 2003. Game Resources, Social Interaction, and the Ecological Footprint in Southwest New Mexico. *Journal of Archaeological Method and Theory* 10:69–110.

Neves, W. 2005. A new early Holocene human skeleton from Brazil: implications for the settlement of the New World. *Journal of Human Evolution* 48:403–14.

Newsom, L., and E. S. Wing. 2004. *On Land and Sea: Native American Uses of Biological Resources in the West Indies.* University of Alabama Press, Tuscaloosa.

Nield, R. 1995. *The English, the French and the Oyster.* Quiller Press, London.

Nishida, Paula. 2007. A coisa ficou preta: estudo do processo de formação da terra preta do sitio arqueológico Jabuticabeira II. Tese de Doutoramento, Museo de Arqueologia e Etnologia, Universidade de Sao Paulo.

Noah, A. C. 2005. *Household Economies: The Role of Animals in a Historic Period Chiefdom on the California Coast.* PhD Dissertation, Department of Anthropology, University of California, Los Angeles.

Nunley, M. C. 1991. Contemporary Hunting and Gathering: the Foraging Ethos and the Mexican Kickapoo. In *Between Bands and States*, edited by S. A. Gregg, pp. 341–58. Occasional Paper No. 9. Center for Archaeological Investigations, Southern Illinois University, Carbondale.

O'Brien, C. S., R. B. Waddell, S. S. Rosenstock, and M. J. Rabe. 2006. Wildlife Use of Water Catchments in Southwestern Arizona. *Wildlife Society Bulletin* 34:582–91.

Odell, G. H. 1996. Economizing Behavior and the Concept of Curation. In *Stone Tools: Theoretical Insights into Human Prehistory*, edited by G. H. Odell, pp. 51–80. Plenum Press, New York.

Oetelaar, Gerald A., and David Meyer. 2006. Movement and Native American Landscapes: A Comparative Approach. *Plains Anthropologist* 51(199):355–74.

Oetelaar, Gerald A., and D. Joy Oetelaar. 2006. People, Places, and Paths: The Cypress Hills and the Niitsitapi Landscape of Southern Alberta. *Plains Anthropologist* 51(199):375–97.

O'Gara, B. W., and R. Dundas. 2002. Distribution, Past and Present. In *Elk: Ecology and Management*, edited by G. Toweill and J. G. Thomas, pp. 67–119. Smithsonian Institution Press, Washington, D.C.

Okada, Yasuhiro. 2003. Jomon culture of Northeastern Japan and the Sannai Maruyama site. In *Hunter-Gatherers of the North Pacific Rim*, edited by J. Habu, J. M. Savelle, S. Koyama, and H. Hongo, pp. 173–86. Senri Ethnological Studies 72. National Museum of Ethnology, Senri, Osaka.

Okumura, M., and S. Eggers. 2005. The people of Jabuticabeira II: reconstruction of the way of life in a Brazilian shell mound. *Journal of Comparative Human Biology* 55:263–81.

Oldfield, Frank. 2008. The role of people in the Holocene. In *Natural climate variability and global warming: a Holocene perspective*, edited by R.W Battarbee and H.A Binney, pp. 58–97. Wiley-Blackwell, Hoboken, New Jersey.

Oliver, Symmes C. 1962. Ecological and Cultural Continuity as Contributing Factors in the Social Organization of the Plains Indians. *University of California Publications in American Archaeology and Ethnology* 48(1):1–90.

Orr, P. C. 1968. *Prehistory of Santa Rosa Island*. Santa Barbara Museum of Natural History, Santa Barbara.

Ortmann, Anthony L. 2010. Placing the Poverty Point Mounds in their Temporal Context. *American Antiquity* 75:657–78.

Orton, J. H. 1937. *Oyster biology and oyster culture*. Arnold, London.

Panter-Brick, C., R. Layton, and P. Rowley-Conwy. 2001. Lines of Enquiry. In *Hunter-Gatherers: An Interdisciplinary Perspective*, edited by C. Panter-Brick, R. H. Layton, and P. Rowley-Conwy, pp. 1–11. Cambridge University Press, Cambridge.

Parmenter, R. R., and T. R. Van Devender. 1995. Diversity, Spatial Variability, and Functional Roles of Vertebrates in Desert Grassland. In *The Desert Grassland*, edited by M. P. McClaran and T. R. Van Devender, University of Arizona Press, Tucson.

Patterson, T. 1994. Towards a properly historical ecology. In *Historical ecology; cultural knowledge and changing landscapes*, edited by C. L. Crumley, pp. 223–37. SAR Press, Santa Fe.

Pauketat, Timothy. 2001. A New Tradition in Archaeology. In *The Archaeology of Traditions: Agency and History before and after Columbus*, edited by T. Pauketat, pp. 1–16. University Press of Florida, Gainesville.

———. 2004. *Ancient Cahokia and the Mississippians*. Cambridge University Press, Cambridge.

Peck, Trevor R., and Caroline R. Hudecek-Cuffe. 2003. Archaeology on the Alberta Plains: The Last Two Thousand Years. In *Archaeology in Alberta: A View from the New Millennium*, edited by J. W. Brink and J. F. Dormaar, pp. 72–102. Archaeological Society of Alberta, Medicine Hat.

Pennings, S., M. Albers, C. Alexander, and V. D. Thompson. 2010. *Comparing Ecological Legacies of Human Activity on Coastal Ecosystems*. Grant Submitted for review to the National Science FoundatPergams, O.R.W., and M. V. Ashley. 2001. Macroevolution in island rodents. *Genetica* 112–13: 245–56.

———. 2002. California Island Deer Mice: Genetics, Morphometrics, and Evolution. In *Proceedings of the Sixth California Islands Symposium*, edited by D. Garcelon and C. Schwemm, pp. 278–88. National Park Service Technical Publication CHIS-05-01, Institute for Wildlife Studies, Arcata.

Pergams, O.R.W., R. C. Lacy, and M. V. Ashley. 2000. Conservation and Management of Anacapa Deer Mice. *Conservation Biology* 14:819–32.

Petersen, K. S. 1993. Environmental changes recorded in the Holocene molluscan faunas from Djursland, Denmark. *Scripta Geologica* 2 (Special Issue):359–69.

Petit, J. R., Jouzel, J., Raynaud, D., Barkov, N. I., Barnola, J.-M., Basile, I., Benders, M., Chappellaz, J., Davis, M., Delaygue, G., Delmotte, M., Kotlyakov., V. M., Legrand, M., Lipenkov, V. Y., Lorius, C., Pépin, L., Ritz, C., Saltzman, E., & Stievenard, M., 1999. Climate and atmospheric history of the past 420,000 years from the Vostok ice core, Antarctica, *Nature*, 399:429–570.

Picton, Harold, and Irene Picton. 1975. *Saga of the Sun: A History of the Sun River Elk Herd.* Game Management Division, Montana Dept. of Fish and Game, Helena.

Porcasi, J. F. 1995. *Trans-Holocene Marine Mammal Hunting on San Clemente Island, California: Additional Data to Assess a Prehistoric "Tragedy of the Commons" and Declining in Mammalian Foraging Efficiency,* Master's Thesis, Department of Anthropology, California State University, Northridge.

———. 2002. Updating Prehistoric Maritime Subsistence at Little Harbor, Santa Catalina Island, California. In *Proceedings of the Fifth California Islands Symposium,* ed. D. Browne, K. Mitchell, and H. Chaney, 580–89. Santa Barbara Museum of Natural History, Santa Barbara.

Potter, James. 2004. The Creation of Person, the Creation of Place: Hunting Landscapes in the American Southwest. *American Antiquity* 69:322–38.

Pozorski, S., and T. Pozorski. 1986. Recent excavations at Pampa de las Llamas-Moxeke. *Journal of Field Archaeology* 13:381–401.

Prentiss, William C., and James C. Chatters. 2003. Cultural diversification and decimation in the prehistoric record. *Current Anthropology* 44(1):33–58.

Price, T. D. 2000. Lessons in the transition to agriculture. In *Europe's first farmers,* edited by T. D. Price, pp. 301–18. Cambridge University Press, Cambridge.

Prous, A. 1977. Les sculptures zoomorphes du sud bresilien et de l'Uruguay. *Cahiers d'Archeologie de Amerique du Sud* 5. Paris: Ecole des Hautes Etudes en Sciences Sociales.

———. 1992. *Arqueologia Brasiliera.* Universidade Federal de Brasilia, Brasilia.

Quitmyer, I. R., D. S. Jones, and W. Arnold. 1997. The Sclerochronology of Hard Clams, Mercenaria spp., from the Southeastern U.S.A.: A Method of Elucidating the Zooarchaeological Records of Seasonal Resource Procurement and Seasonality in Prehistoric Shell Middens. *Journal of Archaeological Science* 24:825–40.

Quitmyer, I. R., H. S. Hale, and D. S. Jones. 1985. Paleoseasonality Determination Based on Incremental Shell Growth in the Hard Clam, *Mercenaria mercenaria,* and its implications for future analysis of three Georgia Coastal Shell Middens. *Southeastern Archaeology* 4:27–40.

Quitmyer, I. R., and E. J. Reitz. 2006. Marine trophic levels targeted between AD 300 and 1500 on the Georgia coast, USA. *Journal of Archaeological Science* 33:806–22.

Rapp, J. M. (editor). 2006. *Prehistoric Landscape Use Along the Western Bajada of the San Simon Valley: The US 191 Project, Graham, County, Arizona.* LSD Technical Reports in Prehistory No. 2. Logan Simpson Design, Tempe, AZ.

Rappaport, Roy A. 1984. *Pigs for the Ancestors.* 2nd edition. Yale University Press, New Haven.

Rauth, J. 1986. O Sambaqui do Gomes. *Arquelogia* 4. Curitiba: Conselho de Pesquisas da Universidade Federal do Paraná.

Rea, A. M. 1983. *Once a River: Bird Life and Habitat Changes on the Middle Gila.* University of Arizona Press, Tucson.

———. 1998. *Folk Mammalogy of the Northern Pimans.* University of Arizona Press, Tucson.

Redman, C. L. 1999. *Human Impacts on Ancient Environments.* University of Arizona Press, Tucson.

———. 2004. Environmental Degradation and Early Mesopotamian Civilization. In *The Archaeology of Global Change: The Impacts of Humans on Their Environments,* edited by C. L. Redman, S. R. James, P. R. Fish, and J. D. Rogers, pp. 158–64. Smithsonian Institution, Washington, D.C.

Redman, C. L., S. R. James, P. R. Fish, and J. D. Rogers. 2004. Introduction: Human Impacts on Past Environments. In *The Archaeology of Global Change: The Impacts of Humans on Their Environments,* edited by C. L. Redman, S. R. James, P. R. Fish, and J. D. Rogers, pp. 1–8. Smithsonian Institution, Washington, D.C.

Reeves, Brian O. K. 1993. Iniskim: A Sacred Piikáni Religious Tradition. In *Kunaitapii: Coming Together on Native Sacred Sites,* edited by B.O.K. Reeves and M. Kennedy, pp. 194–247. Archaeological Society of Alberta, Calgary.

Reeves, Brian O. K., and Sandra Peacock. 2001. *"Our Mountains are Our Pillows": An Ethnographic Overview of Glacier National Park.* Submitted to Glacier National Park.

Reitz, E. J., I. R. Quitmyer, and R. A. Marrinan. 2009. What are we measuring in the zooarchaeological record of prehispanic fishing strategies in the Georgia Bight, USA? *Journal of Island and Coastal Archaeology* 4:2–36.

Reitze, William, and María Nieves Zedeño. 2009. *From Rock Rings to Regional Systems: Late Prehistoric Social and Ritual Architecture on the Two Medicine River, Glacier County, Montana.* Paper presented at the 69th Plains Anthropological Conference, Norman.

Richards, M. P., and R.E.M. Hedges. 1999. Stable isotope evidence for similarities in the types of marine foods used by late Mesolithic humans on the Atlantic coast of Europe. *Journal of Archaeological Science* 26:717–22.

Richards, M. P., R. J. Schulting, and R.E.M. Hedges. 2003. Sharp shift in diet at onset of Neolithic. *Nature* 425:366.

Richardson, C. A., S. A. Collis, K. Ekaratne, P. Dare, and D. Key. 1993. The age determination and growth rate of the European flat oyster, Ostrea edulis, in British waters determined from acetate peels of umbo growth lines. *ICES (International Council for the Exploration of the Sea) Journal of Marine Science* 50:493–500.

Rick, T. C. 2004. *Daily Activities, Community Dynamics, and Historical Ecology on California's Northern Channel Islands.* Ph.D. Dissertation, Department of Anthropology, University of Oregon, Eugene.

———. 2007. *The Archaeology and Historical Ecology of Late Holocene San Miguel Island.* Cotsen Institute of Archaeology, University of California, Los Angeles.

Rick, T. C., and J. M. Erlandson. (editors). 2008. *Human Impacts on Ancient Marine Ecosystems: A Global Perspective.* University of California Press, Berkeley.

Rick, T. C., J. M. Erlandson, R. L. Vellanoweth, and T. J. Braje. 2005. From Pleistocene Mariners to Complex Hunter-Gatherers: The Archaeology of the California Channel Islands. *Journal of World Prehistory* 19:169–228.

Rick, T. C., J. M. Erlandson, R. L. Vellanoweth, T. J. Braje, P. W. Collins, D. A. Guthrie, and Thomas W. Stafford Jr. 2009. Origins and Antiquity of the Island Fox (*Urocyon littoralis*) on California's Channel Islands. *Quaternary Research* 71:93–98.

Rick, T. C., P. L. Walker, L. M. Willis, A. C. Noah, J. M. Erlandson, R. L. Vellanoweth, T. J. Braje, and D. J. Kennett. 2008. Dogs, Humans, and Island Ecosystems: The Antiquity, Distribution, and Ecology of Domestic Dogs (*Canis familiaris*) on California's Channel Islands. *The Holocene* 18:1077–1087.

Rick, Torben C., Courtney A. Hofman, Todd J. Braje, Jesus E. Maldonado, T. Scott Sillett, Kevin Danchisko, and Jon M. Erlandson. 2012. Flightless Ducks, Giant Mice, and Pygmy Mammoths: Late Quaternary Extinctions on California's Channel Islands. *World Archaeology* 44:3–20.

Rindos, D. 1984. *The Origins of Agriculture: An Evolutionary Perspective*. Academic Press, Orlando.

Rohr, J. 1984. Sitios arqueológicos de Santa Catarina. *Anais do Museu de Antropologia* 17:77–168. Florianópolis: Universidade Federal de Santa Catarina.

Roosevelt, A., M. Imazio, S. Maranca, and R. Johnson. 1991. Eighth millennium pottery from a shell midden in the Brazilian Amazon. *Science* 254:1621–24.

Rosen, M. D. 1980. Archaeological investigations at two Santa Catalina sites: Rosski (SCAI-45) and Miner's Camp (SCAI-118). *Pacific Coast Archaeological Society Quarterly* 16:22–60.

Rosenthal, J. E., S. L. Williams, M. Roeder, W. Bonner, I. Strudwick, and S. G. Shahinian. 1988. The Bullrush Canyon project: Excavations at Bullrush Canyon Site (SCAI-137) and Cactus Camp Road Site, Santa Catalina Island. *Pacific Coast Archaeological Society Quarterly* 24(2&3):1–104.

Roth, B. J. 1989. *Late Archaic Settlement and Subsistence in the Tucson Basin*. Unpublished Ph.D. Dissertation, Department of Anthropology, University of Arizona, Tucson.

———. 1992. Sedentary Agriculturalists of Mobile Hunter-Gatherers? Recent Evidence of the Late Archaic Occupation of the Northern Tucson Basin. *Kiva* 57:291–314.

———. 1995. Late Archaic Occupation of the Upper Bajada: Excavations at AZ AA:12:84. *Kiva* 57:189–207.

Roth, B. J. and A. Freeman. 2008. The Middle Archaic Period and the Transition to Agriculture in the Sonoran Desert of Southern Arizona. *Kiva* 73:321–53.

Rowley-Conwy, P. 1984. The laziness of the short-distance hunter: the origins of agriculture in Denmark. *Journal of Anthropological Archaeology* 3:300–324.

Ruddiman, William F. 2003. The Anthropogenic Greenhouse Era Began Thousands of Years Ago. Climatic Change 61:261–93.

———. 2005. *Plows, Plagues & Petroleum: How Humans Took Control of Climate*. Princeton University Press, Princeton, New Jersey.

———. 2007. The Early Anthropogenic Hypothesis: Challenges and Responses. *Reviews of Geophysics* 45:RG4001.

Ruddiman, William F., Zhengtang Guo, Xin Zhou, Hanbin Wu and Yanyan Yu. 2008. Early rice farming and anomalous methane trends. *Quaternary Science Reviews* 27:1291–95.

Russo, Michael. 2004. Measuring Shell Rings for Social Inequality. In *Signs of Power: The Rise of Cultural Complexity in the Southeast*, edited by J. Gibson, and P. Carr, pp. 26–70. University of Alabama Press, Tuscaloosa.

Sahlins, Marshall. 2003. *Stone Age Economics*. Routledge, London.

Sakatsume, Nakao. 1961. *Nihon Sekki Jidai Shokuryo Sosetsu* [An Outline of Stone Age Food in Japan]. Doyokai, Tokyo.

Sassaman, Kenneth. 2001. Hunter-gatherers and Traditions of Resistance. In *The Archaeology of*

Traditions: Agency and History before and after Columbus, edited by T. Pauketat, pp. 218–36. University Press of Florida, Gainesville.

Sato, Yo-Ichiro, Shihsuke Yamanaka, and Mitsuko Takahashi. 2003. Evidence for Jomon plant cultivation based on DNA analysis of chestnut remains. In *Hunter-Gatherers of the North Pacific Rim,* edited by J. Habu, J. M. Savelle, S. Koyama, and H. Hongo, pp. 187–97. Senri Ethnological Studies 72. National Museum of Ethnology, Senri, Osaka.

Saunders, Rebecca. 2004. The Stratigraphic Sequence at the Rollins Shell Ring: Implications for Ring Function. *Florida Anthropologist* 57:249–68.

Savage, J. N. 1967. Evolution of the Insular Herpetofaunas. In *Proceedings of the Symposium on the Biology of the California Islands,* edited by R. N. Philbrick, pp. 219–27. Santa Barbara Botanic Garden, Santa Barbara.

Scarborough, V. 2003. The Flow of Power: Ancient Water Systems and Landscapes. School of American Research, Santa Fe.

Schaeffer, Claude. 1934. *Field Work Among Blackfeet Indians, Montana.* Correspondence and field notes. On file at the Glenbow Museum, Calgary, Alberta.

Scheel-Ybert, Rita. 2000. Vegetation stability in the southeastern Brazilian coastal área from 5500 to 1400 14C yr BP deduced from charcoal analysis. *Review of Palaeobotany and Palynology* 110:111–38.

Scheel-Ybert, Rita, Sabine Eggers, Verónica Wesolowski, Cecília Petronilho, C. H. Boyadjian, M. D. Gaspar, M. Barbosa-Guimaraes, M. C. Tenório, and P. DeBlasis. 2009. Subsistence and lifeway of coastal Brazilian moundbuilders. *Treballs D'etnoarqueologia* 7:37–54. Madrid.

Schlanger, Sarah H. 1992. Recognizing persistent places in Anasazi settlement systems. In *Space, Time, and Archaeological Landscapes,* edited by J. Rossignol and L. Wandsnider, pp. 91–112. Plenum Press, New York.

Schmidt, K. M. 1998. *Logistical Mobility and Faunal Remains: A Diachronic Study from the San Simon Valley of Southeastern Arizona.* Unpublished Master's Thesis, Department of Anthropology, University of Oklahoma, Norman.

———. 1999. The Five Feature Site: Evidence for a Prehistoric Rabbit Drive in Southeastern Arizona. *Kiva* 65:103–24.

———. 2008. *An Assessment of Settlement and Subsistence in Emergent Agricultural Economies In the Tucson Basin, United States, and Chihuahua, Mexico,* Unpublished Ph.D. Dissertation, Department of Anthropology, University of New Mexico, Albuquerque.

———. 2011. Faunal Resources and Human Environmental Impacts in the San Simon Valley, Southeastern Arizona. *Kiva* 76:297–315.

Schoenherr, A. A., R. C. Feldmath, and M. J. Emerson. 1999. *Natural History of the Islands of California.* University of California Press, Berkeley.

Schoeninger, Margaret J. 2009. Stable Isotope Evidence for the Adoption of Maize Agriculture. *Current Anthropology* 50:633–40.

Schulting, R., and M. P. Richards. 2002. The wet, the wild and the domesticated: the Mesolithic-Neolithic transition on the West Coast of Scotland. *Journal of European Archaeology* 5:147–89.

Schultz, James Willard. 1962. *Blackfeet and Buffalo: Memories of a Lifetime among the Indians.* University of Oklahoma Press, Norman.

———. 2002. *Blackfeet Tales of Glacier National Park.* Reprinted by the Montana Historical Society and Riverbend Publishing, Helena, Montana.

Schurr, M. R., and D. L. Gregory. 2002. Fluoride Dating of Faunal Materials by Ion-selective Electrode: High Resolution Relative Dating at an Early Agricultural Period Site in the Tucson Basin. *American Antiquity* 67:281–99.

Schwemm, C. A., and T. J. Coonan. 2001. *Status and Ecology of Deer Mice (Peromyscus maniculatus subsp.) on Anacapa, Santa Barbara and San Miguel Islands, California: Status of Monitoring 1992–2000.* Channel Islands National Park Technical Report # 01–02, National Park Service, Ventura.

Schwemm, C. A., J. T. Ackerman, P. L. Martin, and W. Perry. 2005. Nest Occupancy and Hatching Success of Xantus's Murrelets (*Synthliboramphus hypoleucus*) Breeding on Santa Barbara Island, California During a Twenty-year Period. In *Proceedings of the Sixth California Islands Symposium,* edited by D. K. Garcelon and C. A. Schwemm, pp. 385–94. National Park Service Technical Publication CHIS-05–01, Institute for Wildlife Studies, Arcata.

Schwemm, C. A., and P. L. Martin. 2005. Response of nest success of Xantus's Murrelets (*Synthliboramphus hypoleucus*) to native predator abundance, Santa Barbara Island, California. In *Proceedings of the Sixth California Islands Symposium,* edited by D. K. Garcelon and C. A. Schwemm, pp. 373–84. National Park Service Technical Publication CHIS-05–01, Institute for Wildlife Studies, Arcata.

Shelley, S. D. 2001. *Archaeological Evidence of the Island Fox (Urocyon littoralis) on California's Channel Islands.* Technical Report pp. 98–12. Statistical Research Inc, Tucson.

Shott, Michael J. 1986. Technological Organization and Settlement Mobility: An Ethnographic Examination. *Journal of Anthropological Research* 42:15–51.

Shiner, Justin. 2009. Persistent places: an approach to the interpretation of assemblage variation in deflated surface stone artefact distributions from western New South Wales, Australia. In *New Directions in Archaeological Science,* edited by A. Fairbain, S. O'Connor, and B. Marwick, pp. 25–42. Australia National University Press, Canberra.

Simões, M. F., and C. G. Correa. 1971. Pesquisas arqueológicas na região de Salgado (Pará)—a fase Areão do literal de Mariparim. Boletim do Museu Paraense Emílio Goeldi 48:1–30. Belém.

Sliva, R. J. 2005. Developments in Flaked Stone Technology During the Transition to Agriculture. In *Material Cultures and Lifeways of Early Agricultural Communities in Southern Arizona,* edited by R. J. Sliva, pp. 47–98. Anthropological Papers No. 35. Center for Desert Archaeology, Tucson.

Smith, B. D. 2001. Low Level Food Production. *Journal of Archaeological Research* 9:1–43.

———. 2007. Niche construction and the behavioral context of plant and animal domestication. *Evolutionary Anthropology* 16:188–99.

———. 2011. General Patterns of Niche Construction and the Management of "Wild" Plant and Animal Resources by Small-scale Pre-industrial Societies. *Philosophical Transactions of the Royal Society B,* 366:836–48.

Smith, C. S. 1978. *Summer-Fall Movements, Migrations, Seasonal Ranges, and Habitat Selection of the Middle Fork Elk Herd.* Master's Thesis, Department of Wildlife Biology, University of Montana, Missoula.

Smith, I. P., P. J. Low, and P. G. Moore. 2006. Legal aspects of conserving native oysters in Scotland. *Marine Pollution Bulletin* 52:479–83.

Smyth, D., D. Roberts, and L. Browne. 2009. Impacts of unregulated harvesting on a recovering stock of native oysters (*Ostrea edulis*). *Marine Pollution Bulletin* 58:916–22.

Sowers, T., M. Bender, L. Labeyrie, D. Martinson, J. Jouzel, D. Raynaud, J. J. Pichon, and A.

Korotkevich. 1993. A 135,000 year Vostoc-Specmap common temporal framework. *Paleoceanography* 8:737–766.

Stahl, P. W. 1996. Holocene Biodiversity: An Archaeological Perspective from the Americas. *Annual Review of Anthropology* 25:105–26.

———. 2000. Archaeofaunal Accumulation, Fragmented Forests, and Anthropogenic Landscape Mosaics in the Tropical Lowlands of Prehispanic Ecuador. *Latin American Antiquity* 11:241–57.

Steward, J. H. 1977. *Evolution and Ecology: Essays on Social Transformation*. University of Illinois Press.

———. 1997. *Basin-Plateau Aboriginal Sociopolitical Groups*. University of Utah Press, Salt Lake City.

Stojanowski, Christopher M. 2005. *Biocultural Histories in La Florida: a Bioarchaeological Perspective*. University Press of Florida, Gainesville.

Struiver, Minze, and Pieter M. Grootes. 2000. GISP2 oxygen isotope ratios. *Quaternary Research* 53(3):277–84.

Sullivan, B. 2001. Early days on the Georgia tidewater: the story of McIntosh county & Sapelo. 6 edition, Darien, Georgia.

Sweitzer, R. A., J. M. Constible, D. H. Van Vuren, P. T. Schuyler, and F. R. Starkey. 2005. History, Habitat Use, and Management of Bison on Catalina Island, California. In *Proceedings of the Sixth California Islands Symposium*, edited by D. K. Garcelon and C. A. Schwemm, pp. 231–47. National Park Service Technical Publication CHIS-05–01, Institute for Wildlife Studies, Arcata.

Szuter, C. R. 1991. Hunting by Prehistoric Horticulturalists in the American Southwest. Garland Publishing, New York.

Szuter, Christine, and Paul Martin. 1999. War Zones and Game Sinks in Lewis and Clark's West. *Conservation Biology* 13:36–45.

Szuter, C. R., and F. E. Bayham. 1989. Sedentism and Prehistoric Animal Procurement among Desert Horticulturalists of the North American Southwest. In *Farmers as Hunters: The Implications of Sedentism*, edited by S. Kent, pp. 80–95. Cambridge University Press, Cambridge.

———. 1996. Faunal Exploitation During the Late Archaic and Early Ceramic/Pioneer Periods in South-Central Arizona. In *Early Formative Adaptations in the Southern Southwest*, edited by B. J. Roth, pp. 65–72. Monographs in World Archaeology No. 25. Prehistory Press, Madison.

Tews, J., U. Brose, V. Grimm, K. Tielborger, M. C. Wichmann, M. Schwager, and F. Jeltsch. 2004. Animal species diversity driven by habitat heterogeneity/diversity: the importance of keystone structures. *Journal of Biogeography* 31:79–Thacker, Paul T. 1996. Hunter-Gatherer Lithic Economy and Settlement Systems: Understanding Regional Assemblage Variability in the Upper Paleolithic of Portuguese Estremadura. In *Stone Tools: Theoretical Insights into Human Prehistory*, edited by G. H. Odell, pp. 101–27. Plenum Press, New York.

Thomas, David Hurst. 2008a. Synthesis: the Aboriginal Landscape of St. Catherines Island. In *Native American Landscapes of St. Catherines Island, Georgia III*, edited by D. H. Thomas, pp. 990–1042. American Museum of Natural History, Anthropological Papers, Number 88, New York.

———. 2008b. Population Growth, Intensification, and the Emergence of Social Inequality on St. Catherines Island. In *Native American Landscapes of St. Catherines Island, Georgia III*, edited by D. H. Thomas, pp. 1046–94. American Museum of Natural History, Anthropological Papers, Number 88, New York.

———. 2008c. *Native American Landscapes of St. Catherines Island, Georgia I, II, III*. American Museum of Natural History, Anthropological Papers, Number 88, New York.

Thomas, David Hurst, and Clark Spencer Larsen. 1979. *The Anthropology of St. Catherines Island 2. The Refuge-Deptford Mortuary Complex*. Anthropological Papers of the American Museum of Natural History 56, New York.

Thomas, William. (editor). 1956. *Man's Role in Changing the Face of the Earth*. University of Chicago Press, Chicago.

Thomas, J. 2003. Thoughts on the "repacked" Neolithic Revolution. *Antiquity* 77(295):67–75.

Thompson, Victor D. 2007. Articulating Activity Areas and Formation Processes at the Sapelo Island Shell Ring Complex. *Southeastern Archaeology* 26:91–107.

———. 2009. The Mississippian Production of Space Through Earthen Pyramids and Public Buildings on the Georgia Coast, USA. *World Archaeology* 41:445–70.

———. 2010. The Rhythms of Space-Time and the Making of Monuments and Places during the Archaic. In *Trend, Tradition, and Turmoil: What Happened to the Southeastern Archaic?*, edited by D. H. Thomas and M. Sanger, pp. 217–27. Anthropological Papers of the American Museum of Natural History, New York.

Thompson, Victor D., and C. Fred T. Andrus. 2011. Evaluating Mobility, Monumentality, and Feasting at the Sapelo Shell Ring Complex. *American Antiquity* 76(2):315–43.

Thompson, V. D., M. D. Reynolds, B. Haley, R. Jefferies, J. K. Johnson, and L. Humphries. 2004. The Sapelo shell ring complex: shallow geophysics on a Georgia sea island. *Southeastern Archaeology* 23:192–201.

Thompson, Victor D., and John Turck. 2009. Adaptive Cycles of Coastal Hunter-Gatherers. *American Antiquity* 74:255–78.

———. 2010. Island Archaeology and the Native American Economies of Small Islands along the Georgia Coast, USA. *Journal of Field Archaeology* 35:283–97.

Thompson, Victor D., and John Worth. 2011. Dwellers by the Sea: Native American Coastal Adaptations along the Southern Coasts of Eastern North America. *Journal of Archaeological Research* 19:51–101.

Thurtle, M. C., and B. Roth. (editors). 2008. *Data Recovery at Six Archaeological Sites along U.S.91 from Willcox to Safford, Cochise and Graham Counties, Arizona*. Tierra Archaeological Report No. 2003–38. Tierra Right of Way Services, Tucson, AZ.

Thwaites, R. G. (editor). 1906. *Early Western Travels 1748–1846: Maximilian, Prince of Wied's, Travels in the Interior of North America, 1832–1834*. 2 vols. Arthur H. Clark, Cleveland.

Tilley, C. 1993. Art, architecture, landscape (Neolithic Sweden). In *Landscape, Politics and Perspectives*, edited by B. Bender, pp. 49–84. Berg, Oxford.

———. 1994. *A Phenomenology of Landscape: Places, Paths, and Monuments*. Berg, Oxford.

Torrence, R. 1983. Time Budgeting and Hunter-Gatherer Technology. In *Hunter-Gatherer Economy in Prehistory: A European Perspective*, edited by G. Bailey, pp. 11–22. Cambridge University Press, Cambridge.

Trigger, B. 2006. *A History of Archaeology Thought*. Cambridge University Press, Cambridge.

Trinkley, Michael B. 1985. The Form and Function of South Carolina's Early Woodland Shell Rings. In *Structure and Process in Southeastern Archaeology*, edited by R. S. Dickens Jr., and T. Ward, pp. 102–18. University of Alabama Press, Tuscaloosa.

Tsuji, Sei-ichiro. 1996. Shokubutsu-so kara mita Sannai Maruyama iseki [The Sannai Maruyama site seen from its floral assemblage]. In *Sannai Maruyama Iseki VI* [The Sannai Maruyama Site, Vol. 6], edited by Aomori-ken Kyoiku-cho Bunka-ka [Cultural Affairs Section of the Agency of Education of Aomori Prefecture], pp. 81–83. Aomori: Aomori-ken Kyoiku Iinkai [Board of Education of Aomori Prefecture].

———. 1997. Sannai Maruyama o sasaeta seitaikei [The ecosystems that supported Sannai Maruyama]. In *Jomon Toshi o Horu* [Excavating a Jomon Cty], edited by Yasuhiro Okada and NHK Aomori, pp. 174–88. NHK, Tokyo.

———. 1998. Sannai Maruyama iseki: Jomon jidai zenki no taiseki butsu no naiyo to kankyo fukugen [The Sannai Maruyama site: contents of Early Jomon sediments and environmental reconstruction]. In *Sannai Maruyama Iseki, IX* [The Sannai Maruyama Site, Vol. 9], edited by Aomori-ken Kyoiku-cho Bunka-ka [Cultural Affairs Section of the Agency of Education of Aomori Prefecture], pp. 27–28. Aomori: Aomori-ken Kyoiku Iinkai [Board of Education of Aomori Prefecture] (in Japanese).

———. 1999. Koseido ^{14}C nendai sokutei ni yoru Sannai Maruyama Iseki no hennen [Chronology at the Sannai Maruyama site using a high-precision ^{14}C dating method]. *Gekkan Chikyu Special Issue* 26:32–28.

———. 2002. Hito to shizen no kankyoshi [Environmental history of people and nature]. In *Aomori Kenshi, Betsuhen 3: Sannai Maruyama Iseki* [The History of Aomori Prefecture, Supplementary Volume, No. 3, The Sannai Maruyama Site], edited by Aomori Kenshi Hensan Koko Bukai [The Archaeology Section of the Editorial Board of the The History of Aomori Prefecture], pp. 227–44. Aomori Prefecture, Aomori.

———. 2006. Sannai Maruyama iseki no sojo to hennen [Stratigraphy and chronology of the Sannai-maruyama site, Aomori Prefecture, northern Japan]. *Japanese Journal of Historical Botany* Special Issue 2:23–48.

Tucker, D. B., and J. Ezzo. (editors). 2006. *Five Hours by Stage: Prehistoric and Historic Investigations Along US 191, Greenlee County Line to Three Way.* SWCA Cultural Resources Report No. 03–107. Tucson, Arizona.

Turck, John A., and Clark R. Alexander in review. Coastal Landscapes and their Relationship to Human Settlement on the Georgia Coast. In *Life among the Tides: Recent Archaeology of the Georgia Bight,* edited by V. D. Thompson and D. H. Thomas, (TBA). Anthropological Papers of the American Museum of Natural History, New York.

Turner, D. H. 1979. Hunting and Gathering: Cree and Australian. In *Challenging Anthropology: A Critical Introduction to Social and Cultural Anthropology,* edited by D. H. Turner and G. Smith, pp. 195–213. McGraw-Hill and Ryerson, Toronto.

Tyrrell, J. B. (editor). 1916. *David Thompson's Narrative of his Explorations in Western America, 1784-1812.* Champlain Society, Toronto.

Van Gelder, R. G. 1959. A Taxonomic Revision of the Spotted Skunk (*Genus Spilogale. Bulletin of the American Museum of Natural History* 117:233–392.

———. 1965. Channel Islands skunks. *Natural History* 74:30–35.

Vellanoweth, R. L. 1998. Earliest Island Fox Remains on the Southern Channel Islands: Evidence from San Nicolas Island, California. *Journal of California and Great Basin Anthropology* 20:100–108.

Verbicky-Todd, Eleanor. 1984. *Communal Buffalo Hunting among the Plains Indians: An Ethnographic and Historic Review.* Archaeological Survey of Alberta Occasional Paper No. 24. Alberta Culture, Historical Resources Division, Edmonton.

Vest, Jay. 1988. Traditional Blackfeet Religion and the Sacred Badger-Two Medicine Wildlands. *Journal of Law and Religion* 6(2):455–89.

Vierra, B. J. 2005. Late Archaic Stone Tool Technology across the Borderlands. In *The Late Archaic Across the Borderlands: From Foraging to Farming*, edited by B. J. Vierra, pp. 187–218. University of Texas Press, Austin.

Villagrán, Ximena S., Paulo C.F. Giannini, and Paulo DeBlasis. 2009. Archaeofacies analysis: using depositional attributes to identify anthropic processes of de-position in a monumental shellmound of Santa Catarina State, Southern Brazil. *Geoarchaeology: An International Journal* 24:311–335.

von Bloecker Jr., J. C. 1941. A New Shrew from Santa Catalina Island, California. *Bulletin Southern California Academy of Sciences* 40:163–64.

———. 1967. Land Mammals of the Southern California Islands. In *Proceedings of the Symposium on the Biology of the California Islands*, edited by R. N. Philbrick, pp. 245–63. Santa Barbara Botanic Garden, Santa Barbara.

Walker, P. L. 1980. Archaeological Evidence for the Recent Extinction of Three Terrestrial Mammals on San Miguel Island. In *The California Islands: Proceedings of a Multidisciplinary Symposium*, edited by D. M. Power, pp. 703–17. Santa Barbara Museum of Natural History, Santa Barbara.

Wallace, H. D., P. R. Fish, and S. K. Fish. 2007. Tumamoc Hill and the Early Pioneer Period Occupation of the Tucson Basin. In *Trincheras Sites in Time, Space, and Society*, edited by S. K. Fish, P. R. Fish, and M. E. Villalpando, pp. 53–99. University of Arizona Press, Tucson.

Walne, P. R. 1958. Growth of oysters (*Ostrea edulis L.*). *Journal of marine biology association UK* 37:591–602.

Walne, P. R. 1974. *Culture of Bivalve Molluscs, 50 years of experience at Conwy.* The Buckland Foundation.

Warren, Louis S. 1997. Blackfeet and Boundaries and Glacier National Park. In *The Hunter's Game*, pp. 126–51. Yale University Press, New Haven.

Waters, J. 2001. Faunal Remains: Methods of Analysis and Data Tables. In *The Early Agricultural Period Component at Los Pozos: Feature Descriptions and Data Tables*, edited by D. A. Gregory, pp. 159–65. Technical Report No. 99–4, Desert Archaeology, Tucson, AZ.

Wayne, R. K., S. B. George, D. Gilbert, and P. W. Collins. 1991a. The Channel Island Fox (*Urocyon littoralis*) as a Model of Genetic Change in Small Populations. In *The Unity of Evolutionary Biology: Proceedings of the Fourth International Congress of Systematics and Evolutionary Biology. Volume II*, edited by E. C. Dudley, pp. 639–49. Dioscorides Press, Portland.

Wayne, R. K., S. B. George, D. Gilbert, P. W. Collins, S. D. Kovach, D. Girman, and N. Lehman. 1991b. A Morphologic and Genetic Study of the Island Fox, *Urocyon littoralis. Evolution* 45:1849–68.

Webb, Clarence H. 1982. The Poverty Point Culture. Geoscience and Man, 2nd ed., revised. Geoscience Publications, Department of Geography and Anthropology, Louisiana State University, Baton Rouge.

Wenger, Etienne. 1998. *Communities of Practice: Learning, Meaning, and Identity.* Cambridge University Press, Cambridge.

Wenner, A. M., and D. L. Johnson. 1980. Land Vertebrates on the Islands: Sweepstakes or Landbridges? In *The California Islands: Proceedings of a Multidisciplinary Symposium*, edited by D. M. Power, pp. 497–530. Santa Barbara Museum of Natural History, Santa Barbara.

West, Raymond. 1941. *Elk of the Northern Rocky Mountain Region.* Field Notes on Wildlife II (9).

Whalen, M. E., and P. E. Minnis. 2001. *Casas Grandes and its Hinterland: Prehistoric Regional Organization in Northwest Mexico.* University of Arizona Press, Tucson.

Whitaker, David J., John W. McCord, Philip P. Maier, Albert L. Segars, Megan L. Rekow, Norm Shea, Jason Ayers, and Rocky Browder. 2004. *An Ecological Characterization of Coastal Hammock Islands in South Carolina.* Ocean and Coastal Resources Management, South Carolina Department of Health and Environmental Control, Charleston.

White, J. A. 1966. A New *Peromyscus* from the Late Pleistocene of Anacapa Island, California, with notes on variation in *Peromyscus nesodytes. Los Angeles County Museum Contributions in Science* 96:1–8.

White, J. P. 2004. Where the Wild Things Are: Prehistoric Animal Translocation in the Circum New Guinea Archipelago. In *Voyages of Discovery: The Archaeology of Islands,* edited by S. M. Fitzpatrick, pp. 147–64. Prager, Westport.

Whittlesey, S. M., S. J. Hesse, and M. S. Foster. (editors). 2007. *Recurrent Sedentism and the Making of Place: Archaeological Investigations at Las Capas, a Preceramic Period Farming Community in the Tucson Basin, Southern Arizona.* SWCA Cultural Resources Report No. 07-556 (Draft), Tucson.

Wilson, D. E., and D. M. Reeder. (editors). 1993. *Mammal Species of the World.* Smithsonian Institution Press, Washington, D.C.

Wilson, R. W. 1936. A New Pleistocene Deer Mouse from Santa Rosa Island. *Journal of Mammalogy* 17:408–10.

Winterhalder, Bruce, and Eric Alden Smith. 1981. *Hunter-Gatherer Foraging Strategies: Ethnographic and Archaeological Analyses.* University of Chicago Press, Chicago.

Wissler, Clark. 1910. *Material Culture of the Blackfeet Indians.* Anthropological Papers of the American Museum of Natural History Vol. V(1). The Trustees, New York.

———. 1916. Societies and Dance Associations of the Blackfoot Indians. In *Societies of the Plains Indians,* edited by C. Wissler, pp. 359–460. Anthropological Papers of the American Museum of Natural History Vol. XI. The Trustees, New York.

Wissler, Clark, and David C. Duvall. 1995. *Social Organization and Ritualistic Ceremonies of the Blackfoot Indians.* AMS Press, Inc., New York.

Worm, B., E. B. Barbier, N. Beaumont, J. E. Duffy, C. Folke, B. S. Halpern, J.B.C. Jackson, H. K. Lotze, F. Micheli, S. R. Palumbi, E. Sala, K. A. Selkoe, J. J. Stachowicz, and R. Watson. 2006. Impacts of biodiversity loss on ocean ecosystem services. *Science* 314:787–90.

Worth, John E. 1995. *The Struggle for the Georgia Coast. The Struggle for the Georgia Coast: An Eighteenth-Century Spanish Retrospective on Guale and Mocama.* Anthropological Papers of the American Museum of Natural History, Number 75, New York.

Yasuda, Yoshinori. 1989. Indasu Bunmei no seisui to Jomon Bunka [the growth and decline of the Indus Civilization and the Jomon Culture]. *Bulletin of International Research Center for Japanese Studies* 1:205–72.

———. 2004. *Kiko hendo no Bunmei-shi* [Climate Change and the History of Civilizations]. NTT Shuppan, Tokyo.

Yasuda, Yoshinori, and Jorg F. W. Negendank. 2003. Editorial: environmental variability in East and West Eurasia. *Quaternary International* 105:1–6.

Yasuda, Yoshinori, Kentaro Yamaguchi, Takeshi Nakagawa, Hitoshi Fukusawa, Junko Kitagawa and Makoto Okamura. 2004. Environmental variability and human adaptation during the Lateglacial/Holocene transition in Japan with reference to pollen analysis of the SG4 core from Lake Suigetsu. *Quaternary International* 123–25:11–19.

Yesner, David R. 1980. Maritime hunter-gatherers: ecology and prehistory. Current Anthropology 21:727–35.

——. 1987. Life in the "Garden of Eden": constraints on marine diets for human societies. In *Food and Evolution*, edited by M. Harris and E. Ross, pp. 285–310. Temple University Press, Philadelphia.

Yonge, C. M. 1960. *Oysters*. Collins, London. The New Naturalist Series.

Yoshikawa, Masanobu, and Sei-ichiro Tsuji. 1998. Sannai Maruyama iseki dai 6 tetto standard column no kafun kaseki gun [Pollen data obtained from the Standard column of the Sixth Transmission Tower Area of the Sannai Maruyama site]. In *Sannai Maruyama Iseki ix, dai 2 Bunsatsu* [The Sannai Maruyama Site, Vol. IX, Part 2], edited by Aomori-ken Kyoiku-cho bunka-ka [Cultural Affairs Section of the Agency of Education of Aomori Prefecture], pp. 11–14. Aomori-ken Kyoiku Iinkai [Board of Education of Aomori Prefecture], Aomori.

Yoshikawa, Masanobu, Shigeru Suzuki, Sei-ichiro Tsuji, Kanako Goto, and Taisuke Murata. 2006. Vegetation history and human activities at the Sannai-maruyama site, Aomori Prefecture. *Japanese Journal of Historical Botany* Special Issue 2:49–82.

Yoshizaki, Masahiro. 1995. Nihon ni okeru saibai shokubutsu no shutsugen [The first appearance of domesticated plants in Japan]. *Kikan Kokogaku* [Archaeology Quarterly] 50:18–24.

Zedeño, María Nieves. 2007. Blackfeet Landscape Knowledge and the Badger-Two Medicine Traditional Cultural District. *The SAA Archaeological Record* 7(2):9–12.

——. 2008. Bundled Worlds: The Roles and Interactions of Complex Objects from the North American Plains. *Journal of Archaeological Method and Theory* 15:362–78.

Zedeño, María Nieves, and John R. Murray. 2008. *The Prairie-Mountain Continuum in Blackfoot Culture and Society*. Paper presented at the 68th Plains Anthropological Conference, Laramie, Wyoming.

Zedeño, María Nieves, Lauren Jelinek, and Rebecca Toupal. 2006. *Badger-Two Medicine Traditional Cultural District, Lewis and Clark National Forest, Montana—Boundary Adjustment Study and Traditional Cultural Property Nomination*. Bureau of Applied Research in Anthropology, University of Arizona, Tucson, in collaboration with the Blackfeet Community College and the Blackfeet Tribe.

Zedeño, María Nieves, Samrat Miller, Kacy Hollenback, and John Murray. 2007. *Blackfeet Sacred Site Protection along the Birch Creek Watershed, Lewis & Clark National Forest, MT*. Bureau of Applied Research in Anthropology, University of Arizona, Tucson.

Zedeño, Maria Nieves, Wendi Field Murray, Samrat Miller, and John Murray. 2008. *Blackfeet Sacred Land Recovery Project*. Bureau of Applied Research in Anthropology, University of Arizona, Tucson.

Zeder, M. A. 2008. Domestication and Early Agriculture in the Mediterranean Basin: Origins, Diffusion, and Impact. *Proceedings of the National Academy of Sciences* 105:11597–11604.

Zvelebil, Marek. 1997. Hunter-gatherer Ritual Landscapes: Spatial Organisation, Social Structure and Ideology among Hunter-gatherers of Northern Europe and Western Siberia. *Analecta Praehistorica Leidensia* 29:33–50.

Contributors

William Balée is professor of anthropology at Tulane University. He is currently studying the impacts that societies in species-rich areas have had on
the diversity of flora and fauna and how these impacts are recognized in the
context of traditional knowledge. He has carried out fieldwork since 1979
on relationships between forest-dwelling peoples and their landscapes in
the Amazon region, with special attention to the Tupí-Guaraní–speaking
Ka'apor people of eastern Brazil. His research interests include historical
ecology, ethnobiology, and lowland South American ethnology.

Nicholas H. Beale is a senior archaeologist at the Oklahoma Department
of Transportation and Oklahoma Archeological Survey. His research interests include hunter-gatherer mobility strategies, lithic technology, resource
procurement, and identity. His current research delves into the Late Archaic occupation in Oklahoma's Cross Timbers.

Paulo DeBlasis is professor of archaeology at the Museu de Arqueologia
e Etnologia, Universidade de São Paulo. He has been involved in field research throughout Brazil, particularly in southern Amazonia, Central Pla-
teau, and Southern Coastal areas. His research interests include Paleoindian studies, rock art, and hunter-gatherer societies. Recently he has been
focusing on ritual and religious patterns among pre-Columbian societies.

Chester B. DePratter is an archaeologist with the South Carolina Institute
of Archaeology and Anthropology at the University of South Carolina.
His research has focused on a wide range of topics in Georgia and South
Carolina, including coastal shell rings, Spanish explorations in the southeastern United States, coastal progradation and sea level fluctuation, Span-

ish colonial Santa Elena (1566–87), southeastern chiefdoms, and reservoir archaeology.

Paul R. Fish is professor in the School of Anthropology and curator at the Arizona State Museum, University of Arizona. His field research focuses on middle-range societies in the American Southwest and Northwest Mexico, particularly the Arizona-Sonora borderlands, and southern coastal Brazil. Methodological and theoretical interests include regional analysis, political and social organization, and landscapes.

Suzanne K. Fish is professor in the School of Anthropology and curator at the Arizona State Museum, University of Arizona. Her field research involves the American Southwest, Mexico, and Brazil. She has been co-editor of *Latin American Antiquity* and publications include topics on the organization of middle-range societies, ethnobotany, archaeological palynology, survey, and traditional farming practices.

Maria Dulce Gaspar is professor of anthropology at the Museu Nacional, Universidade Federal do Rio de Janeiro. She publishes widely on shell mounds, rock art, and archaeological method and theory. She was co-editor of *Latin American Antiquity* and has archaeological projects in the states of Rio de Janeiro and Santa Catarina, Brazil.

Patricia A. Gilman retired from the University of Oklahoma as professor of anthropology. She has done southwestern archaeology since 1972 and began her focus on all things Mimbres in 1974. Gilman has concentrated her research in southwestern New Mexico and southeastern Arizona. Her present research interests include Mimbres painted pottery made outside the Mimbres Valley, Mimbres iconography, and macaws and parrots in the ancient Southwest.

Junko Habu is professor of anthropology at the University of California, Berkeley. She has been involved in a number of field and laboratory projects on prehistoric and historic sites in Japan, as well as in the Canadian Arctic. Her publications include *Ancient Jomon of Japan*, *Beyond Foraging and Collecting* (co-edited with B. Fitzhugh), and *Evaluating Multiple Narratives* (co-edited with C. Fawcett and J. M. Matsunaga). She is currently researching long-term changes in the prehistoric Jomon hunter-gatherers of Japan.

Mark E. Hall is an archaeologist and Native American coordinator with the Bureau of Land Management in Winnemucca, Nevada. He has conducted field and museum research in California, Ireland, Northern Ireland, Japan, Mongolia, and Nevada. Archaeometallurgy, Bayesian modeling, and geochemical studies of pottery are just a few of his interests.

Tristram R. Kidder is professor and chair of the Department of Anthropology at Washington University in St. Louis. He does fieldwork in the American Southeast as well as in China. His research spans the Holocene and focuses on environmental archaeology, the archaeology of climate change, and the archaeology of hunter-gatherer complexity. He has published in *Science, American Antiquity, Southeastern Archaeology, Journal of Field Archaeology, Quaternary Science Reviews,* and *Geoarchaeology,* among others, and he has received grants from NSF, NGS, NASA, and private foundations.

Nicky Milner is professor at the University of York, United Kingdom. Her research interests focus on European archaeology, particularly the Mesolithic period and the transition to the Neolithic, and her work is divided across three key themes: palaeodiet and consumption practices, settlement and mobility, and death and burial. She has worked on many field projects, and has recently published the results of her excavations at the Early Mesolithic site of Star Carr (http://www.starcarr.com). She has also carried out research into coastal shell middens and agricultural origins in Europe, as part of a major AHRB project.

Steven C. Pennings is professor at the University of Houston. He is co-project director of the Georgia Coastal Ecosystems Long-Term Ecological Research program, which focuses on the ecology of coastal habitats in Georgia. His research interests include plant community ecology, plant-herbivore interactions, and latitudinal variation in ecological processes.

Torben C. Rick is curator and research scientist of the archaeobiology program at the National Museum of Natural History, Smithsonian Institution. His research focuses on the archaeology and historical ecology of the California Channel Islands, North American Pacific Coast, and the Chesapeake Bay. He is interested in coastal and island archaeology, hunter-gatherers, human-environmental interactions, and the antiquity and evolution of coastal peoples.

Victor D. Thompson is professor at the University of Georgia. His primary interests are in the Native American societies that occupied the coastal and wetland areas of the American Southeast. The majority of his work has taken place in Florida and along the Georgia Coast. Specifically, his research centers on the ritual and ceremonial landscapes, subsistence systems, and political development of societies that occupied coastal and island ecosystems. This work encompasses time scales that cover the latter part of the Holocene (3000 BC to AD 1700). As part of the larger framework of this research, he explores how the actions of individuals, groups, and communities factor into societal trajectories and how such historical processes influenced and articulated with local and regional ecosystems and climate change.

Elizabeth M. Toney graduated with a Master's degree in anthropology from the University of Oklahoma in 2012. She is currently employed as an archaeologist for the Francis Marion and Sumter National Forests in South Carolina. Her interests include small architectural sites in the Mimbres area, the application of Geographic Information Systems to look at landscape scale trends through time, and the transition from foraging to farming in prehistory.

John A. Turck is an archaeologist/GIS specialist for the National Park Service at Valley Forge National Historical Park and Hopewell Furnace National Historic Site, focusing on section 106 and public archaeology. His research concentrates on the dynamic interactions between people and the environment, especially in coastal settings. Turck specializes in geographical and geological methods (GIS, remote sensing, modeling, sedimentological analysis, etc.) as well as quantitative methods to address questions of past human behavior and landscape change.

James C. Waggoner Jr. was an anthropological archaeologist who conducted research in the southeastern United States. His primary research focused on understanding the intersections among Native use of fire, mobility, and the pine-dominated ecosystems of southwest Georgia. Additionally, he examined hunter-gatherer interaction through ceramic analysis along the Georgia coastal plain. He participated in field research in the southeastern United States, Mexico, and Hungary.

María Nieves Zedeño is professor at the University of Arizona. She is a North Americanist, with interests in archaeology, ethnohistory, and ethnography, and an emphasis on hunter-gatherer societies. Her main theoretical focus is on human-land interaction, and she has published extensively on the topics of landscape and territory. Her research projects have covered the Southwest, Great Basin, Great Lakes and, currently, the northern Plains.

Index

www.ingramcontent.com/pod-product-compliance
Lightning Source LLC
Chambersburg PA
CBHW031428270326
41930CB00007B/609